CH00709236

BUSINESS INFORMATION TEC....OLOGY SERIES

Series Editor: TONY GUNTON

An Introduction to Computer Integrated Business
LESLEY BEDDIE AND SCOTT RAEBURN

End User Focus
TONY GUNTON

Infrastructure: Building a Framework for Corporate Information Handling
TONY GUNTON

Inside Information Technology: A Practical Guide to Management Issues
TONY GUNTON

Management Strategies for Information Technology
MICHAEL J. EARL

Managing the Human Resource
JOHN WESTERMAN AND PAULINE DONOGHUE

Organizational Structure and Information Technology
JON HARRINGTON

Professional Systems Development: Experience, Ideas and Action
NIELS ERIK ANDERSEN *et al*

ABOUT THE SERIES

The existing literature about information technology (IT) places heavy emphasis on the *how*? and less on the *why*? and the *what*? Meanwhile the rapid and apparently never-ending improvements in the cost/performance of IT is steadily creating new opportunities for its use. Senior managers already know that IT may be the key to their future ability to compete or to operate effectively, while all departmental managers need to appreciate how IT may affect the way they run their part of the business operation.

The **Prentice Hall Business Information Technology Series** aims to fulfil two related tasks:

- to help specialists and non-specialists to understand *what* they should be doing with IT and *why* various problems arise.
- to help specialists to adjust to the changes made necessary by the advances in information technology and by the closer involvement of non-specialists in the process of technology management.

Explaining in realistic and practical terms what IT can (and cannot) contribute in a business context, what problems it is likely to raise and how it should be planned for and managed, the **Business Information Technology Series** embraces the three resources on which systems based on IT draw:

- the **information** that is handled – what can IT do for a particular business in its particular circumstances today
- the **technology** used – controlling and maximising the potential of this complex and dynamic technology
- the **people** who build, operate and manage systems – what can be realistically achieved through the available human resources.

Different books concentrate on different aspects of the overall task, but all of them approach it from a similarly broad perspective, making the series both accessible and of wide-reaching significance.

Organizational structure and information technology

Jon Harrington
Newcastle Business School

Prentice Hall
New York   London   Toronto   Sydney   Tokyo   Singapore

First published 1991 by
Prentice Hall International (UK) Ltd
66 Wood Lane End, Hemel Hempstead
Hertfordshire HP2 4RG
A division of
Simon & Schuster International Group

© Prentice Hall International (UK) Ltd, 1991

Typeset in 10 pt Sabon
by Columns of Reading

Printed and bound in Great Britain
by BPCC Wheatons Ltd, Exeter

Library of Congress Cataloging-in-Publication Data

Harrington, Jon, 1950–
   Organizational structure and information technology / by Jon Harrington.
     p. cm. – (Business information technology series)
   Includes bibliographical references.
   ISBN 0–13–465162–6
   1. Corporate culture. 2. Organizational behaviour. 3. Information
technology. I. Title. II. Series.
HD58.7H3693 1991
302.3′5–dc20   91–35517
                                     CIP

British Library Cataloguing in Publication Data

Harrington, Jon
   Organizational structure and information technology.
   1. Organizations. Management. Applications of computer systems
I. Title II. Series
   658.05

   ISBN 0–13–465162–6 (cased)
   ISBN 0–13–465147–2 (paper)

---

2 3 4 5   95 94 93 92

Contents

For Ann

Preface

The purpose of this book is two-fold. Firstly to analyse the impact of information technology upon organizations. Secondly to develop a new model of organization and, in so doing, to present a more appropriate framework in which to understand how business organizations in particular change the potential impact of computer installation.

To date, such an approach has suffered from inattention since much of the discussion and policies have reflected a macro interest, often giving a colourful account of the potential impact of installation but failing to identify the realities to be found in the organizations themselves. There is a growing suspicion that the macro level has been covered too extensively, to the point that an impasse on the way ahead seems to have developed.

The time is certainly ripe for new thinking on the subject and this book suggests a possible alternative. It not only emphasizes the importance of micro analysis in determining the impact of technology upon organizations, but also discusses the relevance of existing models in this process of determination. Much has been presented in terms of a relationship between technology as a resource and organizational structure, but the distinction between technology *per se* and information technology has to a great extent been ignored: the latter, though, may be important in fundamentally altering organizations.

The dialectical base of this book is of necessity fairly broad. It is anticipated, therefore, that this breadth will also be reflected in the readership. For both student and manager alike, it is intended to portray an interdisciplinary analysis. Those with experience in management studies, sociology, industrial psychology, organizational behaviour or BIT (business information technology) will all find something of interest here.

Acknowledgements

My thanks to all those who suffered and helped me with this book. Especial gratitude must go to Valerie Leyland for her invaluable comments, to Paul Lee for his patience, to Ed Sciberras for his insight, to Stuart Maguire for his humour and timely corrections, and to other anonymous readers for their advice and assistance.

CHAPTER 1
An overview

1.1 Background

I started my industrial career at a time of rapidly increasing computerization of organizations. During those years (the early 1970s) I worked mainly in a corporate audit function, reporting to senior management on the effectiveness of their strategy, particularly in the area of computer technology implementation. It was at this time that I began to formulate my first ideas about virtual organization.

Management teams were grasping eagerly at the new computer technology as a solution to their efficiency problems. There were at that time forces in the environment – market, political, social or economic – with which the traditional methods of organization could not cope; it was believed that the computer would provide all the answers.

In the space of that time many colleagues began to discover that the impact of computer technology seemed to be contradictory. On the one hand, it did tend to improve efficiency, whilst on the other it was not always so certain that an improvement in effectiveness followed. It seemed that underlying, and as yet not understood, forces were at work. Departments employing the same technology were more or less successful than others. Business organizations with all the ingredients of success and implementing computers to further fuel their growth quite often experienced failure a few years later.

Since those early days there has been considerable discussion and research on the impact of information technology. It seemed that the perceptual aspects of organization were not merely misunderstood but often ignored, and thus we were not able to understand fully the implications of introducing information technology. We now realize that not only does it have an impact on the way we run organizations, it also has an impact on our behaviour. There is a readily understood physical aspect of any firm and a more abstract, perceptual aspect which arises from the way that people behave as a collective.

Information technology is not the only agent in this process, but because of its particular characteristics it can have an extraordinarily powerful effect on both these aspects.

One of two main objectives of this book, therefore, is to underline the importance of the relationship between information technology (and to a lesser extent general technology) and its organizational structure. The two are inseparable. Models that seek to understand either technology or organization must do so within the framework created by this relationship. Otherwise an essential factor leading to an appropriate analysis will be missed.

The other main objective is to produce a model which can do this. Unlike many of its predecessors, the model will not concentrate on the functional or hierarchical nature of organizations but rather on the dichotomy between the physical and perceptual aspects. This exists whether or not there is information technology present, but in many cases the implementation of such technology can exacerbate potential dysfunctional forces existing between the two. In effect there are two organizations – a physical organization and a perceptual or virtual organization. The impact that information technology can have on the sometimes tenuous relationship existing between the two can be quite profound.

The model explores thoroughly this relationship. It proposes virtual organization as the antithesis of physical organization. That is abstract, unseeing and existing within the minds of those who form a particular organization. The point being that because the framework of virtual organization is often subjective and open to many different perceptual interpretations, it is difficult for anyone to establish an appropriate response to it. This makes it no less real; nor does it reduce the need to respond to it. Left unattended the effects of virtual organization can be quite catastrophic, especially if stimulated by the impact of information technology.

This has considerable significance for the practitioner, especially those who have introduced, or are thinking of introducing, information technology. The model suggests that for a firm to survive there would ideally exist a dynamic equilibrium between the two organizations which has been termed the organizational balance. Anything which upsets this balance, such as the introduction of information technology, has to be compensated for by proactive action of management. If managers do not understand, nor indeed perceive the existence of virtual organization, then they will not be able take the appropriate measures. Long-term structural weaknesses or even total failure of the business can result.

Demonstrating the existence of virtual organization can be

problematic. By definition it cannot be observed directly since it exists only in the mind. At best one could ask a selection of staff for their impressions and make certain deductions, but these are likely to be dubious and tainted with the researcher's own perceptions. As such there has deliberately been no direct empirical research to establish the foundations of this model. Support for its validity has been sought in three other areas.

Firstly, there is indirect empirical data gained from several research projects conducted at the Newcastle Business School. This comprises a study over two years by Stuart Maguire and myself into eighty-five small to large firms in all sectors of the North East (Figure 1.1). We examined particularly the strategy that firms employed to implement and control their information technology. The data were gathered through a series of observations, interviews and involvement in the process. Other data were obtained from one or two firm studies on the impact of information technology by a group within the Newcastle Business School called AMBIS (Advanced Manufacturing and Business Information Systems). The argument for using these data rather than dedicated data is that they should be less contrived.

Secondly, there is support to be gained from relevant personal experience. Although many would find this approach invalid because it

Industry	Number
MANUFACTURING	
Heavy engineering	8
General engineering	10
Chemical process	8
Foodstuffs	12
Textiles	2
Pharmaceuticals	4
Electronics	4
Total manufacturing	48
SERVICES	
Business services	14
Entertainment	6
Computing	4
Transport	6
Retail	6
Local government	5
Total services	41
TOTAL SAMPLE	89

Figure 1.1 NBS transectoral study of North East Region

does not comply with traditional or conventional ideas about research data, there is an increasing acceptance that such data can prove useful. In the social sciences, for example, Duke argued that such an approach (amongst others) would make a valuable contribution to the understanding of social experience.[1] It is accepted that it cannot provide the only data, but the data that it does provide should be considered no less valid than any other.

Lastly, this book proposes that we return to a more traditional style in support of the main arguments. That is, rather than gathering empirical evidence first and then developing a model, we should develop the model first from experiential instincts and then support it with data. This is put forward in the belief that to pursue the traditional methods of data-first research would not produce the generic model necessary to achieve the objectives set above. We have become unimaginative in our ideas about organization because we have been blinkered by too many sets of data.

How the book is structured in terms of presenting a logical argument takes on a greater significance than if it were based merely upon direct empirical data. It requires presentation of basic argument, counter-argument and a compromise position which leads the reader forward to the logical conclusion. This is the dialectic which involves thesis, antithesis and synthesis.

This overview, therefore, should not only cover the background to the book's major arguments and supportive material, but also provide the reader with a basic chapter plan.

1.2   The book, chapter by chapter

1.2.1   *What is information?*

To explain the impact of information technology we must look beyond the functional aspects of business organizations. Chapter 2 establishes the first stepping stones by providing a definition and detailed discussion of information, a major component of both organization and information technology. The importance of information is reflected in its ability, through the appropriate technology, to corrupt departmental boundaries. This chapter, therefore, proposes that it is better to understand an organization as a network of information flows, which is itself set within other network flows of region, market, industry and so on.

Such a perspective is underlined by many firms accessing information beyond their established functional boundaries. Within the organization, this could involve different departments accessing a common pool of information from the company database. Externally, employees can gain entrance to public databases such as Prestel, which are run by autonomous bodies.

The drive is towards centralization and hence better management control. Paradoxically, the opposite is being encouraged, whereby every user has the potential to access information which enables them to operate more efficiently, and also to do so outside the control of their manager.

Under these conditions it is difficult for managers to control not only who reads and writes what but also, and perhaps more importantly, who knows what. Large amounts of information can be processed and communicated via a network without managers ever being able to determine whether it runs contrary to their own policy. Security has, as a consequence, become an extremely important issue. The more the dissemination of information is allowed, the more likely control mechanisms will become corrupted. Case Study 1.1 demonstrates this.

In simple terms, data are facts, whilst information is the consequence of interpretation. What is information to some is not to others, and it is the subjective interpretation of what is and is not valuable which has caused managements considerable problems. The

---

CASE STUDY 1.1

The management is implementing a computer aided manufacturing process, and is indeed a long way towards this goal. They are achieving technological integration by networking the 'islands of technology' already existing in the line. To further that process they have centralized control, but at the cost of decentralizing the political process.

Managers from the individual departments have lost their ability to control completely their own sets of information and have thus found their ability to act considerably weakened. Their departments, successfully isolated under the manual system by traditional functional controls, have now all but dissolved into the company-wide network whereby the individuals from different departments link up in response to work needs and thus short-cut their managers. As a consequence the management team has become more fragmented through continual conflict in an effort to maintain disintegrating departmental boundaries.

The centralization of data can quite easily lead to the decentralization of functional control. How an organization interprets its information, and in particular how it distinguishes between data and information, is an important element in formulating an effective response to information technology.

control parameters on the organization's database are based upon managers' own perceptions of its value as information which may not coincide with that of a potential intruder or misuser. But more than this, individual employees' perception of their information stock widens because of their greater accessibility to the information network. As a consequence, their perception of their own job parameters also widens beyond what management might think desirable.

1.2.2   What is information technology?

In so far as control over information forms the basis of managerial authority, the technologies which process it are inherently political. Indeed, business organizations are under pressure to change their decision-making structures as a direct consequence of information technology implementation.

These 'subversive' effects on organizational structures are not immediately obvious to management. They arise as the new technology changes established work practices and consequently creates different relationships on the organization's information network. Management is then faced with a dual threat:

1. A new pool of knowledge outside its formal control structures. Employees are able to access information without hindrance.
2. Power is shifting from line managers to those who control the information technology, such as the technicians in the DP departments or knowledgeable users.

Management's response has been weak and incremental.[2] The control of information generated by computer technologies increasingly reflected the new power structures that these technologies established. On the one hand, functional control (allocation, budget, etc.) remains with general management. On the other, operational control (how and what is processed) is left to the technicians in the DP departments. The pervasive nature of the technology spreading through all levels of the organization established those who controlled it as important power-brokers or gatekeepers.[3] Newcastle Business School research has shown that senior managers are often unwilling to become involved. They served their apprenticeship in computerless or, at best, early mainframe-driven organizations and therefore do not always fully understand or appreciate the new technologies. Despite the obvious need for new control structures the traditional methods are adhered to. The dichotomy between the established management structures and the changed (and changing) technological structures is therefore maintained and often worsened.

Such opposing forces create a complex environment and place considerable constraints on management action. The dichotomy quickly becomes institutionalized. Lack of management action causes other user employees to perceive themselves as powerless in any dealings with the new technologies. This serves to enhance the influence of the technicians and is built into the organization's structures. Business action then tends to become increasingly inflexible; user managers are reluctant to take risks in an environment they do not understand, and many operational decisions are left to the technicians. This area of decision-taking is also built into the firm's task structure. Meanwhile the new networked systems demand increasing flexibility in order to work but are instead being faced with increasingly inflexible and decision-shy managements.

To appreciate the nature of this threat and how profound its impact can be on the organization, it is essential to grasp the characteristics of technology, in particular its integrative nature with any social entity whether it be an organization or something else. Chapter 3 explores this area, but it also then distinguishes between different types of technology, highlighting the perceptual characteristics of information technology. It concludes that to control information technology we must realize that we cannot treat it as just another piece of machinery.

1.2.3 The importance of organization structure

The relationship between technology and an organization has, indeed, been thoroughly explored. For example, Pugh and his colleagues noted in the early 1970s that amongst other contingents such as size, technology is of primary importance in influencing the structure and functioning of an organization.[4] It is obvious that a firm's structure is characterized by the many forces emanating from its operating environment. What is perhaps not so obvious is that technology is one of those forces. This is because it is quite often seen as a locally owned, physical resource. The machine on the shopfloor is just that and not part of a more complex social process. Within the framework of this perspective technology is a tool, totally predictable and controllable by management.

The physical technology alone (e.g. machinery or computers) will not explain how organizations are affected by it. As Weizenbaum suggested, a computer or telecommunication system (or any form of technology) is merely junk without the people to relate to them.[5] It is how those people relate to their technology, how they use it, their perceptions of it and so on, that are important. These aspects govern not only the technological process but also the characteristics of the organization structure.

In the same way, structure should not be seen merely in a physical sense. The dividing of a firm into departments and functions, although of interest, does not capture the essence of an organization, which is to be found within the minds of its employees. The relationship between technology and structure is thus not physical but perceptual because it is within people's minds that the links are made.

Our understanding of such techno-behavioural forces is not great. This is partly because of the hegemonic view of business organizations as hierarchies in organization theory. It would seem, therefore, that we have not as yet learnt to examine organizations in an appropriate dimension which can highlight the effects of information and its technology.

The traditionalist's view of an organization is typically presented by Schein as a rational co-ordination of activities.[6] This emphasizes the hierarchical and functionally-bound aspects. Butler, on the other hand, discussed the lack of understanding of such models determining that all the interrelationships are not adequately identified.[7] They tend to portray firms as static entities without the turbulence of opposing forces. In particular, technology is seen as a side issue, if at all, and not central to the fundamental mechanisms of an organization. Models such as Pugh's (see above) recognize technology's deterministic qualities but go no further. It is seen as an external force influencing the characteristics of an organization, but not as an essential of the organization itself.

A more appropriate model in Butler's mind is Udy's, which puts technology at the centre of an interactive environment of production objectives, social setting, physical exigencies and work organization.[8] Technology, not the structure, sets the constraints ('trade-offs' as Butler calls them) upon an organization. Thus a certain structure can be considered suitable for a given technology. For example, a company using mass production techniques, such as Ford, will best be structured to suit the needs of mass production technology. The relationship does not end there, however, as in Pugh's model, because he suggests that it is technology which drives the organization.

Where this model fails is in not identifying with sufficient clarity the perceptual aspects of an organization's technology. It is only within this domain that useful links can be established between technology and structure. The perceptual aspects of structure must also be emphasized for this to be successful since within any physical domain technology can only be seen as a resource and structure as a functional framework.

Chapter 4, therefore, presents important underpinning for this proposal by seeking an acceptable definition of structure. It will then demonstrate that employees' perception of their structure determines the consequent structural characteristics. This chapter also suggests, however, that the relationship is two-way, in that an established structure can itself influence and change the perception of the employees. The impact of information technology is then again introduced. Previous chapters will already have established that such technology can change the way that individuals perceive their environments. A link with the present chapter is that since an employee's perception of the environment can be changed through information technology, his/her perception of the firm's structure must also change. The post-implementation structure that emerges may be profoundly different from any previous structure.

1.2.4 The right methodology

This control-theoretic view of information technology's impact is particularly relevant to the devolution of management authority. The impact of the new technology may radically affect the power structure or the political relationships between management and staff (but not the functional relationships) thus creating an imbalance between the perceptual and physical aspects of the organization.

Through the perceptual domain, information technology has also infiltrated the cultural base of organizations and has thus had the potential to alter cultural objectives, which are the consequence of existing value systems. For example, it may be the formal objective of one firm to produce good quality products at the expense of higher profits. This objective has arisen from the organization's culture, but any form of technology, especially information technology, is not sensitive to cultural requirements. Managers may try to fit the technology into their companies but it is generally within a framework provided by the physical domain. The objectives suitable for the technology do not always match existing cultural needs.

To seek an explanation of the technological impact, therefore, we should no longer look at organizations in terms of departments and divisions. Any boundary established by such a definition may be rendered irrelevant. It is more sensible to consider an organization as a network of perceptual maps, dependent on an information network which is itself part of a wider network within the region, market, industry and so on.

The need for such an outlook is underlined by the number of firms accessing information beyond their established functional boundaries. Internally, this involves different departments accessing a common pool from the company database; externally, employees gaining entrance to public databases such as Prestel. It is increasingly difficult to understand these organizations as physically controllable entities.

The problem, however, extends beyond management. If it is accepted that our models of organization are also too limiting because of their inability to highlight the dichotomy between the perceptual and the physical, then we must develop new models, which is one of the major proposals of the book. In order to do this we must first establish an appropriate methodology. Chapter 5 presents a systems approach as that methodology.

The analysis which must be pursued is wide-ranging. It extends beyond the convenient boundaries that traditional theory has established. The tidy logic of an organization reaches only into the physical domain, beyond that is a vast perceptual arena which can be understood only as a network of relationships. Chapter 5 argues that a systems methodology is the best analytical tool for this purpose and then describes how it can be used to understand technological impact.

1.2.5　The dynamic element

The first five chapters are devoted to establishing a perceptual and theoretical foundation for the proposed model of virtual organization. Before its presentation, however, there are other factors which must be addressed. The point has already been made that an organization is a fluid and ever-changing entity. The components so far discussed form the framework of the organization but they are no more than boxes in an analyst's model. Other forces exist which breathe life into these concepts. They can be termed as the dynamics of an organization. Chapters 6 to 9 attend to these important aspects and in so doing form the second part of the book.

People are the organization, and as such their perceptions, aspirations, alliances and conflicts form an important dynamic. Chapter 6 examines people firstly as an entity of the firm and then places them in a dynamic role. It suggests that the outcome for any organization is not through a rational process, although that may seem to be apparent within the physical domain, but rather as a consequence of perceptual interaction between individuals or groups. These can be dysfunctional as well as functional.

For managers the issue is how such diverse forces can be controlled. They can only directly access the physical domain and therefore have to attempt to manipulate this in some way to have any impact upon the perceptual domain. One area, however, which allows a controllable linkage between the two domains is the information network. The quality, quantity and content of information, amongst other factors such as historicity, will determine an individual or group perception. On the other hand, the network itself can be physically manipulated thus affecting the quality, quantity and content of information. Its control is therefore of considerable importance to management.

Chapter 7, in recognition of this, is entitled information management. Its particular emphasis is on the use of computer technology to generate information. Other forms of generated information through manual methods can also be controlled as information management, but because of the computer's ability to generate so much information other important forces come into play which are not present in a manual system. This chapter, therefore, explores the different approaches to computer generated information management. As such it is particularly integrated with the ideas established in Chapter 2. The ways in which employees regard the characteristics of their information will determine in part the nature of their information network and ultimately the organization structure itself. Management must be aware of this and develop strategies through training and computer technology implementation which are sensitive to this.

Information, however, is only part of the process. On its own it is not particularly a dynamic of the organization. Individuals may receive information and do nothing with it. A firm, therefore, does not change because of information. Information must be used. Action or behaviour is the consequence of information being used in the physical domain. In the perceptual domain, information being used is manifest through the decision process. There are no actions without decisions, no matter how minor or simple they may be, so that an organization, which can be analysed in terms of its actions, is driven by its decision processes.[9]

In any context there is no such thing as an individual decision, even if the person involved is on a deserted island. Especially within a complex social process such as an organization, a decision is based upon a range of perceptual and physical influences. A person's experience coming to bear in a decision, for example, is the consequence of previous interactions with other people and institutions. Therefore one cannot fully control the decision process by controlling those individuals who are seen to own it. Their actions might be constrained but the source of their decisions is to be found in the perceptual domain. This is particularly important when such processes are affected by computer technology. Managers tend to develop mechanisms around the physical aspects of the technology and ignore the wider perceptual impact. Chapters 8 and 9 explore this relationship.

Chapter 8 lays the theoretical foundation by defining the decision process and demonstrating its relevance to understanding organizations and the impact of their technology. It then places these ideas in the context of the other major components of a firm, in particular the information network, by highlighting the close relationship between a decision and information. Chapter 9 takes this further by examining the decision as a dynamic and determining how this focus can change our view of the impact of information technology.

1.2.6 The final model

The third and final part of the book comprises Chapters 10 to 12 in which the completed model is presented and discussed. We have so far developed the framework of an organizational structure dominated by two domains: the physical and the perceptual. In a similar fashion to matter and anti-matter, their forces conflict and contradict one another. Management must maintain the narrow ground between the two, because it is only here that long-term stability is established. At this point the forces of both domains are in equilibrium, which for the purposes of the model has been termed balance. Chapter 10 examines the concept of balance and discusses its importance to the viability of the model.

The achievement of such a state is one of the key outcomes to be identified. The domination of one domain over another could lead to long-term instability, the degree of which depends upon a range of factors unique to specific organizations. For example, if there is no balance and an organization is dominated by its physical domain, then its short-term survival, at least, will depend upon how effective that domain is in dealing with the firm's particular environment. In the longer term, however, all firms must achieve an equilibrium whether the dominant domain is in tune with the environment or not. This is because the cost of not achieving equilibrium will be manifest in the dysfunctional relationship between the two domains. Forces will come into play that will undermine stability.

Chapter 11 formally presents the model of virtual organization in this spirit. It shows a complex social entity driven by an abstract relationship between two sets of forces. Much of this arena exists within the minds of the employees, of course, but like other societal phenomena its logic extends beyond them. The forces can exist independently of particular individuals in that they are perpetuated by culture, technology and training. Individuals may come and go, some people may contribute more than others, but the logic of the organization as a separate entity remains consistent. It is proposed that an organization can pass a significant point, the virtuality point, whereby its survival does not depend upon a particular set of individuals.

This is a different world from the one portrayed by established theory. It comprises many of the same elements, such as structure and technology, recognized by conventional wisdom, but it is the perspective, the way in which those elements are arranged, that is different. The emphasis is upon a force field relationship rather than the aspects of one domain or another. By having this different framework, we can also analyse the effects of change in other ways. In particular, the impact of information technology is shown to have a far wider effect upon organizations than the traditional models may lead us to suppose. Chapter 11, therefore, demonstrates the model's application to information technology and shows that in many cases organizations would have done better to have refrained from its implementation.

Chapter 12 places the model in the context of the debate about information technology and how we use it. There is recognition that empirical evidence for such a model is far from complete. Much of it is common sense, gleaned from the working environment and from those in it. Other aspects are taken from established models and applied to a new framework through research conducted at the Newcastle Business School. Nevertheless, the model is placed before all management as a challenge: to use the ideas this book presents as a basis for analysing the worth of their information technology. Some interesting outcomes may result. To ignore such a challenge may well court disaster in the long run.

REFERENCES

1. Duke, James. *Conflict and Power in Social Life*. Brigham Young University Press, 1976.
2. Lindblom, Charles. 'The science of muddling through', *Public Administration Review*, vol. 19, 1959. Although an old paper, it gives an interesting exposition of incremental management.
3. Pettigrew, Andrew. 'Information control as a power resource'. *Sociology*, vol. 6, issue 2, 1972.
4. Pugh, Derek, *et al.* 'The context of organization structures'. *Administrative Science Quarterly*, vol. 14, issue 1, 1969.
5. Weizenbaum, Joseph. *Computer Power and Human Reason*. W.H. Freeman, 1976.
6. Schein, E. *Organizational Psychology*. Prentice Hall, 1970.

7.   Butler, Gathorne. *Organization and Management*. Prentice Hall, 1986.
8.   Udy, Stanley. *Work in Traditional and Modern Society*. Prentice Hall, 1970.
9.   Simon, Herbert. *Administrative Behaviour*. Free Press, 1976. Provides an interesting discussion on the links between decisions, structure and strategy.

FURTHER READING

Heirs, Ben and Pehrson, Gordon. *The Mind of the Organization*. Harper & Row, 1982.

Weizenbaum, Joseph. *Computer Power and Human Reason*. W.H. Freeman, 1976.

CHAPTER 2
What is information?

2.1 Introduction

Information is one of those misunderstood concepts. Yet it is at the same time one of the most used. We go to the bus station to seek information from timetables. We obtain information from government offices such as the DSS and the DVLC. Banks, supermarkets, leisure centres, libraries and even the police ply us with more. Newspapers, television and the radio present us with their own ideas of what information should be.

In many instances, however, we may not agree with their conclusions. McLeod termed its subjectivity as being one person's junk and another's treasure.[1] We all understand and deal with this accordingly when extracting news from the media, for example. Yet many of our organizations consider information to be something more. They see it as a vital resource, to be managed like any other valuable resource.[2] How it is used and disseminated through the available technology can determine how efficient, and indeed effective, an organization is. Peter Drucker sees information acquired in a systematic and purposeful way as enhancing an organization's productivity.[3]

2.1.1 Changed perceptions

Information is important, we cannot operate without it. But more than this, we are discovering that our ability to process it by increasingly sophisticated technological means is fundamentally changing the way that employees perceive their organizational environment. The consequences of this could be either to break down established functional controls or indeed to enhance them by becoming super-efficient. Much will depend upon the characteristics of the organization before implementation.

RESEARCH 2A

1   Discussion with line managers within the framework of NBS research revealed that:

(a) Eighty per cent of them felt that their control over their departments had diminished subsequent to the computerization of their systems.

(b) Twenty per cent of them considered that they had more control and were thus more effective.

2   Research by Wightman tends to underline the implication that to take advantage of IT implementation, organizations must have certain characteristics.[4] The 'common themes' which he identifies relate quite strongly to the established manual information systems being sufficiently robust to withstand impact.

3   Action research by Newcastle Polytechnic over a period of two years in two major local firms also supports this view. In one where the control of information was weak, a subsequent computer-driven system worsened the situation. In the other, where control was much stronger, the situation improved.

Merely gaining the ability to process more information more quickly does not guarantee success. If the present system cannot cope with the amount of information passing through it, then exposing it to yet more through computerization can only worsen matters. How an organization responds to this new challenge can often affect its position in the marketplace.

2.2 Two paradigms

As firms become increasingly 'information dependent'[5] we need to identify the perceptual relationship between ourselves and the information we use. How, for instance, can we possibly design an adequate information system if we do not understand the nature of information?

The answer to this lies, in part, with the conventional wisdom of the day. Managers, like everybody else, develop their views through exposure to established ideas. Thus the way in which they understand information will influence the way in which they treat it.

Such conventional wisdom is coloured by the technicians on the one hand and the user's own experience on the other. Anecdotal prescriptions abound as guidelines to the way forward for all who care to listen. These arise from a blanket of professional and academic thinking which surrounds the business environment and provides remedies for action. We could categorize all these ideas into two bodies of thought, two paradigms.

The first could be termed the resource-driven paradigm. This is because its central theme in understanding information is the continuity and consistency of the information itself. It is very much in vogue at present.

The second body of thought is the perception-driven paradigm. Information is seen as an abstract concept, the product of individual perception. It is a temporary phenomenon and as such belongs only to the receiver.

The difference is not merely one of academic debate. Managements adopting one or the other can affect the design of their organizations. If information is considered to be a resource then resulting systems are usually more centrally controlled, the assumption being that all information is corporate property. Whereas information considered to be personally owned is seen as being outside the formal structure.

2.2.1 Resource-driven paradigm

Within the framework of this paradigm the view of information is coloured by its use as a resource. Like any other resource it can be tapped at any time with the certainty of achieving a predictable value from it. Information is regarded as unchanging, and therefore can be easily accommodated into a firm's formal procedure. There is a range of propositions available which seeks to explain information. Each proposition has a consequence for organizational design. Listed below are those major themes and what their implications might be on business.

Proposition. Information exists independently from its receiver.

Herbert A. Simon took the view that information, along with energy, constitute the two basic currencies of our society.[6] We need energy to breathe, to move, to think, to live. But this alone is not enough. We need to know when to breathe, when to move and how to think. Information provides us with that knowledge.

To adopt this perspective is to interpret information as an independent entity. It is all about us waiting to picked up and used. There may be minor variations in its interpretation by different individuals, but consistency can be easily achieved through better training.

Consequence. Information systems are designed on the assumption that information has a predictable and consistent value.

Specific sets of information, such as finance information, are given a unique value by organizations which is usually based upon departmental rather than individual need. Particular information is thus attached to particular departments. This allows information to be generally accessible because perceptions of it are bound by the formal departmental framework. Information is then tied into that framework and cannot be used legitimately within any other context, thus guarding its consistency.

What is excluded, therefore, is an important role for the individual receiver. This is not to suggest that information cannot be perceived by individuals. Psychologists such as Anderson and Bower have long been aware of the importance of information reception in determining an individual's behaviour.[7] However, information can be received automatically without an individual having to understand it. For example, through training an employee could process production statistics without knowing what they mean. In this case it is the functional process (through its formal procedure) that is acting as the receiver rather than the individual. An accounting process, for instance, responds to specific inputs without anyone having to understand them. A motor car responds to certain information transmitted through mechanisms such as the throttle, steering wheel or brake. Both of these examples are designed to act as receivers to specific information.

By implication, information can be transmitted to any receiver that logs into the particular transmission.[8] In the same way as a radio picks up a station when it is switched on, the right form will pick up the right information. And like radio waves, information is omnipresent, only needing the correct tuning. Such a view allows information the continuity and consistency required to be regarded as a resource. It also allows a further proposition.

Proposition. Information does not legitimately change during transmission.

The design of any formal information system must assume that information does not change during transmission. It can, however, be transformed from data or other information sets before transmission.

Within such a framework it is the transmitting functions (departments, processes, etc.) which are considered to be the main determinants. The information receiving functions (also departments, processes, etc.) are designed to link into the operational needs of the transmitter functions.

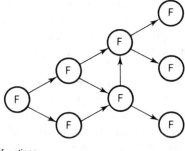

F = functions

Figure 2.1   An information network between functions

Each function, however, can be both transmitter and receiver of information, and together with other functions will form part of a integrated network. The functions are tied by their simultaneous roles as information receivers and transmitters (see Figure 2.1), thereby being prevented as much as possible from deviancy in their information usage.

> Consequence. Business organizations are driven by those functions which transmit information. The higher the value that a particular set of information is given, the more important will be its relating transmitter function.

For example, the finance department could both transmit and receive information. Indeed, each job function within that department could also do the same. A cost clerk, for instance, receives information from the factory floor which he then processes into other information and transmits to some other source, perhaps management. The value of the information he processes will depend upon the utility his organization has placed upon it. If the utility is high, then the prestige attached to the transmitting function will also be high irrespective of job complexity. In the same way, if a department has a great number of important information transmitters within its control, then it too will be prestigious and possess influence. Why certain sets of information are prestigious and others are not will depend, amongst other things, upon the organization's political processes.[9]

Conclusions

The resource-driven paradigm determines that information is constant in value and a resource of the organization. This enables information systems to be a practical proposition. The existence of these systems depends upon those within them perceiving the information they handle as having general application. Information can subsequently be altered by the system but in a controllable and predictable manner; the new information is then added to the resource.

Any information system, therefore, is not only underpinned by its driving technology but also by the perceptions of those within it. They must view their information as accurately reflecting a particular truth. They may not agree with that truth and may seek to change it. What is not questioned is the information about the truth.

Such trust in the accuracy of information is based upon the propositions which make up this paradigm. Once formed, a set of information must remain unchanged; if it is further processed then it becomes different information. Once formed it also becomes part of a consistent and identifiable stock of knowledge.

Within those organizations that apply information as a resource, the emphasis is placed upon its transmission since it is at this point that information is created. Therefore those functions which are generating further resources in the form of increased information sets are seen to be more significant than those that are not. Consequently their influence tends to be greater.

2.2.2 Perception-driven paradigm

The perception-driven paradigm does not consider information to be a resource. Individuals or groups are seen to own their information. What belongs to the organization are the data sets, the facts and figures specific to certain functions. For instance, data on how an organization is performing in its market quite obviously belong to that firm. How well that data is used is dependent upon the individual's own competence in interpreting it. Management can control this indirectly through training, but they cannot directly control the thought processes which turns data into information.

Once again, there is a collection of propositions or ideas about information which formulate a general approach. Adherence to this paradigm, as in the previous paradigm, may not necessarily be by conviction but rather by default because people not treating information as a resource automatically form part of this group. However, there are others who are members by conviction.

> **Proposition. Information does not exist beyond the perception of the receiver.**

Information is said to be receiver-dependent in that any set of information can be considered to be information only if it is recognised as having value by a particular individual. Thus a river flooding may be information to someone who lives on its banks but of no consequence to someone living several miles away.

It would be difficult, therefore, to understand information as group or organization property since its determination is subjective. This can be overcome by training individuals to think in a similar fashion, so enabling them to interpret data in a manner consistent with their fellows.

Consequence. Because information is individualistic it is not appropriate to treat it as a resource.

NBS research has shown the experience described in Case Study 2.1 to be common. Management teams have implemented computer technology and in so doing also developed their information sets into a resource. They experience problems, usually some time after a

---

CASE STUDY 2.1

A public development corporation introduced a computer-driven administrative system. They expected employees to use the information it generated as a resource. This allowed the managers to design a system which assumed consistent interpretation. Thus an accounts clerk was expected to perceive a certain piece of information just as readily or in the same way as a marketing manager.

Once the system had been operating for about a year it became clear that it was not working. Time and workload had not been reduced. Indeed, many had complained that these had increased, with the additional burden of increasing complexity.

It was found that individuals within different departments were understanding the information sets in contradictory ways. In one particular process a cost clerk was sitting on a printout vital for the engineering department. He believed the information contained therein to be useless. For his part, he was still supplying the necessary information but in another format which in turn was not recognized by the engineers. What seemed to have happened was that the complexity of the new system had forced employees back to manual methods. They understood its information in different ways. To make what was not going to work work they had to reconcile their different perceptions by creating manual links, such as documents, over and above the formal structure, which, of course, added to the complexity. It also meant that despite their efforts the system still did not work.

---

successful launch, and then abandon using their technology in an integrative manner, returning to the 'islands' approach (that is, a computer system, perhaps physically integrated through networks, etc. but perceptually segregated into different functional areas). Information is no longer seen as a resource; indeed its treatment as such is often seen as the culprit and not the technology itself.

Proposition. Information is more than processed data.

Both paradigms recognize a difference between data and information. Computer personnel, for example, have long known of the distinction. Information is seen by them as processed data. The two are interrelated, data being the input to a process, and information the output. In the same way that an output of one system can form the input of another, information from one system can form the data of another. This is consistent with treating information as a resource.

Perceptually-conceived information on the other hand is not the consequence of a formalized process. Data are a factor, but then so are other aspects such as individual traits, culture, structure and political processes. The relationship between data and information is, therefore, not so strong.

Consequence. To work effectively, systems (whether computerized or manual) should be designed to produce data and not information.

This contradicts the objectives implied by the creation of management information systems and data processing. The former allows the individual access to established information, whilst the latter converts data into information. Since the production of information cannot be formalized there is no point in trying to achieve it. Systems should, therefore, be designed to produce the most accurate and readable data in order to enhance easy conversion into information.

The following proposition is a logical consequence of this.

Proposition. It is data, and not information, which is absolute.

When Ligomenides (see above) describes information as a fundamental force, he should be referring to data. Levitan, on the other hand, is correct in claiming information to be dynamic and continuously evolving.[10] The logic of these two views can be seen when data and information are differentiated. It is only data which is time-independent, and therefore unchanging and static – a fundamental force. By this we mean that data retains a constant empirical value: a fact is a fact and cannot be altered. Information, on the other hand, can be altered and changed. It is time-dependent and thus its value can alter from one moment to the next. It is dynamic and evolving because it is determined by an individual's perception. Only data therefore can be absolute.

> Consequence. The integrity of information produced as a resource must be questionable.

It is, indeed, time and utility which transform data into information. If at a particular time a set of data is useful to an individual then it can be described as information. Equally, at another time the same set of data may not have utility and therefore not be information. The data themselves have not changed in any way, remaining always constant. What has changed is the individual's perception of those data. Information is in reality the consequence of a complex psychological process which transforms perceived data into usable thought inputs.

It is, therefore, data which the individual receives from the environment, the brain which transforms these data into information. No formal system can directly pre-empt this stage; thus no formal system can transform data into information.

> Proposition. Information can never be transmitted.

Data can be transformed into different data, transmitted and received. For example, production data submitted to the cost department and processed into second generation costed production data, which are in turn submitted to the financial director.

Information is transformed, in part, from data; it can only be received and never transmitted. The financial director may attach value to costed production data and thus receive it as information. If he/she passes it on, it will once again be as data, perhaps refined into third generation data. The managing director might then receive this data as information and so on.

> Consequence. There is no such thing as an information system.

There cannot be information systems because information is so transient. The individual's subjectivity, which can be developed by training and formal procedure, determines what is information. At another time that perception may be different. Information systems cannot work in this way. Their assumption must be that information is not transient but consistent.

Conclusions

The propositions within this paradigm deny organizations the ability to process their information. Those within it would argue, if they do so at all, that functions exist to produce an output which will have specific data attached to it. Thus a production function produces a good, for example, along with the facts about that particular good. An accounts function produces completed accounts, in one form or another, with relevant attached data. The conversion of this data is done by the individual when they find it of value and act as a consequence.

Such proponents would also argue that this perception of information is the more common one. The typical organization before the emergence of the computer would have been designed in keeping with these ideas. It is the domination of information technology which has forced management into seeing information as a resource. Its integrative nature can only work if the validity of information itself is not questioned.

2.2.3 Why the debate?

Quite obviously information systems do exist in one form or another. They may not be what they claim to be but they are nevertheless working. Is it worth arguing the difference?

The answer to that lies within ourselves. Our actions and behaviour, and consequently our organizations, are governed by our perceptions. If, therefore, we understand information to be permanent rather than transient then how we organize ourselves will be coloured by that. We will design systems which use information as a resource and expect it to be totally consistent.

2.2.4 Structural implications

The difference between these two paradigms may seem subtle, and in terms of information usage it may well be. However, NBS research indicates that the effects upon organizational design can be major. Structural characteristics consequent upon individually-owned information, for instance, can adopt two extremes.

On the one hand they can be organic and informal (adhocracies) whereby all members are seen as contributing equally, each possessing a particular range of techniques to interpret data, whilst at the other extreme there are formal and mechanistic organizations (bureaucracies).

The rigidities of structure stifle any use of information as a resource, so by default such processes are left to the individual.

These contrast with the resource-driven paradigm in which the structural characteristics of organizations are seen to be centrally orientated, with spheres of influence at the periphery, their importance dependent upon the perceived value of particular sets of information.

2.3 The wider implications of information

The development of an organization orientated toward the resource-driven concept of information is well known, and many large firms are aligned in that direction. A sophisticated network is established, more than likely computerized, accessing and distributing information. Particular attention is paid to ensuring standardization of information sets. For example, a piece of costing information is so devised that it can be used by accounts, marketing and production.

These organizations treat all information as their property, attaching to it a value like any other asset. This denies the employee any sense of ownership and tends to detach them from the work process with consequential inefficiencies evolving.

It is asserted that a motivated staff is a contented and efficient staff. One important way to motivate is to give the individual responsibility within their job.[11] Such responsibility is manifest in how much ability a person will be given to determine the information need of their particular function. To standardize information in the way that many corporate systems do, takes away that fundamental element of responsibility. Levitan, on the other hand, would claim this to be an inevitable consequence of increasingly sophisticated corporate structures.[10]

In addition, Karen Levitan and others imply that information which is not used as a resource is inferior. On the contrary, one could argue that giving the individual ownership could result in a greater entrepreneurial drive. Standardization is the killer of innovation.

It is difficult to conceive of any substantial organization, however, where such a degree of individuality could be tolerated. Their size demands a need for cohesion through standardized practice. Therefore it is only in the smaller establishments where such freedom would work. Large organizations which do not treat their information as a resource still exist. Their mechanisms of control, however, are not informal or organic. Indeed, the realities are the converse. Individuality is stifled by greater control, rather than less. No-one is trusted to use information for the organization's good without formal control procedures. Classic examples of such organizations are to be found within the civil service or large quasi-government institutions such as the post office.

2.3.1　A matrix of information control

It has been suggested that there is a relationship between the way in which a firm uses its information and its structure. A matrix can be established differentiating organizations in terms of how they treat their information and the consequential structural characteristics. If, for example, information is plotted against size (another important contingent of organization) four major structural types could be identified (see Figure 2.2). Each is the outcome of the way a particular firm uses its information.

2.3.2　The detail

On the vertical axis of the matrix are the two extremes of information. On the horizontal axis are the two extremes of organizational size. Both information and size are considered to be contingents, that is variables

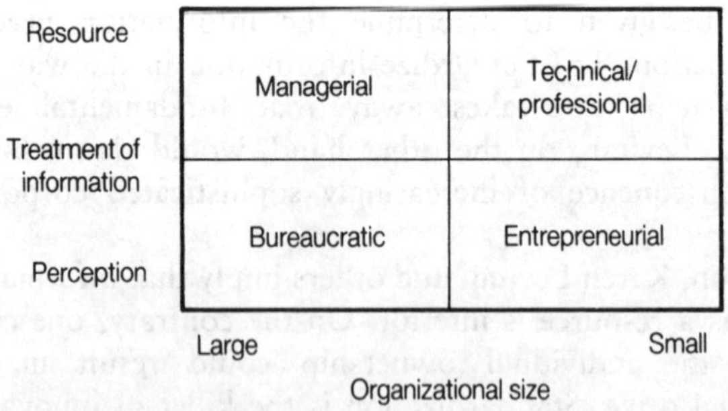

Structure parameters:
    Managerial: larger in size with central/top control
      but with more departmental integration
    Bureaucratic: larger in size with formal structure
      and a diversified control
    Technical/professional: smaller in size with a
      professional body and formal structure
    Entrepreneurial: centrally controlled but with less
      formal structure and smaller in size

Figure 2.2　Information/structure matrix

which affect the characteristics of an organization. The four possible combinations of these two variables determine four organizational structures. Thus each structure is an ideal for each of the four combinations. For example, a managerial structure is the appropriate structure for a large firm using information as a resource.

Research into the validity of such a matrix is by no means complete. There is evidence from the NBS regional survey, for example, that such a correlation does indeed exist. In general, the more successful managerial-style firms tend to treat their information as a resource, whilst the more successful entrepreneurial organizations tend to treat their information as a perceptual phenomenon, and so on. It is not yet certain whether the matrix is predictive, that is implying combinations which are not successful. There is sufficient evidence, however, to support the claim that information usage affects organizational structure.

2.3.3 Not just a resource

The issue of information is much more than whether or not it is a resource. Information is indeed the essence of an organization, shaping and determining its structure. For example, bureaucratic organizations could not effectively treat information as a resource because their mechanisms could not control it that way. A technical/professional organization, on the other hand, is better able to handle its information as a resource because of its structural characteristics.

The implication is that there should be a natural balance between the design of an organization and its information structure. Where this has not been achieved it is because managers are not matching the structure of their organizations with an appropriate usage of information (see Case Study 2.2).

NBS research has also shown that the implementation of computer technology can worsen any potential for imbalance. This is perhaps because of two factors.

Firstly, the characteristics of the technology itself do tend to enhance resource-driven rather than perception-driven information.

Secondly, the greater volume of information generated makes the problem more apparent.

If the matrix in Figure 2.2 is valid then there is neither a right nor a wrong way to control information: much depends upon the individual circumstances. Resource-driven information and perception-driven information are opposite extremes of one continuum. The appropriateness of one or the other will depend upon whether the organizational

CASE STUDY 2.2

The management of a local government organization tried to implement a more client/market-led task environment. This required the client to contact departments, such as housing and engineering, to disseminate information about 'out there' to all the other departments so that everyone could appreciate the current issues concerning the public.

Much of their information as a consequence had been transformed into a resource. User departments were encouraged to implement this information into their operating strategies. On the other hand, the old formal structure was maintained: rigid controls and lines of demarcation where a hierarchical information network was actively enforced.

Problems were soon to appear. In particular the line managers were finding it increasingly difficult to control their departments. Their ability to influence departmental decisions and action was being eroded by information generated outside their boundaries. In many instances their staff were making decisions which affected their department without them being involved. The structures in place did not allow the managers to respond appropriately.

structure is orientated towards an individual or corporate use of information. Thus if information is treated as a resource there is the emphasis on its collective use. If it is not then it is seen as being individually owned.[12]

2.3.4 Information cannot be isolated

Such aspects cannot be seen in isolation. There are other phenomena within an organization which have considerable impact upon information usage and its characteristics. Technology, particularly information technology, is one. It can be a constraint or a determinant. The nature of their relationship can have a bearing not only upon themselves but upon other organizational aspects such as structure. In Chapter 3, therefore, technology is considered and a framework provided for further analysis.

2.4 Summary

There are two perspectives of information, and which one is employed by an organization will have consequences for its design. The first views information as a resource that is easily transportable from one source to the next and possesses consistency in its meaning. The second perspective regards information as the outcome of an individual's own judgement. This tends to make it far less transportable and thus less controllable by management.

NBS research has indicated that the way in which firms utilize their information can determine many of their structural characteristics. Thus if management were to use information as a resource then the necessary structure to control it would be different from one required by the more individualistic view of information. Even without the evidence of a direct causal link between information usage and organizational structure, there is an indirect one through our behaviour. More or less information, good or bad information can affect decisions and hence actions. The outcome of such actions within the context of the organization can affect its structure.

Either way, directly or indirectly, information is a determinant of structure. By implication, the characteristics of the two must be in harmony, otherwise the structure would not be the most appropriate. Simple deduction, therefore, tells us that certain structural types are a better match for a particular information usage than others.

The organizational system in place, whether manual or computerized, has important implications. This is especially so when considering the impact of information technology since the amount of information produced becomes greater thus exacerbating any dysfunctional relationship caused by a mismatch.

REFERENCES

1. McLeod, Raymond. *Management Information Systems.* SRA, 1983.
2. Daniel, Evelyn. 'Information resources and organizational structure', *Journal of the American Society for Information Science,* 1983.
3. Drucker, Peter. *The Age of Discontinuity.* Harper, 1968.
4. Wightman, D.W. 'Competitive advantage through information technology', *Journal of General Management,* vol. 12, no. 4, 1987.
5. Borko, Harold. 'Information and knowledge worker productivity', *Information Processing and Management,* 1983.
6. Simon, Herbert. 'What computers mean for man and society', *Science,* vol. 195, March 1977.
7. Anderson, J.R. and Bower, G.H. *Human Associative Memory.* Winston, 1973.
8. Ligomenides, Panos. 'Notions and dynamics of information', *Journal of Information Science,* 1985. For further details of this perspective, see reference 9.
9. Pettigrew, Andrew. *The Politics of Organizational Decision Making.*

Tavistock, 1973. This book provides an interesting view of the relationship between politics, information and decisions.
10. Levitan, Karen. 'Information resources as "goods" in the life cycle of information production', *Journal of the American Society for Information Science*, 1982.
11. Maslow, A. H. *Motivation and Personality*. Harper & Row, 1970. Provides a sound basis for ideas on motivation.
12. Cullen, Andrew. 'Electronic information services – an emerging market opportunity?', *Telecommunications Policy*, 1986. This paper provides a useful perspective in identifying differences in information.

FURTHER READING

Boisot, Max. *Information and Organisation*. Fontana/Collins, 1987.
Dretske, Fred. *Knowledge and the Flow of Information*. Basil Blackwell, 1981.

CHAPTER 3

Technology and information technology

3.1 What is technology?

If information allows man access to his humanity, then technology has allowed its achievement. Technology is a historical process reflecting the interface between man and his perception of the environment. All societies, no matter how primitive they may appear, possess technology. But how it manifests itself will depend upon how each society views the need for it. Within western culture, for instance, technology has achieved a predominant role in which the technological process and the social process are quite often alienated. Whereas within primitive cultures, much like those still to be found in many parts of the Third World, technology is far more integrated. It is the consequence of those people's lifestyle rather than the driving force behind it. Since the technologies found in these two worlds are so different, a problem can arise when they meet.

Technology appears to be a curious concept which can determine the characteristics of different societies. And yet to the lay person, technology concerns physical attributes, such as machinery and computers, which cannot change but are merely used. This view recognizes only the physical attributes and ignores other more abstract factors. A machine, for instance, is useless to a person without the knowledge to use it. Such knowledge is gained through activities like training, which are in turn elements of the techno-social awareness unique to every society.

This chapter will, therefore, place these difficulties in the context of business and by so doing establish a framework for the analysis of its impact. It will begin by identifying three perspectives of technology based upon traditional wisdom and then demonstrate how they do not easily convert to information technology. It will show that the problem is to be found in the difference between technology *per se* and information technology. That difference is manifest in the ways individuals use and organize their information networks.

3.2   Seeking a definition

Although the Collins English Dictionary (1982 edition) defines technology as 'the total knowledge and skills available to any human society for industry, art, science', it is a difficult concept to define in a single sentence. There are indeed four generic perspectives which must be taken into account. One, the scientific perspective, can be quickly disposed of, not because it lacks importance but because it is not relevant to the objectives of this book. Within this perspective technology is seen as a machine, predictable and controllable, to be analysed and designed, finite and physical. It is also the perspective which is probably the closest to the lay view.

The remaining three perspectives are listed below. Each determines the characteristics of technology from a different academic and experiential basis. Together they provide the background to our present ideas about information technology.

3.2.1   A sociological perspective

Technology within this perspective is seen as a societal phenomenon. It is believed to be an interface between man and his world. It can be a simple tool or a complex production process. The physical aspects, however, are not as important as the behavioural/perceptual aspects. For the sociologist it is the relationship between man and technology, and its effect on social function which are important.

Earlier theorists were particularly interested in production technology. Although relatively late in arrival, Blauner's work is an example of this.[1] He and others, especially Marxists, believed that whoever owned the production processes had the power. Technology did not reflect the need of the worker to produce, but the need of the dominant class to dominate. Divorced from the workforce, and quite often an instrument of oppression, technology had become detached from the social process. This view typically highlighted technology as an alienating factor. Its importance was in terms of production and as such it was a worthwhile prize in the class conflict.

Others in the sociological tradition are not so extreme. Goldthorpe and Lockwood[2] are one example, Wedderburn and Crompton[3] another. They reject this positivist approach and through their extensive studies of mass production workers, suggest that worker behaviour is not determined by technology alone. More important are their expectations of work, which in turn affect their attitudes towards their technology:

the higher their expectations, the more positive their attitudes.

For example, the workers assembling Aston Martin cars are more respected than those assembling Fords. The formers' expectations about their work are consequently higher. They consider themselves to be craftsmen owning their technology, whereas those working for Ford are seen as part of a mass production line in which they could be drilling holes one day and screwing nuts the next. They work as machines and as such their expectations are low. They feel no ownership for what they do, believing that the technology they use belongs to management.

In reality both technologies are owned by the respective managements. However, in Aston Martin's case the more positive attitudes of its workers are reflected in a more organic structure. The negative attitudes of the Ford workers, on the other hand, are reflected in the formal, mechanistic structure of their production line.

There are obviously more factors determining structure than worker behaviour. However, this view's proponents do at least agree with the Marxists on the importance of technology in organizational design. The relationship is not one of confrontation but rather one of social integration. That is, technology allows individuals to have a productive input into society. The capitalist system may have transferred the ultimate ownership of production but its technology is still closely tied to those using it.

The study of worker attitudes and behaviour thus gained increasing importance; the assumption being that those who feel in harmony with their technology, whatever the realities, are likely to be more motivated to use it effectively than those who do not. The Hawthorne Studies conducted by Mayo and his associates in the period between the wars has always been an important source of evidence for this.[4] Although now dated, they did demonstrate how worker attitude could be changed to increase productivity. The right technology was important, but it had to be accompanied by the right attitudes to be used effectively.

Mayo's emphasis on worker behaviour rather than organizational structure did lead the way to a more innovative perception of technology. Until then workers were seen as something apart from the structures of their firms, as they were also separated from their technology. They were related but they were not integrated. Mayo showed that these three elements could not be examined in isolation. The technology and the structure existed only in the minds of the employees and therefore it was ludicrous to attach to them an independent form. As such, it would be more appropriate to see worker behaviour, the technology used and the structure of the firm in which they worked as a single entity. This was subsequently called a sociotechnical system.

One of the first and major exponents of this model was Trist.[5] He conducted a famous study into the effects of new technology in the UK coal mines. He showed how the new machinery and work methods implemented, far from increasing productivity, quite drastically reduced it. His argument was that Coal Board management ignored how the traditional technology formed part of the miner's culture. He concluded that technology must be fully integrated with the social and psychological properties of any workgroup. In doing this he had presented technology as an integrated social process.

Others such as Burns and Stalker,[6] Lawrence and Lorsch[7] and Woodward[8] have also successfully pursued this methodology, but in so doing recognized technology as an important contingent (amongst others such as the environment and size) in influencing organizational design. Theirs is a refined socio-technical perspective in that technology is part of the social process but it may not be the sole determinant of an organization's structure.

In summary, there are three major themes attached to this perspective of technology. Firstly, the theme of technology as an alienating factor driving a wedge between owner and worker. Secondly, the theme of technology as an integrating force cementing together disparate elements of an organization. Thirdly, the theme of technology as a social process whereby an organization's elements are far from being disparate but fully integrated within one system. Whichever is believed – and each has its own advantages and disadvantages – they all have the same contribution to make: to highlight the impact that technology has on our lives.

3.2.2   A political perspective

Technology is seen as an important element in the political processes of nation-states. This is manifest not only in sophisticated armaments, but also in its use as a means of domination. For example, in the so-called cold war each side used its vast stocks of weaponry as a threat. The intention was not to conquer but to force others to do their will.

A typical example of this approach is to be found in Von Clausewitz's classic book.[9] He determined diplomacy particularly to be the technology of peace, and war to be the consequence of its failure. Smoke[10] or McNeill[11] are more modern examples of this tradition. They and others see war as a social process (albeit rather extreme) with identifiable elements such as technology which play a role in its continuity. Yet more have a softer view. Stoessinger for example, is representative of a group interested in the world as an international arena.[12] Nation-states have influence in the world because they possess powerful technologies. Within a nation-state itself, governments have control because they own the military technology.[13] On the other hand, H.M. Drucker talks of ideology as a political technology.[14]

The common denominator in all these perspectives is to see technology, in whatever form, as a political weapon. This is not necessarily confined to national and military aspects. Indeed, governments are increasingly using 'civilian' technology in their international manoeuvres by calling on the technological muscle of their business organizations. A classic example of this is the US government's control of computer technology. Since most of this technology is either US-owned or licensed, they are able to refuse access to it for countries identified as hostile.

The idea of technology as a political weapon has taken on greater significance in the past few years, especially in terms of an organization's competitive strategy. Technological innovation, for example, is seen by people such as Galliers[15] or Porter[16] in political and strategic terms. Managements use their technology not only to produce but also to aid them in the pursuit of their objectives. One firm in north-east England implemented a computer integrated manufacturing system to increase efficiency. They hoped that a useful side-effect to this, however, would be to eliminate the competition through a more complex production process. If their competitors were to compete successfully they too would have to adopt the process. Unfortunately the expertise to do this took years to develop, which was too long to prevent their being driven out of the market themselves.

In this case the technology was not solely a production process but also a political weapon aiding management in their strategy. With the emergence of information technology, in particular, the scope for managements to use their technology in both external and internal strategy has considerably increased. Pettigrew, for example, viewed information and its technology as determining the political processes of an organization by its positioning on a network.[17] In this instance technology is more of an abstract force affecting the way employees interact.

To summarize, the political perspective views technology as a tool rather than a process. Its contribution has been to show that technology is not merely to do with production or social processes, it can be used as a weapon.

Once again there are three major themes which can be identified. Firstly, the traditional idea that technology is an instrument of conflict. Governments use it to control and defeat others. It is spatially identifiable, in that it is a phenomenon and not a process.

Secondly, the view that technology is a political weapon in either the national or international arena. Governments use their national technologies to bend other nations or groups to their will. Once again it is spatially identified but more abstract in form.

The third form is a refinement of the second. Technology is a political weapon but one that is more integrated into a social process and thus not so easily identifiable in spatial terms. This is no longer purely a political perspective but one which developed from that in order to accommodate the information technologies.

3.2.3   An economic perspective

The economist considers technology to be a resource: that is, factors of production to be exploited by the market or industry. Their prime objective is not to analyse how it and the individual interact but rather how it can change the market, industry or the national and international economy. On the micro level of analysis, for instance, technology is considered to be given, even exogenous. In any analytical framework a firm has a fixed technological stock which in the short term it could not change. Only through investment in the long term could that situation change. Work by Kogiku[18] on microeconomic models, or Leibenstein[19] on the firm and Meyer[20] on decisions, are typical of this approach.

In terms of technological analysis the more interesting perspective is on a macro level. Technology has always been seen as important for innovation, and innovation itself is the fuel for social and economic change. Schumpeter, in particular, demonstrated how important these aspects are by identifying clusters of innovation which form the foundation for an economy's next stage of development.[21] Technology has become more than a resource, it is a societal phenomenon, almost a process, allowing for nothing less than survival itself. This idea has been utilized by others, such as Whynes,[22] in their analysis of economic development. To achieve the transformation from an underdeveloped to a developed economy, it is necessary to have the right technology (see also Hoogvelt[23]). Dicken,[24] amongst many others, sees this not only as a problem for the Third World but for everyone, in terms of getting the technology right. Too many fossil fuel burning power stations, or too many cars and so on could lead to our early demise.

In recent years the interest in technological change has shifted from a global to a national level. The economic slump of the 1970s made the problems of the Third World seem of secondary importance. This was also coupled with the increasing emergence of information technology as a social and economic force. The elation of earlier years that this new technology was going to solve all our problems soon gave way to concern about how it could be most appropriately utilized.

Williamson's work on organizations, their information and technology heralded the popularization of an alternative approach based upon institutional analysis.[25] It also allowed for a positive contribution by the economist in understanding technology as a social and organizational force. The Centre for Urban and Regional Development Studies (CURDS), for example, has been at the head of this thrust by recognizing both the social and resource consequences of technology, in particular information technology.[26]

To summarize, the economic perspective is more cohesive than the other two. Most economists see it as a resource and a phenomenon rather than a process. The difference lies in how they subsequently integrate that into their models. The earlier economists generally saw it as a given in the short term which could be changed in the long term only by investment. Other themes are a development from this. These describe technology as less an exogenous factor and more a controllable and usable force of change. This view is manifest in development economics or technological change. In the past few years, in particular, such ideas have been applied increasingly to information technology.

3.3 Information technology

Information technology, although technology *per se*, is nevertheless something quite radically different. When sociologists and economists talk of technology they refer more often than not to the production process of a society or industry. It is seen as the interface between humanity and the environment or as a useful resource, and in many cases as an agent of change. With the advent of the computer, however, such perspectives were no longer appropriate. The effects of the computer and its accompanying systems went well beyond any societal interface by possessing a range of capabilities which could directly change social structures.

3.3.1 What is the difference?

Computers are not as crucial to our survival as the plough or indeed the typical production process. They can create employment like any utilized technology, but their importance is more as an enabling mechanism allowing a greater power to understand the environment, as opposed to interacting with it. Through such understanding humanity may be more effective. For example, space travel became a possibility only after the development of the computer. The environment in which agencies such as NASA have to operate are so complex that no manual system could have coped.

This difference is the essence of any discussion on the attributes of information technology. Other technologies will help an individual to achieve a better wheat crop or to get from A to B. These forms quite obviously utilize some technique or knowledge, but their subsequent users need only possess a knowledge sufficient for their use, they do not have to understand why they work. So, too, with information technology many would argue.

General technology, however, is restricted to a knowledge base constrained by its own design parameters. For example, if I drive a car I do not expect to end my journey considerably more knowledgeable than when I started it. I have at my disposal a range of information, some of which I can obtain independently through observation, more through the use of other technology such as the speedometer, etc. All of this combines to enable me to interact with my environment. The anticipated outcome is to move at speed over a certain distance. I may well perceive the world slightly differently at such a speed, but the knowledge I have gained is directly attributable to the operating environment of my technology. In other words I am tied into a particular knowledge base from which there is no escape until other forms of technology and their corresponding knowledge bases are used. Since, therefore, my actions and knowledge are governed by the nature of this interaction, my perception is also bounded by it.[27] (See Figure 3.1.)

Information technology, on the other hand, transcends the knowledge base constraints of general technology and gives the user access to a theoretically limitless perceptual field. Whether the user utilizes this effectively will depend upon the abilities of the individuals and the structural constraints of their organization. In ideal conditions, at least, information technology gives us access to large integrative databases allowing construction of knowledge which is not achievable in traditional manual systems. No longer constrained by the technological and social process, our understanding of the environment significantly increases.

Some business organizations, for example, may not have become so large without the processing power of information technology. Their environments would have been so complex, in terms of information flow and decision requirements, that there would not have been the necessary support from manual systems. In other words, until the

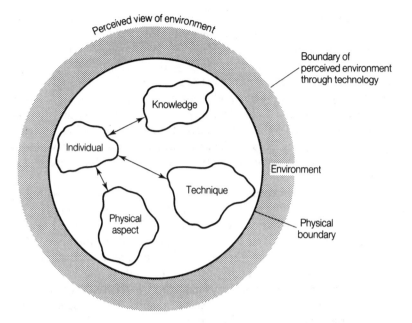

Figure 3.1 Technological framework

emergence of the computer, firms were constrained by the capabilities of inefficient systems. The computer allowed them to expand beyond these constraints and achieve growth hitherto unseen.

3.3.2 A model proposed

A distinction, therefore, has to be made between general technology and information technology. General technology is constrained by its physical domain. That does not mean it has to be a machine or something physically tangible, it can be an abstract process such as management technology. What it does mean is that the technology, machine or process, cannot generate perceptions beyond its own design parameters. Information technology, on the other hand, can. And yet, like all technology, it does have physical attributes. The interface between people and these knowledge structures is the physical equipment: to access them we have to use hardware and software.

There are, therefore, two dimensions for all technology: the physical domain and the perceptual domain. The physical constraints of general technology make it biased towards the physical domain, whilst the converse is true for information technology.

We focus on information technology. Firstly, there is the physical dimension of the machines themselves – the hardware. When we use information technology, we do so through physical technology such as computer keyboards, modems and printers. We are interacting with our environment through a technological process, as we do with any other form of technology. To this extent our information technology is just as much governed by the laws of the physical domain, so that it would be foolish to expect this technology to do anything else but process data and information.

Secondly, the perceptual dimension gives information technology greater power by giving it the ability to tap into and manipulate our perceptions through its knowledge structures. This is profound because firms are themselves driven by the perceptions of its members. Thus information technology has the potential to change the characteristics of our organizations by changing our perceptions.

The split between the physical and perceptual domains of technology is not a simple one. Some general technologies have a greater perceptual domain than others. For example, a complex machine has a greater perceptual domain than a simple tool. In the same way, some information technologies have less perceptual power than others. A standalone microcomputer, for example, has less perceptual power than a network. This can be represented by a continuum (Figure 3.2) with the physical domain and the perceptual domain as its extremes.

Information technology in general, therefore, would be positioned towards the latter end of this continuum. However, such an approach would also allow us to differentiate between different information technologies, or indeed to differentiate between differing usage configurations of the same hardware.

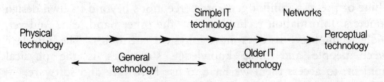

Figure 3.2 Physical/perceptual continuum

3.3.3   Old and new

This analysis clearly identifies differences in terms of perceptual impact between the simple information technologies (such as a compass), the older complex information technologies (such as standalone mainframe and minicomputers) and the new information technologies, which include sophisticated communication networks. The difference between the first two – simple and older complex information technologies – is the latter's ability to attain a degree of environmental independence and consequently to process information quickly (and beyond the immediacy of the particular interaction). The difference between the second two – older complex information technology and communication networks – is an even greater environmental independence (although not necessarily greater processing speed) through network communication systems. The more complex forms of information technology (both older and newer), therefore, differ from the simpler forms by the latter possessing no environmental independence. Thus all technology can be differentiated by whether it possesses environmental independence, and, if it does, in having such independence, the scale of that independence.

3.3.4   The human element

Information technology is thus defined in terms of both the physical and perceptual aspects. However, there is also the human element, without which the two domains are meaningless. At some stage the data and information sets must be understood and related to in the form of knowledge. This does not have to be a continuous process since the points of particular interest are only those where the knowledge base is accessed and acted upon. Fully automated processes, for example, can easily operate control systems without too much intervention. And yet their interest for us lies not in the production but rather in how they affect people's behaviour. Interaction, therefore, takes place at points along a historical continuum which can and does govern individual or group perception of the environment. What is perceived and created yesterday can and does have an impact upon the information people perceive and create today. As such, the organizational knowledge base is accessed by input or output at particular times in the process which can then determine future relationships. This may be termed historical interaction.

   An example of historical interaction could be found in accessing a database. The basis of this has been determined by past decisions. It is then used in the creation of both present and future decisions which themselves change the database to some extent. What makes a computerized system more powerful than any manual system is its interactive capability.

General technology, by contrast, has no historical interaction since it is contained within, and thus constrained by, its physical parameters. The interaction generated in this case between man and machine is translated through the present. (Accessing a knowledge base is an interaction of sorts in terms of techniques, but such a process is not a stored transformation nor time-independent.)

Production process technology, for example, is organized into a unique operating line which produces a predetermined output. There is interaction between the technology and the labour of that line, if only to press a button or to download raw materials as required. Knowing when or how to interact is catered for by labour's own knowledge gained from experience and the technology itself. But the ability to manipulate information into knowledge constructs within the physical parameters of the technology is limited to the particular process. To do anything beyond that context would be meaningless since the logic of the physical application and its information flow is constrained by the boundaries set through its relationship with the specific environment.

3.4   The importance of perception

Much of the power, therefore, from the complex information technologies arises out of their ability to change our perception of environments, so enabling us to act differently within them. The world we see is one coloured by our own perceptions and experiences, molded by a complex and continual process of socialization.

We live successfully because we are able to translate relevant data into an understanding of our environment. What is or is not relevant depends upon our perception. The weighting that each of us put on different sets of environmental data will affect our view of the world. Indeed, on many occasions we may well misinterpret data or be unable to understand them, so that our perception differs from other times when we have more complete data. But who is to say which is right and which is wrong? No matter how uniform we try to be within the framework of an organization, for example, no two of us will see it in exactly the same way. There is, therefore, no ultimate reality, no ultimate truth we can all fall back on to assess the accuracy of our knowledge. The best we can do is to identify a consistency of many perceptions within a given tolerance and call that 'the norm', against which deviancy is judged.

3.4.1 Physical and perceptual aspects

To operate more effectively we try to simplify the complexity which confronts us by assuming what we perceive is absolute. We can, after all, touch a door or a typewriter, and therefore regard such physical things as the norm by which to judge our total perception. The abstract, intangible interaction we see between two people, for instance, which we cannot touch but only observe, is translated in the same physical and absolute terms. We thus regard such a perception as concrete and indisputable. What we receive through our senses governs only part of our perception, and yet our social constructs are built upon the premise that they are all there is. We have a legal system based upon bearing witness, we have an educational system based upon empirical evidence, and we have a business system based upon the perceived physical constraints of our environment. There seems to be no recognition in any of our institutions for the perceptual part which is every bit as real.

This, then, is where our difficulty lies in understanding the characteristics of information technology. If we interpret our world in terms of physical reality and relate all in it to that concept, then we would have difficulty in accepting a purely abstract form as being real because it does not conform to our norm. We therefore dismiss those aspects as being irrelevant and concentrate upon something which can provide us with what we seek, or indeed ignore it completely. The classic example of this is to be found with information technology. Because our view of the environment cannot cope with complete abstraction, we tend to ignore the perceptual aspects of information technology and concentrate upon its physical side such as hardware organization and data processing. The perceptual factors, we would argue, cannot be real because we cannot see or touch them.

But they are real. Indeed, taking into account the way in which our perception works they are perhaps more real than our physical environment. If we accept that the power of information technology is derived from the perceptual dimension, then it is an easy step to conclude that information technology might drastically colour our view of the environment.

This is, of course, much more than the bounded perception of the general technological process we have already discussed. It is concerned with the creation of completely new knowledge structures which, rather than bound our perception and rationality, expand them beyond our physically constrained environment. As such our perception and our consequential action, through the organizational dynamics such as the decision process, can be altered.

A possible example of this effect could be the experience of the Stock Exchange after the 'Big Bang' when all the systems were computerized. An internal report suggested that the financial collapse a few months later was in part generated by the information technology. The inefficiencies of information transfer in the old manual system allowed 'thinking' time between transactions. The super-efficient computer system started to generate a completely different perceptual environment in which no one had time to think. Prices of stocks were being hyped up by the quick responses of the network, and it was only a matter of time before it all came tumbling down.

3.4.2 Computers as experts

Weizenbaum has conducted detailed studies on how we interact with the new technologies and how they might change our perception.[28] He describes situations where volunteers have been seated before a microprocessor in a predefined role in which the computer is given the status of an expert and they the client. A typical example was a medical scenario where the computer, through application software, adopted the role of a doctor and the volunteer was the patient. The expert system processed by the computer questioned the patient closely as to the state of his/her health and then made certain subsequent recommendations dependent upon outcome. Weizenbaum was primarily interested in the operation of his piece of software. He nevertheless observed that even though the volunteer was placed in an artificially constrained situation by the technology, after initial hesitation the patients began to develop a pseudo-personal relationship with the computer. Despite it being no more than a machine they were prepared to treat it as a person – in particular as a doctor, an expert.

Their perception of the environment was being changed by the technological process. So that rather than interacting with it in terms of the physical technology (the computer and the application software), they found themselves creating a perceptual domain which tried to mirror what they expected a normal relationship with such an expert to be. For the purposes of the experiment this particular perceptual world determined their action. However, it was limited. The technology itself was isolated in laboratory conditions and confined to limited information. The individuals themselves were not part of an organizational or informational network which could be tapped or manipulated, they were on their own.

Weizenbaum, however, saw beyond the limitations of this experiment to far wider implications. Complete formal decision processes of organizations turned over to 'complex computer systems' which only a few could understand. This was the scenario he saw all too often in many of our business enterprises: the illusion that we are in control of an environment which is far from controllable and created by our perception of the expertise of the technology, in a similar vein to Weizenbaum's experiment. In effect the perceptual dimension of organization is no longer in tune with the physical aspect of it.

This has implications other than Weizenbaum's own interpretation which link in with the subject matter of the next chapter. Individuals are spatially and temporally positioned within the organization by their perception of it. Therefore, how they act, what roles they adopt, the alliances or enmities they pursue will to some extent depend upon the nature of such perception. If indeed we agree that information technology can alter perception of the environment, then we must also accept that people will act differently within that environment as a consequence. This, in turn, will have ramifications upon the structure of organizations.

3.5 Summary

There four major perspectives of technology which have contributed to our understanding of its impact. Firstly, the scientific perspective which regards technology as machines and not much else. Secondly, the sociological perspective which portrays technology as a social phenomenon. Thirdly, the political perspective which views technology as a tool in a political process. Lastly there is the economic perspective which sees technology as a resource to be managed. Together they give us the ability to analyse technology in all its forms, except, that is, information technology.

Information technology's peculiar characteristics require a different form of interpretation. A promising way forward is by understanding all technology in terms of its physical and perceptual domains. General technology is orientated in the physical domain. It does have perceptual aspects but the way it is used and understood is in terms of the constraints placed upon it by the environment. Information technology, on the other hand, has physical aspects which are immediately obvious when we use a printer or tap a keyboard, but its real power lies in the perceptual domain. Through the knowledge constructions that it builds it has the power to change the way we see the world and ultimately the way we act in organizations.

The implication from all this seems to be that we are implementing technology which we do not really understand. The criteria we use to determine whether information technology is successful or not is efficiency-driven and based upon the physical domain. In other words, since it produces more output more quickly it must be successful. We are evaluating our computer systems as if they are production processes. What we are not doing is looking to the wider effects: because we cannot see its impact upon our perceptions we ignore it. Yet there are, no doubt, many situations where it would have been better had information technology not been implemented in the first place because of its dire effects on the organization's perceptual domain.

We need not only new ideas about the technology, but also new concepts of organization for them to relate to. This is dealt with in the following chapter.

REFERENCES

1. Blauner, Robert. *Alienation and Freedom*. University of Chicago Press, 1964.
2. Goldthorpe, J.H. and Lockwood, D. *The Affluent Worker: Industrial Attitudes and Behaviour*. Cambridge University Press, 1968.
3. Wedderburn, D. and Crompton, R. *Workers' Attitudes and Technology*. Cambridge University Press, 1972.
4. Mayo, George Elton. *The Human Problems of an Industrial Civilization*. Harvard Business School, 1933.
5. Trist, Eric, *et al. Organizational Choice*. Tavistock, 1963.
6. Burns, T. and Stalker, G. *The Management of Innovation* (2nd edn). Tavistock, 1968.
7. Lawrence, P. and Lorsch, P. *Organization and Environment*. Harvard Graduate School of Business Administration, 1967.
8. Woodward, Joan. *Industrial Organization: Theory and Practice* (2nd edn). Oxford University Press, 1980.
9. Clausewitz, Karl Von. *On War*. Modern Library, 1943.
10. Smoke, Richard. *War*. Harvard University Press, 1977.
11. McNeill, William. *The Pursuit of Power*. University of Chicago Press, 1982.
12. Stoessinger, John. *The Might of Nations* (4th edn). Random House, 1973.
13. Alford, Robert and Friedland, Roger. *Powers of Theory*. Cambridge University Press, 1986.
14. Drucker, H. *The Political Uses of Ideology*. Macmillan, 1974.
15. Galliers, R. 'Information systems and technology planning within a competitive strategy framework', in *Information Management. State of the Art Report*, P. Griffiths (ed.). Pergamon, 1986.
16. Porter, Michael. 'From competitive advantage to corporate strategy', *Harvard Business Review*, vol. 65, issue 3, 1987.
17. Pettigrew, Andrew. *The Politics of Organizational Decision Making*. Tavistock, 1973.

18. Kogiku, K. *Microeconomic Models.* Harper & Row, 1971.
19. Leibenstein, Harvey. *Beyond Economic Man.* Harvard University Press, 1980.
20. Meyer, Robert. *Microeconomic Decisions.* Houghton Mifflin, 1976.
21. Schumpeter, Joseph. *The Theory of Economic Development.* Oxford University Press, 1961.
22. Whynes, David. *Comparative Economic Development.* Butterworths, 1983.
23. Hoogvelt, Ankie. *The Sociology of Developing Societies.* Macmillan, 1976.
24. Dicken, Peter. *Global Shift.* Harper & Row, 1986.
25. Williamson, Oliver. *Market and Hierarchies: Analysis and Antitrust Implications.* Free Press, 1975.
26. Amin, A. and Goddard, J. (eds). *Technological Change, Industrial Restructuring and Regional Development.* Allen & Unwin, 1986.
27. Simon, Herbert. *The New Science of Management Decision.* Harper, 1960.
28. Weizenbaum, Joseph. *Computer Power and Human Reason.* W.H. Freeman, 1976.

FURTHER READING

Drucker, Peter. *The New Realities.* Heinemann, 1989.
Gunton, Tony. *Infrastructure: Building a Framework for Corporate Information Handling.* Prentice Hall, 1989.

CHAPTER 4
Organization and structure

4.1 Introduction

It is only since the Second World War that interest in organizational structure has developed, culminating perhaps in Woodward's survey of manufacturing firms between 1953 and 1957.[1] It is not coincidental that interest in both technology and organizational structure developed at the same time. Woodward's identification of a deterministic relationship between the two only confirmed what many had long suspected. With increasing information technology implementation in our organizations the linkage is considered by people such as Michael Porter to be even stronger.[2] Structure has thus become a central theme in organization theory, encouraging a less reductionist and more holistic view.

The sociologist has long been aware of structure as an important societal concept. Merton[3] and Parsons,[4] for example, are indicative of this. But their concern was not particularly for the organization but rather general social institutions, of which the organization is one. The explanation of organizational structure was, therefore, left to two mainstream approaches. The first was the economic model whereby the business organization was subsumed into the market. Structure was thus defined as an extension to the market. The second was through the Taylorist and management science movements, where organizations were seen as no more than vehicles for management control. In neither case was sufficient analytical sensitivity provided to appreciate the close relationship between structure and its technology.

Today, different ideas about organization are prolific. The traditional views are still around but there are many others which have greater sophistication and which span a range of academic disciplines. They can be condensed into three major perspectives or metaphors.

Scott, for example, identified these as follows.[5] Firstly, organizations are rational systems, based upon some collective rationale such as profit maximization or growth. This perspective also embraces the two approaches already mentioned above. Secondly, organizations are natural systems; arising from the behaviourist movement of Elton Mayo this perspective views organizations as a living organism. Thirdly, organizations as open systems which are seen as processes being open to the environment.

Watson, on the other hand, identified 'waves' of organization theory.[6] The first sees organizations as machines, portraying the view that, like machines, they are predictable. The second wave sees organizations as organisms to demonstrate that they are as complex and unpredictable as a living organism. The final wave sees organizations as processes, thus highlighting their dependence upon interactive behaviour. Others, such as Gareth Morgan,[7] have gone further in identifying metaphors of organization (brain, machine, psychological prison, etc.) that we use to aid our understanding of them.

Whichever perspective is supported, they all agree that organization structure provides some form of framework. Using the headings provided by Tony Watson, this chapter assesses each of them. It pays particular attention to their suitability to provide a sound foundation for an understanding of the impact of information technology. In order to do this, however, structure itself must first be defined.

4.2 What is structure?

Mintzberg's book places considerable emphasis on structure and his definition proposes it as the summation of the ways in which a firm's labour is directed and co-ordinated into tasks.[8] Although this definition's simplicity is appealing, it leads us to view an organization in terms of a division of labour and the co-ordination of management control to maintain that. It is an outlook typically portrayed by the firm's organization/management chart, which identifies quite precisely who is responsible for what and to whom. This merely lists a functional relationship, which although important, reveals only part of the organization structure.

Handy hints that there may be more when he talks of linking mechanisms between roles and co-ordinating structures.[9] Although the elements of line control and co-ordination are still present, Handy extends his definition to cover the perceptual domains of an organization. This can lead to a more open definition. The concept of linkages increases our awareness of both interdependence and independence between factions; of how resource groupings can either contradict or complement other resource groupings. Linkaging is, therefore, necessary to cement the otherwise contradictory elements to prevent dispersal, or to reaffirm the complementary to prevent them becoming contradictory. Linkaging, therefore, provides the organization with its completeness, establishes a boundary (perceptual or physical) which can be identified as being the domain of a particular organization.

The idea of a boundary is an important aspect of structure since it enables us to determine how integrated the structure is with both its internal and external environments. For managers also, the boundary is useful since it enables them to identify their area of control.

However, with the increasing implementation of information technology the issue has taken on greater significance. Boundaries can no longer be so easily identified. Modern technological systems directly link organizations into other organizations, thus merging in part their established boundaries. For example, a major retail outlet requires all its suppliers to link into their own stock control network. Those firms have thus become tied into their customer. In this situation it is difficult to determine where the supplier's boundary ends and the customer's begins.[10]

4.2.1 The perceptual constraints of a boundary

Robbins proposes a traditional view of the relationship between a structure and its boundary.[11] He determines the structure being defined by its boundary in the same way that a human skeleton defines a person. However, by equating boundary with human skeletons he has missed an important point. The body of a person is a finite concept in that it is spatially bounded within the physical domain. On the other hand, an organizational structure, although providing a framework, is as much perceptual as physical. That is, it exists because its members perceive it to do so. To someone who does not understand the concept of an organization, the distribution of its physical resources has no significance and thus they will not see an organization.

This problem is not as remote as it may appear. It is common, for example, for small business organizations to share resources such as office space, equipment and even staff, therefore possessing the same physical structure. There is no suggestion, however, that they are the same organization. Their differentiation is thus established by the perception of the actors (employees, suppliers, customers, etc.) and not the physical aspects.

Organizations are not like people even though they comprise them. They are not necessarily spatially bounded; their buildings, for example, do not represent their outer edges. Indeed, some organizations have no formality about them or physical structure, such as some political or religious institutions, but they are just as real as a small business enterprise. Organizations are not bounded by a temporal framework in the same way that people are. Individuals have their historicities which influence their behaviour, but they are creatures of the here and now. Their socialization has made them believe that all there exists is the physical domain which is governed by the present. The operational levels of organizations are also bounded by time and the physical domain. However, the structure is not. It exists in the minds of its members and therefore is in the present, but it is also equally valid in the past because its existence is just as dependent upon past interaction.

For example, a firm's production process, which forms part of its structure, is physically bounded by time. It can produce only so many items within an hour or a day. This is its operational level – the dimension of doing. But the same process is time independent because how it can produce is and will be determined by decisions taken in the past, the present and the future.

Structure, therefore, has to be more than a static framework of functional and co-ordinative hierarchy, because organizations themselves are fluid, perceptual entities and as such could not be supported by a rigid framework. Robbins' model of complexity, formalization and centralization does suggest a certain fluidity in structure, but only to the extent of differentiation between particular organizations and not within the unit itself. In other words, Robbins recognizes an infinite variety of structures befitting the mode of operation, but once set they provide a rigid framework in the short term which can be changed only in the longer term. This definition would certainly not suit Watson.[6]

4.2.2 Complexity and vagueness

Watson's ideas about an organization's structure provide a better match for a considerably more complex form of structure than so far developed. He does not see structure as a given framework but rather as a fluid, abstract entity which is the outcome of ever-changing employee interaction. Such a view can present no definitive solution to the quest for perfection, because the outcome is dependent upon so many variables.

With such a cost comes also a benefit. There is a freeing of structure from the constraints of 'conventional wisdom', by allowing greater flexibility in organization design and therefore enabling a more appropriate framework to be established for the analysis of the impact of other forces such as technology.

CASE STUDY 4.1

A medium-sized service company visited during the NBS research project had implemented an integrated, networked computer system. Managers quickly found that their established organizational structure was under threat. This was formal and hierarchical in that there was a rigid demarcation between functions and roles. The maintenance of such depended upon physical boundaries and control mechanisms constraining individual worker perceptions.

Managers found, however, that the computer network short-cut these management-imposed boundaries. Particular individuals were discovered doing job functions which belonged to other areas. The reason always given was that it was logical for one person to follow a process through since they had access to all the information and it required no further effort. The task structure had been reorganized almost by default.

The structure was changing because the employees' perception of it was changing. In effect there were two structures in place: the one imposed by management and the other arising naturally from interactions developing from the computer implementation. As these managers soon discovered, the structure is not owned solely by them. It is the consequence of everyone and its boundaries can never be permanently fixed, and are therefore difficult to control.

Watson's words reflect a school of thought which considers the only reality of an organization is to be found within our minds (see Morgan[7]). The structure we put on that organization is also within our minds. It will change as people's actions and perceptions change, and can never be completely controlled. Innovating forces like information technology, for example, can have the greatest impact upon an organization's structure through the minds of its participants. Structural change could occur through differing actions/perceptions of the employees, which may be beyond the control of management (see also Case Study 4.1).

4.2.3   Organizations may not be definitive

Structure, therefore, must be seen to be more than a rigid framework. It may well be that some organizational structures have become increasingly flexible in the past few years as a consequence of their information technology systems. However, it would also seem likely that structures have never been as rigid as many would suggest. Some are more stable than others within a given period. Others are more responsive to certain situations such as crisis or particular market conditions. They may all have areas of rigidity within them which can subsequently cause problems.

Whatever their apparent characteristics they are manifest not because of the way we organize our physical resources but rather as a consequence of the way we relate to those resources. Structure is indeed in our minds. As such any boundaries which are obvious to us are there only because we perceive them to be. If we then introduce a technology with a strong perceptual impact, such as information technology, it is not surprising that a change occurs in the way we view our organization. Such changed perception may lead to a changed structure.

4.3 The waves of organization theory

The idea that organizations are perceptual maps has implications for their analysis and design. How we view them, and hence how they manifest themselves, will depend upon the particular organizational model we use. Thus in a self-determining way we align our particular organization's characteristics, as far as possible, to those found within the model which matches our own opinions. For example, if I believe along with my colleagues that the most realistic metaphor for an organization is a machine in terms of formality and controllability, then our behaviour would be governed by that belief. The organizational structure would then be affected and to a limited extent changed by such perceptions if there is not a match (see Morgan[7]). Problems can occur, of course, if these perceptions are not fully disseminated throughout the organization.

The models of organization we have, therefore, are themselves affecting the environment which they are attempting to analyse. From this aspect alone it is worth while determining what these models are. However, we need to also consider them in terms of their suitability for the impact analysis of information technology.

4.3.1 Organizations as machines (first wave)

The mechanistic view of organization is the first wave of theory, which comprises the metaphor of organization as a machine. Like a machine, its characteristics are determinable and controllable. The degree of its formality is not considered because all actions and behaviour within it are considered to be purposeful and co-ordinated. In other words, organizations are rational processes. Therefore the underlying assumption is one of an organization as a formalization of a need to meet certain objectives. Such objectives are seen as rational in that they are based upon an obvious range of criteria suitable for the type of organization. Thus a business organization's objectives could be to maximize profits, to grow or to dominate a particular market or industry. The emphasis is on goal attainment and its management. The profound question presented by this metaphor is, why are some managements better at achieving their objectives than others?

This metaphor evolved from the economic model in which organizations are perceived to be unitary entities pursuing the same collective objective, controlled and driven by market forces. As such, organizations do not have any analytical value other than as a unit of the market.

From this, however, four softer perspectives developed, each a response to the demand of business managements at the time for better understanding. The first is Taylor's scientific management. The second is administrative principles proposed by people such as Henri Fayol. The third is Weber's theory of bureaucracy, and lastly Simon's discussion on administrative behaviour. There are many books which cover these areas quite adequately (see Watson,[6] Morgan[7] and Scott[5]). Apart from an introduction below, these will not be dealt with in detail. The emphasis will be placed on examining their approaches to technology.

The scientific approach

The founding father of the scientific movement is claimed to be Frederick Taylor[12] and subsequently developed by others such as Lillian Gilbreth. Their perspective is an extension of the economic model by recognizing that organizations are not determined solely by market forces but can be molded by management activity. They prescribed a methodology for action through a scientific analysis of tasks in a firm so that formal procedures could be established for optimum efficiency. The approach, in short, is prescriptive in that it presents patterns for management behaviour.

Although lacking in fundamental academic support the traditions of scientific management are still reflected in many of our management training programmes. The 'modern' view is more developed in its recognition of greater uncertainty but nevertheless still portrays a controllable environment.[13] The elements of that environment are also controllable. Thus the notion of technology is coloured by the certainty of its predictability.

Technology in all its forms is a management tool. The original exponents of scientific management thought this, as do their followers. There is no relationship between a structure and its technology because neither is seen as a social process but rather as building blocks for management use. Thus the impact of innovations such as information technology is not seen to affect the organizational structure as such, but rather the relationship between management and workers: any impact is regarded as an input to be controlled. Innovation, therefore, changes only the way in which management operates (although this might have an indirect effect upon the organization itself).

Impact assessment of information technology is in terms of functional analysis or efficiency criteria (how good or bad its contribution is to management objectives), the assumption being that the technology will always fit into existing organizational structures with the appropriate implementation strategy. The emphasis, therefore, is on performance measures and the ability of information technology to meet them. There is a range of literature which explores the scientific management viewpoint of information technology.[14] Its presentation is prescriptive and consultative.

Administrative principles

The remaining three perspectives within this metaphor are dealt with under the one heading. They are the models initiated by Fayol,[15] Weber[16] and Simon.[17] Their collation is not because the themes they support are necessarily in agreement, although they do cover broadly the same principles, but rather because their implications for the analysis of technology are similar.

The major difference between these and the previous approaches is that scientific management sought to establish the organization as a management phenomenon whereas Fayol, Weber and Simon sought to establish the organization as an administrative process. The immediate implication of this is that, as an administrative process, the organization is less controllable and less predictable. It is no longer a tool but a set of administrative interactions. The objective of this group, therefore, was to identify such interactions and then to determine their appropriate control.

Fayol was perhaps the first to recognize the importance of the administrative process in understanding organization. However, his work was not translated until the late 1940s and thus not widely known. The initiation of such an approach in the English-speaking world was left to Gulick and Urwick.[18] In about the same period (between the wars) a sociologist, Max Weber, was also developing an ideological set of administrative principles.[16] He identified bureaucracy as being the ideal form of organization. The formal and impersonal structural characteristics allowed for the most appropriate administrative processes and for an efficient achievement of objectives coupled with a certain humanity.

Although advances were being made in other areas, it was not until the late 1950s, with the appearance of Herbert Simon's ideas, that advances in this area were made. He sought to portray a more open administrative process in which the actors are not machine-like in their rationality but more human in pursuing their own interests and in many ways ignorant of their total environment. He saw their rationality bounded by the complexity of the environment and thus their decision-making was not perfect or indeed predictable. Simon, along with others such as Cyert and March,[19] perhaps provided the link between this metaphor and the second wave (see below). They viewed people as being less predictable than did their forebears, but still nevertheless determined the organization itself to be of machine-like stature.

As a consequence of a wider perspective, however, the view of technology was softer. It is regarded as part of the process, still a tool but one which affects the efficiency of the process. Perhaps by default, technology is, therefore, more integrated into the administrative mechanisms of the organization. There is concern about technological fit, thus the approach is directed away from one of expert handling to one of greater integration. This is particularly evident in this view's handling of information technology. The literature which reflects it concentrates upon the user end: it is here that a controllable interface exists between the administrative process and the machine.

A classic example of this view is to be found in a book by Whisler, although it is becoming dated.[20] In the 1980s, with the increasing power of computer technology, many other books found their way onto the market.[21] They all sought to merge the computer with the work processes of the organization rather than to allow it to dominate them, but stopped short of seeing it as a social process. The latest work to appear is by Michael Earl, which may well supplant Whisler's book as a classic.[22]

Conclusion

The academic foundation of this metaphor's approach to technology is an economic one in that all perspectives within it see technology as a resource. Depending upon their view of organization (e.g. scientific management or administrative principles) is whether they see such a resource as needing to fit into the work processes or to dominate them. Either way it has important implications for the management of information technology in terms of the policy adopted. Ownership of the computer system is seen to be in the hands of management and therefore controlled by them rather than by the workforce itself.

4.3.2 Organizations as organisms (second wave)

Peter Blau determined that it is irrational to view an organization as rational in the way that the machine metaphor does because it does not take account of the non-rational behaviour of people.[23] Such a perspective summarizes the natural or organismic metaphor, in that organizations are seen as complex, living entities which do not have machine-like qualities. They are no longer reified, cohesive units which act in harmony and with total rationality towards a common set of goals. In the same way that a living organism is a collection of competing and interacting forces, some living and some not, so too the organization comprises individuals and social forces which compete with and contradict each other. The consequence is that the organization cannot be so easily prescribed for management action, being at best a rather fuzzy area for common agreement. Technology, therefore, as an element of organization, cannot be so predictable in terms of a resource.

Neither is there agreement on how to model the metaphor. With some justification it is claimed that Elton Mayo (along with Harvard Business School colleagues such as Roethlisberger and Dickson[24]) provided a foundation with his Hawthorne experiments.[25] As social psychologists, their contribution was in recognizing the importance of behaviour in organizational design. Their work initiated the behaviourist school for the explanation of firms. The offshoots are many and are still very much in vogue today. The works of Maier,[26] Katz and Kahn,[27] Argyris[28] and Blake and Mouton[29] are but a few.

Since Weber's work[16] the sociologists have also been major contributors to this metaphor, particularly through the work of Selznick[30] and Parsons.[31] Rather than placing the emphasis upon the people element of an organization as the behaviourists did, these and other theorists who followed were interested in the complete entity and how it worked. In true functionalist tradition they identified various component parts and studied interaction between them. Selznick highlighted the relationship between these and the organization's employees, whilst Parsons developed a dynamic model in which people were an integrated part.

The technological tradition which grew from this metaphorical approach is less prescriptive and more analytical than that of the machine metaphor. The earlier ideas are typically represented by the works of Gouldner[32] or Wedderburn and Crompton.[33] Theirs is mainly an examination of production technology and its relationship with the workforce (see Chapter 3). The structure of an organization was a consequence of the way its workforce produced, in particular of the relationship existing between workforce and technology. However, a more formalized development of this took place in the late 1950s and early 1960s which was influenced in part by Elton Mayo and also by considerable empirical research. Although not labelled until much later, the approach became known as contingency theory.

In contrast to the classical approach (whether the machine or natural metaphor) which sought to achieve a universally best structure for a business organization, the contingency theory proposes that there is no one best solution. Different situations demand different organizational structures, which are governed by forces of change known as contingencies. Thus the prevailing contingent would shape the corresponding organizational structure.

For Woodward, after extensive research of over a hundred firms in Essex, the most important contingent is technology.[34] If, for instance, a firm has a mass production technology, then its structure would develop in terms of the other contingents, such as size and culture, which would best suit that. So mass production technology, for example, by its very nature determines that firms generally be large with formal cultures.

Quite apparently, therefore, technology is seen by Woodward as a determinant of organization. Although others, such as Pugh and the Aston Group,[35] do not agree with her upon the extent of the power of technology to determine structure, there is a general consensus on the nature of technology itself. It is no longer a resource as such, but as much an element of organizations as structure, people and their culture (see Chapter 3).

Information technology is perhaps not addressed as positively as it is in the previous metaphor. This is because there is no formal distinction made between general technology and information technology. Both are social processes and therefore to be treated as such. That is not to say there are not writers on the subject. Miles *et al.*,[36] Anderson and Mumford,[37] and Zuboff[38] are typical of the works produced. Information technology is analysed in terms of its ability to integrate into society or business. In general, the conclusions seem to be doom-laden, predicting dire consequences if we do not get it right.

Conclusions

The academic background to the organismic metaphor is both sociological and psychological. It is by no means a cohesive school, ranging as it does from behaviourists such as Mayo to social functionalists such as Parsons. Their only common ground is in seeing technology as a social phenomenon or process. The integration between technology and structure is, therefore, more profound. They do not, however, provide considerable help in the analysis of the impact of information technology because there is no formalized distinction between information and general technologies. Nevertheless, the models provided are more useful than those of the machine metaphor because, through their emphasis on technology's social integration, they can mirror more effectively the impact characteristics of information technology.

The implication of this for the management of information technology is that like every other technology its ownership is with the workforce. Management owns and controls only a part of the technological process – the machinery. The rest is an integrated part of those who use it in terms of their knowledge and technique. In this area, management has only indirect control over technology through better training programmes, etc. Thus the implementation of a new technological system, particularly a computer network, has a greater impact than merely upon a firm's efficiency: it may also change the firm's effectiveness through other, not so controllable factors.

4.3.3 Organizations as processes (third wave)

This metaphor describes the organization as a complex conglomerate of interaction which does not necessarily produce a clearly identifiable form. An organization exists because people are told it does by management teams, corporate identity and so on; although, in reality, apart from resource allocation, members/employees act very much for themselves as individuals or within groups, occasionally forming alliances to get things done. It is the process of doing (production, administration, etc.) which is the major input to organization structure, so that the organization is a series of different or interlocking processes. Its structure is shaped by those processes because it is the arena in which they are actioned.

As with the other two waves there are disagreements, in particular over the identity of the process. Some put forward the decision process as a dynamic which determines the organizational structure.[39] Others view the organization as a political arena in which structural adjustments are made through political mechanisms such as ownership of power.[40] Yet others, such as Johnson *et al.*,[41] regard these processes in terms of their relationships with one another and how open they are to external influence. Contingency theorists Lawrence and Lorsch,[42] on the other hand, determined a particular relationship between the organization and its environment as being the important process, whilst Weick[43] highlighted the processes between the individual and their social formation.

In general, organizations are no longer seen as hierarchical and solid (albeit at times fuzzy) frameworks. Structure is considered not to be as important as the processes themselves because it is a transient thing, created and remolded by the whim of changing interactions. Watson described this organization as being formed in the minds of the employees through their perception of its interactions.[6]

The process or open systems metaphor, therefore, shifts the emphasis of analysis from the design of the organization to the functioning of its elements. It allows these elements (e.g. technology, politics, decisions) a far greater impact than the previous two metaphors. For technology in particular the approach is significant. In the machine metaphor, technology is not part of the organization, whilst in the organismic metaphor technology is part of an organization's social process and a determinant of structure. In the process metaphor, technology can be a process in its own right, determining the perceptions of individuals and affecting their behaviour. Its ability to affect the characteristics of an organization are thus considerably increased because the mechanisms involved (i.e employee perception) form the essence of an organization.

These ideas have been most prevalent in the analysis of information technology. The relationship between the behaviour of people and the technology they use is portrayed by the socio-technical systems theory. This applies a systems methodology to the analysis of information technology and how it affects the way we organize. Its roots can be traced back to Mayo and his Hawthorne experiments[26] in terms of the paradigm's behavioural aspirations. It was Mayo who first formally stated the link between our behaviour and organizational design. But it was Trist and Bamforth who galvanized those ideas into understanding the impact of technological innovation.[44]

With the growth of computer technology as the dominant innovative technology it was, therefore, not surprising that Trist and Bamforth's methodology was quickly taken up by others to analyse its impact. Burns and Stalker produced an impressive model based upon empirical research describing a close behavioural relationship between our technology and the way we organized.[45] If the structure of the firm did not suit the technology employed then pathological responses evolved on the part of management. The works of Beer[46] and Weizenbaum[47] are typical of the deep analysis that this approach has enjoyed. More up to date thought, particularly in terms of networked information systems, can be found in the writings of Buchanan and Boddy,[48] Child,[49] and Checkland.[50]

Conclusions

The basis for this metaphor is to be found in the political and social sciences. The structure of the organization, if it exists at all, is no more than the consequence of human behaviour. The representations of such behaviour are to be found within the organizational processes. Which process is the most successful in determining the organization itself depends upon an individual's perspective. One may believe that decision processes are the most important elements, or that political processes are more significant; or even that there is no one process more important than another. Whatever, the belief allows the analysis of our organizations in terms of their activities rather than their formal structures: it encourages us to view an organization as an arena for continuous action.

It could be claimed that this approach goes too far the other way by tending to place emphasis on perceptual processes without considering the constraints of the physical domain. The consequence of this is rather paradoxical. On the one hand there is this abstract entity, defined by the perceptions of the organization's employees and associates, whilst on the other hand its links with the environment cannot be expressed in physical terms when quite obviously they should be.

The effects of this on the assessment of the impact of information technology is also significant. Through this metaphor's technological paradigm, the theory of socio-technical systems, information technology becomes purely a behavioural phenomenon. Its impact is interpreted in terms of the effects it has on the behaviour of its users. Therefore its management is seen to be most appropriate when directed toward user behaviour.

4.4 Seeking a solution

Just as firms are not merely a collection of resources, human or otherwise, nor are they merely a collection of processes. As with all social entities, they are a combination of physical and perceptual: but it

CASE STUDY 4.2

A manufacturer of high-tech production machinery covered by the NBS research project was suddenly faced by foreign competition releasing a machine more capable than theirs utilizing the very latest in software technology. Despite the obvious gains, this firm could not respond. This was because previous decisions on production line design had precluded any flexibility in that direction. The physical consequences of this were to be found in the way the production line operated. The perceptual consequences were to limit management's view of their market.

is how the relationship between the two is understood which is important. Quite obviously many organizations do have buildings which figure strongly in the image they project but also quite obviously the influence of the organization does not end at a brick wall. They do comprise physical beings constrained by their physical environment but beyond such environments they have resources which can be both physical (machinery, etc.) and perceptual (knowledge). Any complete model of organization must accommodate both domains.

Organizations, however, must be more than the summation of individuals, resources and perceptions within them. Unfortunately the metaphors discussed describe no more than this. Yet organizations tend to develop some sense of being in their own right. This is not in terms of a conscious, spatial positioning, as any individual would have, but is rather a consequence of history. Continuity of an organization, for example, cannot be solely explained as the perception of individuals or the particular allocation of resourcing. There is a logic within it which outlives any temporary input an individual may care to make. It is indeed a process, but one which is at the same time both independent and dependent. For example, previous decisions made by management can constrain and develop the organization's structure in future years.

Both the physical and perceptual aspects of the decision described in Case Study 4.2 are as real as each other. One could be seen in the production line whilst the other, although not seen, is ingrained within the management culture. Together they form an inheritance passed onto subsequent management which constrains their action. It is in this sense that an organization can be said to be existing independently. Decisions and actions are taken all the time which can then exist beyond their initiators and add to a bank of knowledge within the firm. To a certain extent we are referring to the organizational culture,[51] but culture's form relates only to the rules for action and does not express the logic of the actions themselves, as does structure.

Structure can thus be determined by neither domain alone. More probably, it arises as a consequence of a relationship between the two domains continually interacting with one another through a historical process which in turn feeds the logic of the organization.

In the same vein, information technology (or technology in general) cannot be treated as either a physical or perceptual phenomenon. The way in which each of the three metaphors provides analytical tools for the assessment of its impact restricts our being able to see the whole framework. Information technology does have a strong physical impact: it can, for example, turn an inefficient firm into an efficient one. The criteria used to assess such a change are based in the physical domain in that there can be more information output in terms of management reports or invoices billed and so on. It can also change user behaviour, as we see in socio-technical systems, so that employee perceptions of their tasks or indeed their firm change.

In many models the two domains sit either separately or uncomfortably side by side. However, it is not so much the consideration of the individual domains that is important (although obviously for line managers it cannot be ignored), it is the relationship between them which must be analysed and the subsequent effects such interaction has upon organization design. We must, therefore, devise organizational models which not only identify these two domains but also show how they relate to one another.

4.5 Summary

The structure of an organization is seen as providing the framework which turns a collection of people and resources into an identifiable form. The perception of it, however, is not particularly easy because it reflects considerable complexity. Therefore the models which attempt to describe it are better seen in terms of metaphorical association. Depending upon whose ideas are considered, there are generally three major metaphors of an organization. Firstly, those models which portray the organization as a machine. Secondly, those which view the organization as an organism. Thirdly, those which support the process metaphor of an organization.

Since the organizational structure (whichever metaphor is used) provides a framework for the other elements such as technology, there is a logical link between the structure and its particular elements. We can, therefore, determine a causal relationship between the metaphor and the attitude towards technological characteristics. Thus in the machine metaphor, technology is seen as a fully controllable resource, whereas in the organismic metaphor technology is perceived as a social phenomenon and thus a more integrated and less controllable aspect of organization. The process metaphor perceives technology as a behavioural phenomenon and as such lost in the perceptions of the users.

The way in which technology is modelled affects our ideas about how it should be managed. In the first metaphor, because we see it as a resource we believe it capable of being managed like any other resource. The second metaphor encourages us to believe that the management of our technology is difficult because the ownership no longer rests with management but with the workforce. The final metaphor sees technology as being managed by the user, whose perceptions and culture can be changed through training.

The problem is that these metaphors supply us with an extremist, not necessarily simplistic, view of organization. They are based mainly in either the physical or perceptual domains and do not reflect the relationships existing between them. With general technology this may not be too problematic, but with the peculiarly corrosive characteristics of information technology this may mean that we are not managing it as effectively as we should be.

REFERENCES

1. Woodward, Joan. *Management and Technology, Problems of Progress in Industry.* HMSO, 1958.
2. Porter, Michael. 'From competitive advantage to corporate strategy', *Harvard Business Review*, vol. 65, issue 3, 1987.
3. Merton, Robert. *Social Theory and Social Structure.* Free Press, 1957.
4. Parsons, Talcott. *The Structure of Social Action.* Free Press, 1949.
5. Scott, Richard W. *Organizations.* Prentice Hall, 1981.
6. Watson, Tony. *Management, Organization and Employment Strategy.* Routledge & Kegan Paul, 1986.
7. Morgan, Gareth. *Images of Organization.* Sage, 1986.
8. Mintzberg, Henry. *Structure in Fives: Designing effective organizations.* Prentice Hall, 1983.
9. Handy, Charles. *Understanding Organizations.* Penguin, 1987.
10. Work by F.W. McFarlan is useful in this area. For example, 'Information technology changes the way you compete', *Harvard Business Review*, vol. 62, issue 3, 1984.
11. Robbins, Stephen. *Organization Theory: Structure, design, and application.* Prentice Hall, 1987.
12. Taylor, Frederick. *Scientific Management.* Harper & Row, 1947.
13. Examples of the 'modern' strategic management approach are: Cowan, John. *The Self-reliant Manager.* Amacon, 1977; Blake, Robert and

Mouton, Jane. *The Managerial Grid III*. Gulf, 1985; Albert, Michael. *Effective Management*. Harper & Row, 1988.

14. For example: Walsh, Myles E. *Understanding Computers*. Wiley, 1985; Deeson, Eric. *Managing with Information Technology*. Kogan Page, 1987.
15. Fayol, Henri. *General and Industrial Management*. Pitman, 1949.
16. Weber, Max. *The Theory of Social and Economic Organizations*. Allen & Unwin, 1947.
17. Simon, Herbert. *Administrative Behaviour*. Macmillan, 1957.
18. Gulick, L. and Urwick, L. (eds). *Papers on the Science of Administration*. Institute of Public Administration, 1937.
19. Cyert, Richard and March, James. *A Behavioural Theory of the Firm*. Prentice Hall, 1963.
20. Whisler, Thomas. *The Impact of Computers on Organization*. Praeger, 1970.
21. For example: Rowan, T.G. *Managing with Computers*. Heinemann, 1982; Gunton, Tony. *End User Focus*. Prentice Hall, 1988.
22. Earl, Michael. *Management Strategies for Information Technology*. Prentice Hall, 1989.
23. Blau, Peter. *Bureaucracy in Modern Society*. Random House, 1956.
24. Roethlisberger, F. and Dickson, William. *Management and the Worker*. Harvard University Press, 1939.
25. Mayo, Elton. *The Social Problems of an Industrial Civilization*. Routledge & Kegan Paul, 1949.
26. Maier, Norman. *Principles of Human Relations*. Wiley, 1952.
27. Katz, Daniel and Kahn, Robert. 'Some recent findings in human relations research in industry', in *Readings in Social Psychology*, Swanson *et al.* (eds). Holt, 1952.
28. Argyris, Chris. *Personality and Organization*. Harper, 1957.
29. Blake, R. and Mouton, J. *The Managerial Grid*. Gulf, 1964.
30. Selznick, Philip. 'Foundations of the theory of organizations', *American Sociological Review*, Feb. 1948.
31. Parsons, Talcott. *The Social System*. Free Press, 1951.
32. Gouldner, Alvin. *Patterns of Industrial Bureaucracy*. Free Press, 1954.
33. Wedderburn, D. and Crompton, R. *Workers' Attitudes and Technology*. Cambridge University Press, 1972.
34. Woodward, Joan. *Industrial Organization: Theory and practice* (2nd edn). Oxford University Press, 1980.
35. Pugh, Derek and Hickson, D. *Organizational Structure in its Context: The Aston programme I*. Gower, 1976.
36. Miles, Ian, Rush, Howard, Turner, Kevin and Bessant, John. *Information Horizon*. Edward Elgar, 1988.
37. Bjorn-Anderson, N. and Mumford, E. (eds). *Information Society*. North-Holland, 1982.
38. Zuboff, Shoshana. *In the Age of the Smart Machine*. Heinemann, 1988.
39. Cohen, M., March, D. and Olsen, J. 'A garbage can model of organizational choice', *Administrative Science Quarterly*, vol. 17, 1972.

40. Pettigrew, Andrew. *The Politics of Organizational Decision Making.* Tavistock, 1973.
41. Johnson, R., Kast, F. and Rosenzweig, J. *The Theory and Management of Systems.* McGraw-Hill, 1967.
42. Lawrence, Paul and Lorsch, Jay. *Organization and Environment: Managing differentiation and integration.* Harvard University Press, 1967.
43. Weick, Karl. *The Social Psychology of Organizing.* Addison-Wesley, 1969.
44. Trist, E. and Bamforth, K. 'Social and psychological consequences of the longwall method of coal-getting', *Human Relations,* Feb. 1951.
45. Burns, Tom and Stalker, George. *The Management of Innovation.* Tavistock, 1961.
46. Beer, Stafford. *Cybernetics and Management.* Wiley, 1964.
47. Weizenbaum, Joseph. *Computer Power and Human Reason.* Freeman, 1967.
48. Buchanan, D. and Boddy, D. *Organizations and the Computer.* Gower, 1982.
49. Child, John. *Organization.* Harper & Row, 1984.
50. Checkland, Peter. *Systems Thinking, Systems Practice.* Wiley, 1981.
51. For a good discussion on the relationship between structure and culture see: Handy, Charles. *Understanding Organizations.* Penguin, 1987.

FURTHER READING

Earl, Michael. *Management Strategies for Information Technology.* Prentice Hall, 1989.
Gunton, Tony. *End User Focus.* Prentice Hall, 1988.
Watson, Tony. *Management, Organization and Employment Strategy.* Routledge & Kegan Paul, 1986.

CHAPTER 5
The systems approach

5.1 Introduction

We can never see our environment as it really is because firstly it is too complex and secondly, our historicities colour and distort our view of it. Therefore in any organizational analysis we should try not only to understand the complexity, but also to understand how we as employees perceive such complexity. This is important because our behaviour as a major identifiable element of an organization is governed by our perceptions. They are not infallible, invariably they are wrong. We might, for example, suffer cognitive dissonance whereby the apparent realities of a situation are ignored in preference for the greater psychological comfort of an already established belief.[1] In doing this, however, we feel worse not better because we know our logic is wrong. Such discomfort could then drive us to pathological behaviour which may in turn affect organizational characteristics. Our social positioning could also determine how we view a particular event. During an industrial dispute both management and employees see their particular stance as the right one, and in many cases deadlock arises because neither side is prepared to move. The facts are the same, but they are interpreted differently. Both sides see the world through their own aspirations coloured by their objectives; they interpret these as fact, and are unwilling to accommodate other views.

We therefore judge people and situations by stereotyping, which is the creation of mental patterns for future reference. What we are doing is simplifying: we are then fooled into believing that our simplifications are fact and thus act accordingly. To stereotype is to aggregate. If we ignore the constituent parts of a disturbance we are more likely to comprehend it. In other words, we try to see as many things as possible in terms of their wholeness.

Any aspect, physical or abstract, can be extremely difficult to understand if reduced. People, for example, comprise a veritable host of bits and pieces from the hair to finger nails, not to mention the elements we cannot see. But we do not attempt to understand a person in those terms; we take what is often called a holistic view by judging them as a complete entity. When we look at a chair we do not see the legs and seat separately, we see the whole chair. If necessary we understand that what we are viewing can be reduced into its constituent parts.

5.1.1 Analysis of organizations

In a manner similar to the above, when we analyse organizations we tend to look at them as whole entities. This does not preclude our examination of their constituent parts, but we do so in relation to the overall wholeness. In Chapter 4 we saw that Morgan[2] identifies this approach in terms of metaphorical creation (organizations as machines, organisms, etc.). It is easier for us to view an organization as a machine for example, than it is to see it in all its complexity.

This is perfectly acceptable as an aid to our performance at work or whatever but it is not so desirable in the development of an organizational model, since to simplify in this way may lead to us missing an essential element. On the other hand, the principle of aggregation as opposed to reductionism is sound in that an organization does have more meaning as a whole rather than as a summation of its parts. What this suggests is that an analyst cannot successfully determine the characteristics of a firm merely by identifying all its basic components. There is a logic to be had which can only be seen when all the parts are working together and not in isolation.

5.1.2 Rigorous approach

The solution it seems lies in the degree of control. With a purely holistic approach we do not possess the rigour to be confident that our models of organization are sufficiently accurate. A reductionist approach, although quite often empirically based, may well miss some vital aspect. A systems methodology on the other hand provides a holistic perspective but regulated by 'laws' of interpretation for greater rigour.

It will be the contention of this chapter that we need such a methodology to analyse successfully the impact of information technology on our organizations. This is because the nature of such technology can be assessed only in terms of its total impact. To understand it in relation to only one aspect of organization does not highlight its greater perceptual impact. However, a purely holistic view is not sufficient because the complexities involved require greater analytical rigour. The importance of information technology is to be found in the way it changes people's perceptions and thus their behaviour. Eric Trist (see Chapter 4) and his socio-technical system was one of the first to see this, and yet it will also be the contention of this chapter that he (and others) missed a vital point as a consequence of their particular methodology.

The change in employee behaviour determines a change in the organizational structure. In Chapter 4 it is suggested that an organization is mainly within our minds, thus any behavioural change will have an impact upon our perception of organization.[40] As we see below, however, the change does not stop here. The logic of the organization itself also changes. Such higher level changes can be modelled only by using a systems methodology. It is successful at doing this because it not only reflects the way we as individuals tend to aggregate, and thus captures the essence of how we organize, but also allows us a glimpse of a change effect in terms of the whole rather than the part.

This chapter will suggest, however, that due to confusion in its use, a systems methodology is not always appropriately applied. In particular, what often purports to be a systems model is no more than a holistic perspective. The difference is important because one is not a methodology and therefore does not itself have rigour, whilst the other, the systems approach, is a methodology. Such a discussion is essential for the objectives of this book because we need to establish an appropriate methodology. In doing so there must be no confusion as to what is or is not a system.

5.2 What is a system?

The common usage of the word system is problematic. We talk of systems when referring to the completeness of a particular concept (e.g. a hi-fi system), or when referring to a process, in particular one which tends to be bureaucratic and inflexible (e.g. 'you can't fight the system'). It is a shorthand which we all understand and as such may help us relate to some complexity or other. A problem arises when we do not agree on what the complexity is. Jordan, for example, identified this situation within a conference on systems.[3]

It seems that systems can be all things to all people. To a certain extent this is true, but in accepting this we need also to provide an analytical framework, otherwise there is no credibility. We need to establish what is a systems methodology as opposed to a holistic perspective.

5.2.1   A whole or a system?

To have a holistic perspective is construed as relating to the wholeness of an entity. More rigorously applied, it indicates a generalistic view in analysis, contrasting to a more specific view in a reductionist perspective.

When we talk of an organization in its entirety we are indeed viewing it holistically. When we attach to it a unity for either theory, analysis or discussion, our perspective is a holistic one. We have ignored all the smaller aspects not as being unimportant but for the sake of simplicity.

Many models of organization, particularly those portraying the organismic or process metaphor, adopt a holistic perspective. Contingency theorists such as Lawrence and Lorsch (see Chapter 4), for example, see their organization operating as a whole entity within its environment. Leavitt[4] defines his organization as a whole with four basic sub-elements. Udy[5] perceives organization in a similar fashion. They, and others, believe that the characteristics of any organization can only be fully understood if they are described as complete entities. The parts are not ignored, their relationships are sometimes examined, but in the holistic perspective their purpose is seen as a part of the whole.

A system, on the other hand, is something else. It does incorporate holistic aspects but it emphasizes interaction rather than wholeness. Johnson, Kast and Rosenzweig[6] define a system as being complex and organized, a collection of parts making up a unitary whole. The perspective is no longer from the outside looking in as with the holistic view but rather the other way. Therefore when we view an organization from a systems perspective we are looking at the parts which make up the whole. We are seeing them as essential elements which determine the characteristics and behaviour of the whole.

An organizational system is portrayed as a collection of parts which act in unison and produce a whole identifiable from the surrounding milieu.[7] A system is seen as a framework in which interactive forces play out predetermined roles, the consequence of which is the system itself. The organization, therefore, is analysed in terms of its parts interacting with one another to produce the organization. The parts and the whole cannot be isolated. There is an integrated and dependent relationship between them, neither can exist without the other.

Parsons (see Chapter 4) is seen as using the systems approach in his analysis of society and organizations. Boulding also translated the world through a systems perspective.[8] Both these authors, however, saw the organization as part of a wider system. Etzioni, on the other hand, interpreted his organizations as a number of psychological control systems.[9] The contingency approach is seen as a systems interpretation whereby the various contingents interact with the structure system of organization.[10] Trist (see Chapter 4) and the socio-technical systems school are also cited as systems models, as indeed their name suggests. The range of people who are portrayed as being systems analysts is immense. Some are appropriately listed as such, others are at best reflecting a holistic view.

We could summarize in the following way. The major differences between the holistic perspective and a system are emphasis and degree of detail. When individuals view something holistically they are concentrating upon its wholeness, in other words the totality of elements comprising the whole is important. A system, on the other hand, is highlighting relationships between the elements which define its total characteristic. The former is also a perspective. The latter is a methodology. As we see later, this difference is important in terms of establishing an analytical framework.

5.2.2 When is a whole a system?

It is the contention of this chapter that many descriptions of organization portrayed as systems models are not that, but holistical perspectives. For example, the socio-technical systems model offers merely a collection of interactions, within previously defined areas, applied to a functional hierarchy of organization. That is, the relationship between technology and the manifest behaviour of an organization's employees is expressed in terms of the roles and job tasks within an organization's structure. This does not make these models systems models, because the analyst is taking only one aspect of organization and viewing that alone in terms of a whole and is, therefore, adopting a holistic perspective.

The argument can also apply to organizational processes. Within the process itself, such as decisions, it could be argued that there is a systems approach. In other words, taking our example, a decision process model could be construed as a systems model of decisions. But it would not be correct to portray it as a systems model of organization because the decision process can only ever be part of organization, as indeed can any process. Thus to examine a process is only to view it as part of the overall concept – it may be perceived holistically but cannot be a system of organization.

To adopt a systems approach is, therefore, to lock into a set of

---

CASE STUDY 5.1

A local manufacturing firm implemented what they called a management information system. Consultants were engaged and an extensive six month project was instigated during which a selected number of managers were involved. After implementation management found that the process did not work as well as was hoped.

NBS research found that apart from the consultants and some of the managers involved, most of the identified users of the process could not properly relate to it in their job tasks. Its validity as a system was in question because, apart from the few, the rest could not identify it as a system from the surrounding milieu. Users did not understand where the boundaries of the system were and thus could not perceive its particular control mechanisms.

---

predetermined relationships between elements of a system, all of which have to be included in any model and none discarded. In other words an analyst cannot pick and choose the elements needed: for a model to work consistently as a system it must not be contrived. A system does not exist as such, it is an abstract declaration of intent on the part of the analyst to portray a particular entity in accordance with a set of universally consistent truths (see Boulding[8]).

Thus, within a holistic perspective we could identify relationships between the elements of our particular model. We could be concerned with how management affects the productive capability of the organization. We may want to see how this in turn affects the organization structure: in other words, to view the organization as a whole. But the viability of our identified linkages are tested only by their consistency within the applied model. For them to be an appropriate systems model those linkages must be consistent not only internally but also externally with the established law. Without this reference point the statement that a particular entity is a system is meaningless because its validity will depend solely upon the subjectivity of any individual.

Case Study 5.1 demonstrates the practical aspects of not getting a system definition right. What the management of this firm failed to do was to establish a generally known set of rules for the system which everyone could relate to and thus identify what was and what was not the system.

The principle is no different when looking at an analytical model of organization. The ground rules have to be established which link the particular entity being examined into the more formal regulatory mechanisms of general systems behaviour. The next section does just that by portraying the organization in the systems perspective and seeking to establish what are exactly the regulatory mechanisms of a system.

5.3 The systems approach

It would seem that just about anything can be a system in the same way that just about anything can be viewed holistically. The difference is that whereas with the holistic perspective it does not matter if the identification is subjective and somewhat contrived, with a system it must be consistently identifiable. The Open University Systems Group provides a definition which underpins this.[11] They see a system in terms of four major aspects.

1. The parts or components are connected in an organized way.
2. They are affected by being in the system and are changed by one leaving it.
3. The system does something.
4. The system must be identified as having special meaning.

The organization, therefore, can be a system in the same way that any identifiable entity can be a system. The point is, however, that to be an appropriately identified system the organization must fit with its lower-level internal processes and its higher-level external forces. This is because an organization can also be a subsystem or an element in other analytical frameworks, depending on the level of perspective. They too may form systems models, but not an organizational systems model. This is the hub of the argument against conventional so-called systems models, in that many of them do not reflect the right level of interpretation for an organizational system and thus do not present a valid interpretation of a firm in terms of a system.

5.3.1 The importance of hierarchy

Hierarchy is an important concept in enabling a model of organization to be fixed at the appropriate level for a systems analysis. Boulding describes a model of the world in terms of hierarchies, whereby different levels of interaction (systems) are linked together in a formal structure.[12] Hierarchy, therefore, formally describes the different levels of any social entity. In an organization, for example, this is seen as a management structure in which the different levels of seniority are highlighted. More importantly, a hierarchy also reflects the functional relationships between each level in terms of dependencies and seniority.

Williamson, in particular, analysed organizations as formalized hierarchies arising from increasing transaction costs in an informal market.[13] Handy, on the other hand, discusses hierarchy and structure.[14] Both authors, and many others, see the formalized relationship established by hierarchy as being an important control mechanism in that it maintains the cohesion of the organization.

In a similar vein, a systems hierarchy is an important control mechanism. It describes the dependencies between high-level and low-level systems within the same entity. For example, if we take an organization as our system then the major elements which comprise that system could be identified as that system's subsystems. Using Leavitt's model (see Leavitt[4]) the organization as a whole is the system which comprises the technology, people, task and structure subsystems. These then can comprise even lower-level subsystems. Through the hierarchy we have established a network of direct and indirect dependencies. We have also stated which of the systems is more important (thus at a higher level) than others (at a lower level).

According to Thompson, however, the expression of dependency and seniority is not the only significance of hierarchy.[15] He believes that the higher the level the more inclusive are the clusters which comprise it. This means that interdependence is greater the higher it is in the hierarchy because the level above is always formed to contain aspects beyond the control of the lower levels and therefore demands a greater degree of co-ordination. An organization system has greater interdependence with its subsystems than with a lower-level finance system, for example, such as a lower-level day ledger system.

This implies that for any system to be valid it has to be linked, in terms of hierarchy, not only downwards but also upwards. Thus the organization system will be affected itself by higher-level super-systems such as the market or industry and so on. To be valid, any systems model must link appropriately into this hierarchy. It must relate upwards as well as downwards, and must cover all aspects of the entity it purports to represent.

The degree of linkage upwards and downwards in a system, thus increasing or decreasing its validity, depends to some extent on the strength of the links identified.

5.3.2   Open or closed?

One of the major contributions of the systems approach for organization theory has always been the differentiation according to whether a system was open or closed to the surrounding environment. Von Bertalanffy was one of the first to not only formally develop a systems concept but also to differentiate between an closed or open system.[16] A closed system is one that does not react to its environment; an open system is one which does. It should be noted that this does not mean that closed systems do not import influences from their surrounding environment, it is just that they do not respond to them in the way an open system does. There are, of course, degrees of openness and closedness.

Living things, for example, are regarded as open systems. They interact with their environment and depend upon it for their existence. They breathe from it and they live upon it. If it becomes hostile they may die, or they may adapt themselves. In other words, they are open to the influences that their normal environment may have upon them and have built-in mechanisms which enable them to respond to any changes.

A fishtank, on the other hand, is generally a closed system. That does not mean to say that there is no interaction with the external environment. Someone has to feed the fish and change the water, but the fishtank system is not particularly sensitive to any change in the environment. It has no built-in mechanisms to respond.

Unfortunately it is not always so simple. Fish live in fishtanks. Fish are open systems, whereas the fishtank is a closed system. So the environment, itself a system, can be either open or closed creating a further dimension of complexity. In general, the higher level the system is, the more likely it is to be a closed system.

Similarly, there are contained within organizations several layers of open and closed systems. Management style, for instance, may make an organization system more or less open to its environment, whilst its subsystems may themselves be determined independently as closed or open. Indeed, the way that analytical methodology is used to examine organizations could result in a different perception of them. A classical management approach, for instance, tends to regard organizations as closed systems; whereas a more organic, behaviourist viewpoint sees them as being open to the environment. The tendency these days, however, is to regard organizations as open systems.

The degree of openness of a system determines, in the sense of Thompson's analysis (see above), the degree of dependency that a particular systems model may have in its relational hierarchy. In

CASE STUDY 5.2

A regional division of a large banking organization included in NBS research implemented a computer information system which was in effect closed. It was controlled centrally by a DP department that did not respond to changing user needs. The obvious effect of this was that the information accessed was out of date and inappropriate in many cases. But we also found tentative evidence for a more fundamental structural impact. The closed system meant the exclusion of the rest of the organization. Other work systems were unable to link into it and therefore by-passed it. Users did not perceive this new, computerized process to be a system and did not behave as if it were a uniquely identifiable entity. As such the system did not work. It was not valid because its closed boundary excluded it from the relational hierarchy.

general, the more closed a system is, the less open it is to its environment which comprises other systems, and thus the less interdependent it is with them. Thus, for reasons stated above, the more closed a system, the more isolated from its hierarchy it is, and therefore the less valid is its description (see also Case Study 5.2).

5.3.3   Subjectivity and laws

It should be apparent that a system is not a reality in the same way that a process or function is, but rather a perspective of reality. It is easy to identify the whereabouts of the finance department within the firm, for example: it is differentiated from other departments by observable job tasks, resource allocation, behavioural activity and so on. These aspects are to be found within the physical domain. They are things which we can all relate to in a similar manner because we can see them, and therefore interpret them, in a consistent way.

A financial system, however, is not so identifiable. There is probably no single manager in charge since its influence can reach into many departments. There are physical resources to be seen, but again they cannot be identified as being solely part of the financial department. Its boundaries are thus invisible, the relationships which cement it are also invisible. It is a perspective created for better perception of an entity and thus achieves greater control of complexity. Therefore consistency in its interpretation depends entirely upon the relevant individuals being able to agree and indeed understand what it is that each other perceives (see also Case Study 5.3).

Subjective interpretation of a system is a problem because it allows

---

CASE STUDY 5.3

A small marketing business experienced considerable difficulty with its financial processes. Its auditors had often complained that they were inaccurate and ineffective. The managers were particularly aggrieved by this because they had within the previous eighteen months introduced a 'number of stand alone micros to run all their administration'. They had not established any training programme and expected the users 'to just get on with it'. The new technology required new job tasks which in effect expanded the elements in the existing systems and thus changed them. The new systems were as a consequence not formally fixed into the existing hierarchy and thus open to many different interpretations. The consultants hired to assess the situation recommended a formal fixing of the new system through training and perceptual marking.

---

an uncontrollable factor to creep into scientific methodology. On the other hand, it is an advantage for a system to create sense out of complexity; in order to do this, subjectivity cannot be denied. All we can hope for is consistency: a framework for interpretation which places limitations on the system's relationships.

A detailed discussion of the systems methodology is beyond the scope of this book. There is not general agreement on what it should comprise. Its characteristics and emphasis, however, can determine completely different views on methodology for systems. The work of Ashby,[17] Beer[18] and Churchman[19] provides useful insight into the development of a systems framework. A more modern view is to be found in Davis and Olson's book.[20] In general we could identify two major schools of thought which congregate around their own interpretation of the regulatory mechanisms of a system. These are known as hard systems or soft systems. Their analysis is important because the perspectives of these two schools affect our understanding of organizations and the impact of their technologies.

5.4   Hard or soft systems?

These two schools of thought present a dichotomy within systems methodology. The hard approach views a system as a machine with definite and identifiable input/output processes and is thus akin to the mechanistic aspects of organization theory. The soft approach, however, is organic in inclination, in that there are many aspects or elements which make up a particular system, which are not easily controlled or defined, and the domination of one set over another may depend upon circumstances.

In both cases, systems methodology is used, but in different ways in order to produce different emphasis. And although one approach (hard or soft) may be more appropriate than the other in one perspective (mechanistic or organic), that does not preclude one or the other from describing any entity.

5.4.1   Hard systems

The hard approach is typified by Siegert when he defined a system as being a way of getting things done.[21] As well as relating to identifiable processes, the implication seems to be that they must also possess some identifiable purpose; whether that purpose is interpreted as good or bad makes them no less or more a system. They have to be doing something, however, otherwise they are not a system.

In pursuit of this productive outcome the emphasis is placed upon the 'doing' aspects of systems methodology: that is, the processes of product transformation. These, in turn, can relate to any firm's basic functions, so that when applied to organization, the hard approach highlights functionality such as departments, hierarchy and processes, and hence emphasizes the physical domain. They are the subsystems within the model and relate quite nicely to the physical operations (i.e. production and administration) of any firm. It is because of this convertibility into an easily recognizable operational form that practitioners have adopted its methodology.

Siegert, amongst many others, formalizes the hard systems view of the appropriate systems methodology. Generally this emphasizes the transforming act by which one system is linked to another in the hierarchy by a sort of production chain. Although the methodology can be almost anything, and indeed worthless, Siegert does believe that a good system is identifiable. A good system by implication, therefore, is one which complies most readily with the systems methodology.

Such a framework requires a system to be effective, efficient, transparent, reliable, repeatable and purposeful (for greater explanation see Siegert's book). The significance of these is not so much what they portray but rather their reflection of the hard systems approach. Within this school the hard system is a scientific phenomenon, something which is easily understood and predictable. It is, therefore, easy to see the link between this and classical management in that the hard systems approach is indeed prescriptive. Thus a valid system is one which effectively and transparently prescribes transformation.

Many of those who analyse the impact of information technology find hard systems methodology appealing. There are many reasons, the major ones being that firstly, such an approach fits neatly with the transforming characteristics of information technology. Secondly, as suggested above, the prescriptive approach of classical management training also suits this approach, and since managers need to understand their information technologies it is reasonable to expect that the books they are likely to read should be in that mode. We saw in Chapter 4 a typical profile of the literature available. For further examples, however, work by Rowan[22] or Sanders[23] is typical. For a more academic and less prescriptive approach, Stewart's classic provides an interesting read.[24]

5.4.2 Soft systems

The soft approach is not so readily prescribable, which to some extent explains why it is not so popular with the practitioner. It proposes more than a physical explanation of an organization in the same way that a hard systems approach does. It encompasses the perceptual domain as well, and draws both aspects into what can only be described as a fluid interactive process. Wholeness and relationships are more important because it is through such a definition that the parts find their purpose. This is in contrast to the hard systems approach which defines its whole through the meaningfulness of its parts.

The soft system only has meaning as a whole. The parts can be examined as parts but only in relation to the whole. For meaning there need not be purpose outside their contribution to the whole. Because of this greater abstraction, individual perception of a soft system is open to greater variation. A soft business system does not have to have an output to have validity. This is its advantage but can also be its disadvantage. Without the constraints of such an output the boundaries of a system are open to subjective interpretation. For example, the hard approach would determine the output of a financial system to be specific financial data which have been previously identified. Other parts of the organization which do not produce these data can be easily excluded from the system. The framework of a hard system is thus set by its output.

The soft system has no such reference. Its boundaries can extend well beyond relationship to any output. This is an advantage. But it also means the integrity of the system is more difficult to maintain because one individual may perceive the actual position of those boundaries to be in a different place from another.

To a marketing specialist, for instance, the financial system's boundary may encroach upon things to do with marketing. An engineer, however, may view the differing perspective of the financial system in a more production line orientated way. Both may not be wrong. But without reference to what is being produced by the system it is difficult to say who is more accurate.

The approach, however, avoids being merely holistic because it still complies with the laws governing systems methodology which take it beyond a perspective. Being based upon individual interpretation does not preclude it from being a useful tool in the analysis of the environment. A hammer can be used in different ways by different people, but that does not mean its potential is any the less.

The definition of Johnson, Kast and Rosenzweig provides a typical indication of this sort of approach.[6] Because the system as a whole is important, and the interaction of its subsystems a necessary part of that, the emphasis has been placed upon maintenance of stability. For Etzioni the control mechanism is vital for the maintenance of his psychological systems.[9] The mechanistic viewpoint does not have this problem since a system is defined by the parts which relate to the physical constraints of the organization. This does not preclude behavioural aspects if they are defined solely by the physical domain, as in socio-technical systems, for example work by Trist *et al.*[25] But if a system's viability is detached from such constraints then there must be substitution from other sustaining mechanisms, otherwise the system may collapse into chaos. Such a state is termed entropy, whereby the wholeness of the system is no longer viable and indeed the entity ceases to be unique from the surrounding 'milieu'.[7]

The sustaining mechanism so identified in any soft system is homeostasis, defined as being the maintenance of equilibrium by a tendency to compensate for disrupting changes. This equilibrium need not be static, it can be dynamic and indeed may well have to be to respond to outside disruptions.[12] As well as reflecting physical law, in that things affected by their environments which do not respond to change tend to die, it is also essential for the soft approach by supplying a necessary framework – a link into physical reality – as well as a predictive capability. It also enables us to distinguish quite clearly between an open system and a closed system. Since the latter does not interact with its environment, we can determine whether such a state exists or not by the absence (or presence) of a homeostatic mechanism.

5.4.3   Summary

A system is a subjective and individual interpretation of an identifiable relationship. The extent of its meaning and validity, therefore, is open to variation because everyone sees the world slightly differently. This subjectivity of a systems methodology is a strength in that it reflects the way we view reality. That is we see our environment not as it is but through a perceptual veil. But if it is a strength, subjectivity is also a major weakness especially when we are trying to use such an approach to model our world. For validity there must be consistency, and yet if there is individuality there is a greater chance of different interpretation.

That is why a systems framework is so important. It sets the rules for consistency and defines each member system's relationship in terms of the hierarchy. There are many different frameworks to be had, however. In general they can be condensed into two major schools of thought – hard and soft systems. A hard system is defined by a framework of rules related to production in the wider sense of the word. Good systems are identified if they achieve appropriate objectives through the enhancement of production. These systems are linked strongly into the physical domain because of their association with the doing aspects and are thus more appealing to the practitioner.

A soft system, on the other hand, is more loosely defined. In comparison with a hard system it is not so strongly linked with the physical domain in that its framework is not defined by production. A soft system's strength is that it spans both the perceptual and the physical domains. It is not required necessarily to produce anything nor indeed to have purpose; it is descriptive analysis whereas a hard system is prescriptive analysis. This strength is also its weakness because the greater flexibility creates greater abstraction. Since a soft system's validity cannot be maintained by production it relies heavily upon internal equilibrium or homeostasis. The cost of this is greater uncertainty and thus less appeal to the practitioner.

The following section will examine how appropriate the systems methodology is to the analysis of a fundamental issue in the relationship between organization and information technology.

5.5   Systems and organizational boundaries

There are many issues involving the impact of information technology upon a business organization. However, the issue of organizational boundary is profound for two reasons. Firstly, an organization has traditionally been defined as a collectivity or a bounded network of social interaction,[26] so that whatever perspective or metaphor is accepted the organization must be contained within an identifiable boundary. The accuracy of its definition will, therefore, determine the validity of the consequent model of organization. Secondly, information technology is seen to break down the traditional organizational boundaries and replace them with a far less identifiable entity.[27] Not only is there a practical implication in the sense of a demand placed upon management to respond appropriately, but also a challenge to the analytical methodology of organization studies. If our models cannot accommodate the issue of a changing organizational boundary then they will no longer be effective.

5.5.1   Systems methodology

It is the contention of this section that a system's methodology offers the greatest promise in understanding organizational boundaries. The analysis of interaction reflects appropriately the aspects of boundary impact. No longer can organizational boundaries be considered stable and unchanging: their fluidity through the impact of information technology can range from inflexibility to total flexibility within the same organization over a given period. In terms of systems methodology this not only means that in some situations a system may be open and in others closed, but more fundamentally, the very nature of the system itself can vary in accordance with circumstance, and that indeed this variation can be time-independent. In other words, the organization could have different boundaries at the same time, dependent upon the perceptions of individuals involved in a particular situation.

For example, employees in the buying department of a firm integrated through an information technology network with their suppliers may perceive their organizational boundary differently from other employees in, say, the sales department with no such integration. Who is to say which is the 'true' boundary, since, as we have already established, organizations are very much perceptual things?

The concept of a boundary is as important in systems theory as it is in organization theory, for very much the same reasons. Pfeffer and Salancik provide a useful link between the two when they talk of an organization ending where its discretion ends and another's begins.[28] Thus when analysing or defining an entity, be it an abstract system such as an organization or a physical system such as a flower, it is essential to understand its uniqueness in the surrounding environment (i.e. to understand where the thing begins or ends). Perhaps in the system's methodology above all others this is important because of the hierarchical interrelationships that exist.

It is this common objective for an absolute definition of boundary in analytical methodology which makes systems methodology eminently appropriate for an analysis of the impact of information technology upon organizations. If the organizational boundary is very fluid then the measure of absolutes which conventional theory provides us with is not sufficient. The boundary is not an absolute but rather a moving abstract thing changed by the perceptions of the employees and their technology. It could be argued that boundaries were never the realities that our models always supposed them to be. Behaviourists such as Mayo assumed organizations to be things of the mind within a solid physical framework, but perhaps that comfort has never been there. The best we can say is that in many cases an organization's boundary appears to be stable because most people's perception of it over a period of time has not varied. All that information technology has done is to heighten the abstraction.

A boundary informs us of what an organization is or is not. Therefore, it is even more essential to define a fluid boundary because otherwise we will not begin to understand an organization or the impact of any change upon it, such as that of information technology.[29]

5.5.2 *Where does an organization start or finish?*

In many instances an organization's boundary may be indistinguishable from the surrounding milieu, but that makes it no less a system. There is a point, however, where the internal control mechanisms of a particular system are no longer effective. It is at this point we can say that one system stops and another starts. Interest in this area is not merely to identify a systems framework. Given the abstract nature of many systems it is quite often only at these boundary points that a clear understanding of their characteristics can be had. This is because at these points there is interaction with other systems and an indication of that system's position in the hierarchy. For example, a finance system may be obscure but its in-built objectives may be clearer seen in relation to outside agents with which it interacts.

An important contributor to the better understanding of the relationship between hierarchy and boundary and system is Williamson.[12] Although he determined transaction costs as the major reason that we organize, the boundaries of organizations are significant because they regulate the relationship between the organization and its market. Simon[30] saw a strong relationship between individual/group perception and boundary in the sense that the complexities of organizational environments created perceptual boundaries which he termed as bounded rationality. Mintzberg has also placed emphasis on the importance of organizational boundary in much of his work. In particular, his examination of the political arena suggests an organization with fluid and perceptual boundaries determined by the degree of political interaction.[31] Peter Drucker sees the boundary of an organization in terms of a two-way relationship.[32] Firstly, in the traditional sense a boundary determined by organizational structure, but also in a less traditional sense whereby the boundary itself, through environmental influence, is changing an organization into a different social entity. One final author to mention, although there are many others, is Koolhaas because he is representative of a new approach to organizational analysis.[33] Within this perspective organizational boundary is almost incidental as a consequence of complex change interactions. A balance between dissonance and harmony results in boundary.

There is, therefore, considerable discussion in the established literature on the concept of a fluid boundary. There is also an increasing acceptance that a boundary in an organization may not necessarily be expressed in physical terms. Indeed it is my contention that an organization's boundary is perceptual and that any physical aspects attached to it are as a consequence rather than a determinant of that. It is to the boundary that we must go in order to understand how organizations change because it is there that we find organizational response, and hence change implications, are developed. For example, an organization's growth in response to an increasing market is first evidenced through the contacts that an organization has with its market.

Our perception of organizations can no longer be as secure as it once was. Hence our management of them cannot be based upon the assumption that they are stable and unchanging. Therefore our models

---

RESEARCH 5A

There is considerable evidence from NBS research of fluid boundaries. Many management teams found their control declining through influence from other trading partners linked into them via some integrated network. Departments that are in the grey area between two firms are generally agreed to be the most difficult to control because of the subversive influence of 'outside' information. Yet it was those departments who were seen generally as the innovators or agents/champions of change.

of organization should not make the same assumptions. Even though many may pay lip service to change (see Leavitt[4]) it is seen as a predictable, physically orientated thing.

The following section analyses the advantages a systems methodology presents in the examination of organizational boundary.

5.6 Systems, organization and information technology

The objective here is to present three models of organization using systems methodology. The purpose is three-fold. Firstly, to demonstrate how systems analysis can be used in understanding organization and also how flexible it is in pursuit of that. Secondly, to determine the methodology's suitability for the analysis of organizational boundary. Thirdly, to highlight and emphasize the impact that information technology has at that point. It should be noted, however, that these three models are by no means definitive of what is available, they are merely demonstrative.

5.6.1 The classical management system

In the first model we could, in the vein of a classical management approach, consider an organization as a machine, whereby the organization is a physically orientated and management controllable entity. It has a collective objective which is attached to some productive output. The systems methodology portraying this type of organizational metaphor would not normally emphasize the functional hierarchy or departments of a firm but rather the major areas of influence. Its purpose then would be to determine and analyse the relationships between them (see Figure 5.1).

There are six major systems identified within this model with one supra-system, the environment. It is an open system with a closed-loop feedback mechanism and is hence potentially able to respond to environmental changes. The management system is determined to be of prime importance in that through control mechanisms it is given the ability to affect the other systems. Their capability in this, however, is hindered or helped by the effectiveness of the information processing system; therefore the management system is directly dependent upon the information processing system.

Studying an organization in terms of general concepts such as management or information enables the possibility of links with other

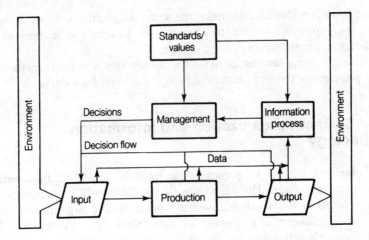

Figure 5.1 A classical management system

organizations. Take, for example, the information processing system: the way in which it is presented within the framework of this model does not preclude it being part of other organizations. If two firms are integrated by the same information network as in the case of a supplier and its customer, then the information processing system would be partially the same in both organizations. It is the same for any of the systems identified: they are not constrained by a rigid boundary.

This ability extends to within the organization. The positioning of systems is determined by their relationships to one another. Managers are constrained by standards but they can affect inputs which in turn affect the transformation process and so on. The lack of boundary definition through a functional interpretation, for example, allows a more organization-wide analysis.

A simple example of the potential impact of information technology can be seen in this model. It is portrayed as part of the information process and a link between management and the line. Its characteristics will thus affect the information process's ability to service the management system.

5.6.2 A socio-technical system

Figure 5.2 depicts a softer view of an organization (a cynic might say a fuzzier view) and is an interpretation of Kast and Rosenzweig's model.[34] The organization is seen as the system with five major

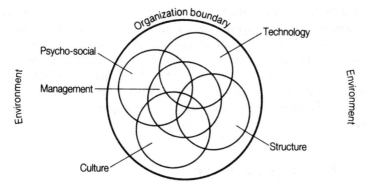

Figure 5.2   A socio-technical system

subsystems. Four of these subsystems – technology, psycho-social, structure and culture – are overlaid by the fifth subsystem, management. This represents the elements of organization still controlled by management activity, but not in such a predictable way as with the classical system. Although not obvious in the diagram, the organization by implication is open to its environment.

There are some interesting differences between this model and the previous one in Figure 5.1. The most obvious is that the identified subsystems are different, the system itself (the organization) and the supra-system (the environment) remain the same. This represents a different view of organization: one which emphasizes interaction or links rather than chains of command or 'doing' as in Figure 5.1. The overlapping of the systems is to demonstrate their dependency upon, their part of a oneness with each other. Circles are drawn to reflect their completeness as systems in their own right, yet at the same time their dependency within the larger system. The space unfilled by the subsystems within the large circle representing the organization depicts the idea that a system comprises more than the summation of its parts. In other words, synergy is achieved through the interaction of a system's subsystems which allows it a greater performance than the total of the subsystems as individuals.

The differing emphasis of this model encourages a differing focus of analysis. We can see this in partic ar when assessing the impact of information technology. There are two aspects to consider. Firstly, technology (of which information technology is a part) is given the status of a subsystem. That means it is an important determinant of an organization.[35] Secondly, technology has been fully integrated into the other subsystems so that it affects their characteristics and is itself affected by them. In Figure 5.1 the links between systems are shown as information flow, in Figure 5.2 the interaction is less definable and more abstract. In terms of the assessment of the impact of information technology, Figure 5.2 reveals a far less predictable environment. Information technology can no longer be kept apart in a box marked information processing, its impact controlled by the management box. The implementation of a computer in an organization depicted by Figure 5.2 would have a far greater impact.

5.6.3   A contingency system

The final model (Figure 5.3) is perhaps the most abstract and yet the most interesting. To begin with, there is no organizational system as such but there is still an environmental supra-system. In effect the organization has been merged with the environment, its boundaries are not well defined and are represented as being fluid (compare this with Figure 5.1). There are three systems: the institutional domain which is a representation of the values and norms in society; the organizational domain which reflects the way society organizes to achieve specific objectives, and the technical core which enables an organization to achieve its objectives. The model can be viewed on two dimensions.

The first dimension is as a general societal expression, that is each system is determined in part by the nature of the society which surrounds it. The second dimension is as a specific organizational expression, that is taken as a model of one particular firm. Consequently the organization cannot be the unique and isolated entity which many models portray it as, but rather a manifestation of our social activity. Its systems are at the same time identifiable as part of an organization and as a much smaller part of society. Therefore each subsystem has, in effect, two master systems: the organization itself and society or the environment.

There are many versions of this model. The main aspect of it is to merge the organization into systems above and below it. In other words to integrate the boundaries in a way similar to Figure 5.2. What can change according to differing emphases are the names of the three (or more) domains. This particular version represents the social functionalist paradigm of organization. Authors like Parsons with his study of society and organization would find sympathy here.[36] Others such as Petit have developed and discussed similar models.[37] The contingency view of organization can also be represented by this model (see Woodward[35]) in that it reflects through input the potential impact of change that different contingencies may have.

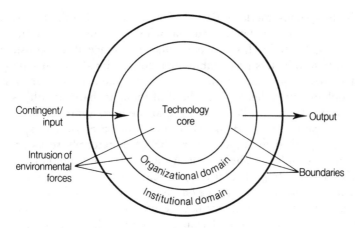

Figure 5.3   A contingency system

One obvious consequence of this model is the lack of management as a major system. Indeed, it is seen to form part of all three systems in terms of a control mechanism. Tannenbaum discusses management in these terms when he examines organizations as a control entity.[38] Another obvious consequence is the important role which technology is now given. It is described as the core of the organization. It is indeed the stabilizing factor of an organization, holding together a collection of social forces in sufficient cohesion for the maintenance of an organization. Part of this core will be information technology.

Once again we are confronted with the potential of information technology impact, but with perhaps even greater effect than in Figure 5.2. It is suggested that technology, not just the physical but also the perceptual aspects, is the organization. A firm's technical processes, in whatever form, are the concrete interpretation of abstract societal forces which gather in our minds. Without technology a firm could not be managed or controlled. Thus the implementation of information technology is not merely a management exercise because it will profoundly affect this technical core. Introducing information technology will undoubtedly affect the technical core and hence the cohesion of the particular organization. Whether that is for the good or not will depend upon other things such as change in management skills.

5.6.4   Conclusions

Systems methodology has been used to analyse three different perspectives of organization. Each perspective had a different emphasis which its systems model reflected. On the other hand, the use of a systems methodology determined that wholeness and interaction would also be highlighted. This has particular advantage if we consider an organization to be less predictable than 'conventional wisdom' suggests.

The main question seems to be not whether we use systems methodology but rather which school of thought (hard or soft) is more appropriate. There can be no doubt that the hard approach fits in very well with the classical management, and hence prescriptive, approach. This has appeal to the practitioner who quite naturally seeks practical solutions to problems. The cost of this is that it oversimplifies what can be very complex. In particular the problem of organizational boundaries is not fully addressed in that they are still presented as fixed features of an organization. Thus our perspective of what makes an organization what it is, stay together and change is limited because forces which generate organizational characteristics are generated at the boundary.

It was Lindblom who pointed out that simplifying complexity for the sake of management action creates more problems than it solves if the complexity is not truly modelled.[39] This argument can be applied to the debate between hard and soft systems schools. Soft systems present a far more complex interpretation and one which does not readily give us solutions. It attempts to describe rather than prescribe and as such enables us better to understand organizations. Its presentation of less definitive boundaries in organizations allows the development of a model which portrays firms as being considerably more integrated with their environments and a greater emphasis on perceptual forces to maintain organizational identity and cohesion.

5.7   Theory or methodology?

When we analyse an organization as a system, therefore, we are applying a formal methodology with a given set of general laws which govern interactive relationships within that framework. In doing so we may take a mechanistic perspective or an organic perspective which emphasize particular aspects of a firm rather than the analytical methodology adopted. This means that the systems approach is not an alternative paradigm.

The alternative to viewing an organization as a system is not to view it in a classical management perspective or whatever, but to view it in reductionist or holistic terms applied to the various established perspectives. In other words, the organization as a system is a methodological statement upon which others may hang their respective interpretations of an organization.

This has particular significance when considering the worthiness of a systems methodology in the analysis of organization. In many cases the system is presented as a unique paradigm of organization and thus interpreted as a theoretical model.[40] The issues concerning its utility become clouded in the ensuing debate about how appropriate it is. The major argument against a systems theory of a firm is that it is not specific enough. This is indeed true. But then what this book is proposing is that systems modelling is not a theory but a methodology.

The difference between a theory and a methodology is quite profound. A theory is an explanation of a phenomenon or process, whilst a methodology is an analytical framework for the production of a theory.[41] The two are not contradictory in the sense that one can replace the other. Nor can one be used instead of the other. A methodology cannot be seen as a theory, for example. Yet the idea of a systems theory seems to project this and as such places an inconsistency in this approach which is to be found by using a methodology as a theory.

The benefit of using systems in organization theory, therefore, is not as an explanation but rather as an analytical framework in order to develop an explanation. Systems methodology can provide us with a useful tool to gain greater understanding but it should not be clouded by a debate about whether it is a theory or not.

5.8 Summary

The concept of a system affords considerable possibilities for the integration of information technology and organization into one model. The main advantage of a systems methodology in the analysis of organization is its ability to integrate all the dimensions of an organization. On the other hand, the interesting feature of the information technologies is their power to link into a perceptual domain which can be more than adequately covered by a systems perspective. Thus it would seem that not only is a systems methodology suitable to develop a model of the impact of such a combination, but, indeed, it is the only methodology which could do it effectively.

It is unfortunate that an argument between hard or soft has developed, because it tends to detract from the utility that the overall approach can provide. Both sides have their advantages. The emphasis on process on the hard side is important because at the end of the day firms are no more than some form of organized process. Soft systems emphasize interaction and hierarchy; this approach highlights how abstract the concept of organization can be: it is more than just the building it is located in, and indeed more than the individuals who form it. The volatile and potentially unstable organization encouraged in our models by the use of systems methodology allows us to focus on areas other than the traditional analytical ones for answers. The interactive emphasis of a soft system in particular leads us to consider the importance of boundaries in the design of organizations. It also enables us to appreciate fully the potential impact a computer system may have because boundaries are easily changed by phenomena such as computer technology. If the boundaries of an organization change, so do the characteristics of the organization.

REFERENCES

1. Festinger, Leon. *A Theory of Cognitive Dissonance*. Row, Peterson, 1957.
2. Morgan, Gareth. *Images of Organization*. Sage, 1986.
3. Jordan, N. *Themes in Speculative Psychology*. Tavistock, 1969.
4. Leavitt, Harold. 'Applied organizational change in industry: structural, technological and humanistic approaches', in *Handbook of Organizations*, James March (ed.). Rand McNally, 1965.
5. Udy, Stanley. *Organization of Work*. Human Relations Area Files Press, 1959.
6. Johnson, R., Kast, F., and Rosenzweig, J. *The Theory and Management of Systems*. McGraw-Hill, 1967.
7. Sutherland, John. *Systems*. Van Nostrand Reinhold, 1975.
8. Boulding, Kenneth. 'General systems theory – the skeleton of science', *Management Science*, Apr. 1956.
9. Etzioni, Amitai. *A Comparative Analysis of Complex Organizations*. Free Press of Glencoe, 1961.
10. Lawrence, P. and Lorsch, J. *Organization and Environment*. Harvard Graduate School of Business Administration, 1967.
11. Open University Systems Group (eds). *Systems Behaviour*. Harper & Row, 1981.
12. Boulding, Kenneth. *The World as a Total System*. Sage, 1985.
13. Williamson, Oliver. *Markets and Hierarchies: Analysis and antitrust implications*. Free Press, 1975.
14. Handy, Charles. *Age of Unreason*. Hutchinson, 1989.
15. Thompson, James. *Organization in Action*. McGraw-Hill, 1967.
16. Von Bertalanffy. *General Systems Theory*. Penguin, 1971.
17. Ashby, Ross. *Introduction to Cybernetics*. Chapman and Hall, 1956.
18. Beer, Stafford. *Decision and Control*. Wiley, 1966.
19. Churchman, West. *The Systems Approach*. Dell, 1968.
20. Davis, Gordon and Olson, Margarethe. *Management Information Systems*. McGraw-Hill, 1987.
21. Siegert, Paul. *Systems and General Management*. American Management Association, 1972.
22. Rowan, T.G. *Managing With Computers*. Heinemann, 1982.

23. Sanders, Norman. *Computer-aided Management.* Woodhead-Faulkner, 1985.
24. Stewart, Rosemary. *How Computers Affect Management.* Macmillan, 1971.
25. Trist, Eric, Higgin, G.W., Murray, H. and Pollock, A. *Organizational Choice.* Tavistock, 1963.
26. Homans, George. *The Human Group.* Harcourt, 1950. Provides a classic debate on the concept of boundary.
27. A useful discussion can be found in two HBR papers: F. McFarlan. 'Information technology changes the way you compete', *Harvard Business Review*, 1984. Porter and Millar. 'How information gives you a competitive advantage', *Harvard Business Review*, 1985.
28. Pfeffer, Jeffrey and Salancik, Gerald. *The External Control of Organizations.* Harper & Row, 1978.
29. Lindblom, Charles. *Politics and Markets.* Basic Books, 1977. Provides a good exposition of how firms use their boundaries in management strategy.
30. Simon, Herbert. *The New Science of Management Decision.* Harper, 1960.
31. Mintzberg, Henry. 'The organization as political arena', *Journal of Management Studies*, 1985.
32. Drucker, Peter. 'The coming of the new organization', *Harvard Business Review*, 1988.
33. Koolhaas, Jan. *Organization, Dissonance and Change.* Wiley, 1982.
34. Kast, F. and Rosenzweig, J. *Organization and Management.* McGraw-Hill, 1986.
35. Consideration of the following work would help to place this point into perspective: Woodward, Joan. *Industrial Organization: Theory and practice* (2nd edn). Oxford University Press, 1980.
36. Parsons, Talcott. *The Social System.* Free Press, 1951.
37. Petit, Thomas. 'A behavioural theory of management', *Academy of Management Journal*, Dec. 1967.
38. Tannenbaum, Arnold. *Control in Organizations.* McGraw-Hill, 1968.
39. Lindblom, Charles. 'The science of muddling through', *Public Administration Review*, Spring 1959.
40. For example: Watson, Tony. *Management, Organization and Employment Strategy.* Routledge & Kegan Paul, 1986.
41. Ansoff, Igor. 'The emerging paradigm of strategic behaviour', *Strategic Management Journal*, 1987. Provides a useful framework for understanding the concept of theory and paradigm.

FURTHER READING

Checkland, Peter. *Systems Thinking, Systems Practice.* Wiley, 1981.
Morgan, Gareth. *Images of Organization.* Sage, 1986.

CHAPTER 6
People and organization

6.1 Introduction

An organization is essentially a creation of the mind and the perceptions of those people who are involved with it, both internally and externally, are important in determining its design. Gareth Morgan's model of organization is driven by the individuals' metaphorical interpretation. We would see them as machines, as human brains or as organisms for example.[1] The particular way we translate our environment will govern the way we act. In such a context it would seem that the individual and groups of individuals are important.

6.1.1 Contradiction of systems analysis

It is curious, therefore, that systems analysis is seemingly so dismissive of the individual. In the previous chapter we established that it is indeed a systems methodology which is the most appropriate way to analyse organization, especially with regard to the impact of information technology. Yet we also established a close relationship between such technology and the mind of the individual.

The apparent contradiction arises not so much from acceptance of whether individuals have an important role to play but rather from the nature of the reductionist approach in the psychoanalysis of people and how they respond to certain stimulation. Its exponents examine an employee almost in isolation, allowing access to outside variables (such as the environment) in a strictly controllable way. A systems methodology, on the other hand, tends to integrate all elements of an organization, whether they be individual or resource.

Therefore both a reductionist and systems perspective regard individuals as being important to any organization. That is not the same, however, as saying that the understanding of an organization must be through the individual, the viewpoint encouraged by the psycho-behavioural models of organization.

Individuals do not live in isolation, but that means more than allowing them interaction with their environment. Any behaviourist could identify an array of outside forces which influence the action of an individual. In doing this, however, those forces are the property of the individual, whose action is attributable solely to them. This allows a predeterminable and prescriptive environment. For example, an individual is given the ability to respond purposefully and rationally to the behaviour of others or his own needs.

6.1.2 Systems approach

Systems methodology perceives the individual being no different from any other interactive force within the system. The relative importance of the individual and the forces is ranked by the hierarchy. Individuals' thoughts, for example, are not just theirs but part of a larger psychosocial system. Their functional roles as managers form part of another system (management) which is independent of each individual who provides an input to it. Again, individuals' knowledge and technology is not solely their own but part of the organization and as such is a force to be reckoned with beyond the individual. The individual is thus an element within the organizational system, part of its many subsystems, feeding into and extracting out of them through the appropriate networks.

Information technology has a significant role to play in determining such interaction. We have discussed how information technology, in particular, affects the behaviour of users through the alteration of their environmental perceptions, the implication being that, once implemented, computer technology, particularly when networked, has such a far-reaching effect upon the fundamentals of an organization that any analytical consideration of them would not be complete without its inclusion. However, the traditional explanation of organizational behaviour, especially in terms of a reductionist perspective, establishes the individual within the organization and then, where necessary, adds the technological layer. It is argued that this does not reflect reality. There are in effect two main types of organization: one before computer implementation and the other after. The reductionists do not seem to grasp the point that the behaviour of people will be different in both.

It is, therefore, interesting to understand how individuals behave as individuals; but this is not essential to the complete understanding of organization. Individuals must be integrated fully with other organizational elements, particularly after computer implementation analysis. The systems, as opposed to the reductionist, perspective allows this to be done, and a systems methodology is the means by which this is achieved. In this chapter we examine the behavioural aspects of the individual and see how they can be integrated into the various subsystems of their organization, all the time relating this to the impact of information technology.

6.2   The individual

The Human Relations Movement, which recognizes the importance of the individual in the context of an organization, is relatively young. Its appearance reflected the increasing scepticism with the economic explanation of organization. As the work environment became increasingly complex the idea that solutions could be found in understanding what made people 'tick' gained prominence. In so doing, management would be able to control their departments more effectively and develop greater motivation in their employees.

Even theorists such as Pugh *et al.*, who are considered to be structuralists, acknowledged that employees are the organization.[2] This is not a rejection of their own position but rather an indication of the differences between the two approaches. The structuralist does not deny the importance of the individual but their action is determined by the structure of their organization and the roles that they play. The behaviourist sees this the other way around, in that employee behaviour through their action determines the organizational structure. The methodologies are not the same. The former tends to encourage force analysis, which is well supported by a systems methodology. The latter regards the individual as the central analytical arena open or closed to outside forces depending on particular model. In this case the reductionist approach is quite often adopted.

The latter is also a spirit of analysis pursued not only by the academic but also by the manager, who found its prescriptive inference considerably more appealing than the broad synoptic emphasis of organization theory hitherto. Specific assessments could be applied from the understanding of an individual which seemingly enabled management to do their job more easily. Until the emergence of Trist and his Tavistock colleagues, however, the relationship between the individual and technology was not particularly emphasized.[3] And despite the increasing popularity of socio-technical systems as an explanation of organizations, many behaviourist models today still do not highlight this link. Thus the true impact of information technology is not clearly identified.

6.2.1   Organizational behaviour

Elton Mayo, with his Hawthorne investigations, is widely seen as the midwife to organizational behaviour.[4] Through a series of experiments with six female operatives isolated from their production line, Mayo determined that individual interactive aspects are more important in achieving motivation than structural aspects. Thus if a group is cohesive and friendly it is likely to be more productive than one which is not, regardless of working conditions. The roots of this go beyond Mayo, however: the understanding of a person's behaviour is based upon traditions to be found both in psychology and sociology.

6.2.2   Individuals will be individuals!

The behaviourist's perspective can cause problems for the analyst, whether manager or academic, because if organizations comprise solely individuals then an element of unpredictability is brought into the equation simply because individuals are individuals. What motivates employees or what makes them work more productively are the behaviourist's roots to understanding the organization. Yet in their solutions and models they can never be certain that the persons whose behaviour they seek to predict will act rationally. The assumption is that they will. The paradox of this is that to act rationally is to act in a predetermined manner in order to meet the criteria set for rationality. Predetermination also implies dependence upon other forces which in case of the organization can be aspects such as structure and technology.

For example, Maslow's model determines that individuals possess an intuitive hierarchy of need, whereby their actions are dictated by a series need fulfilments.[5] However, such an approach presupposes that a person will not seek to achieve higher-level needs such as social recognition or job success until the lower-level needs, such as hunger or safety, have been met. The consequences of this for management are obvious. Before they can motivate their employees through job satisfaction, they have to ensure that the lower-level needs are addressed. On the other hand, this denies the effects a person's particular role or position in their firm may have on their perception and consequent behaviour.

Research 6A is fairly typical of the assessment of the impact of information technology. It demonstrates quite effectively how individuals' behaviour can be changed by their environments but more so

RESEARCH 6A

NBS regional research into information technology implementation found that many firms with newly implemented computer systems worried about the consequential low morale of their workforce affecting performance. One medium-sized manufacturing firm, in particular, tried to remedy the situation through a series of training programmes in order to increase user knowledge of the technology and hence their motivation. The firm was disappointed with the results. Although the training did help, it did not significantly improve resistance to the technology or motivation. Our deeper investigation highlighted structural problems. The computer had changed not only the task structure of the firm but also the reporting hierarchy. This created conflicts that were previously not present and was as such affecting the psychology of employees.

how integrated those individuals are with their surroundings. The behaviourists, on the other hand, try to distance the individual from the context in which they are placed. The problem they then have is to reconcile the normative model of the individual to the unpredictable arena of the organization, the consequence of which is a credibility gap. Maslow's model in particular is criticized in this respect. Robbins is typical in his recognition of Maslow's impact upon management training, but determines that his thoughts have not received convincing empirical testing.[6]

There are, of course, many more contributions to the behaviourist school and they are by no means a unified and cohesive collection. Herzberg's motivation–hygiene theory, for example, was an interesting response to the one-dimensional approach of Maslow as it recognized more formally that individuals are members of differing systems and would thus possess a complex layer of needs which are not necessarily originated with the individual.[7] McGregor recognized to a great extent the weaknesses of this approach by developing a model to analyze general misperceptions of individuals about others (theory X and theory Y).[8] Vroom's[9] expectancy theory, Alderfer's[10] ERG theory or the Hersey–Blanchard[11] situational theory are but a few milestones in an extensive and varied literature which covers aspects from motivation, leadership, group and individual behaviour to communication skills and stress.

6.2.3   A management implication

The traditional theoretical framework for organizations encourages a perceptual dichotomy which is quite often reflected by the practitioner, through management training courses. On the one hand there are the models and theories that emphasize the individual, whilst on the other hand there are those that highlight organizational aspects such as structure or process. These can and do cut across the paradigms identified in earlier chapters.

Management for its part is not only confronted by this analytical debate, where it is encouraged to attend to either the individual or the organization, and which is pushed forward depends very much on their trainers. They are also confronted by the realities of the situation, which perhaps the academics do not always have to face. Such realities determine that there are two visible dimensions which they must manage.

The first is, of course, the individual, whether by themselves or in groups. Here, the understanding of what makes the individual 'tick' is important, but it tells the manager nothing about his organization.

The second dimension is in the structure of the organization, which can tell the manager something about the individual but considerably more about the organization.

All managers, whatever their tasks, should be managing both these dimensions. They should man-manage, but they should also structure-manage. The two dimensions are interdependent and should be treated as such. It is proposed that, as a consequence of our theoretical dichotomy, conventional wisdom does not encourage management to do this. What in fact happens is that this single management responsibility is given to two sets of people. Tony Watson made this

---

RESEARCH 6B

NBS research underpins Watson's conclusion but found a more obvious split. Line managers, on the one hand (perhaps through the type of training they received), concentrated upon individual management. Non-line managers, usually in service departments such as personnel or audit, were split between the individual or structural aspects. Internal audit, for example, manages the structure of the organization; the personnel department manages the people structure (perhaps contrary to Watson's statement). Both may have staff with line responsibility, and thus individual emphasis, inside their own departments.

point in his book; his research revealed that personnel specialists (as an example) tended to emphasize the individual, whereas others, such as output specialists, are more structurally inclined.[12]

The net effect seems to be that the individual and organizational structure are not formally integrated by effective management control. This is because there are different groups of people dealing with the two major vehicles of control: people and structure.

A typical example of this is to be found in the way that firms implement their information technology and establish new and, it is to be hoped, integrating systems of control. Some form of structural analysis is carried out by those who manage the structural aspects of the organization. The impact on people is rarely considered, not because of any callousness but simply because different people are responsible for those aspects, and they do not always involve themselves with computer implementation. There is, therefore, a structural change which is not accompanied in response by a planned, and well managed, people change. The firm's internal balance is upset as a consequence, and the system inevitably fails.

The implementation of the computer changed the structure of the organization which in turn affected the morale of the staff, who are part of that structure. There was a definite cause–effect relationship between the two. Yet the demarcation of management was such that no one was able to identify this relationship. One group of managers was looking purely at the structural problem, while others (personnel and line) were looking at the consequential decline in staff motivation. Both issues were seen as separate when in fact they were not.

RESEARCH 6C

A medium-sized manufacturing firm found that its new computer system was in fact less productive than the manual system it replaced. A structural analysis had been properly carried out; the personnel had been adequately trained, so no-one really understood the problem. The answer was to be found in the subsequently changed relationships between the personnel of the department. Before computerization they were a happy, cohesive unit. After implementation they had been driven into isolated units, albeit linked through a network. Motivation and morale declined as a result.

6.2.4 Theoretical implication

The implication of the above argument is for the integration of the individual and structure into one model. But that does not merely mean that one stops talking about the individual or the structure and starts talking about psycho-social systems. Abstract concepts such as these can be meaningless unless they are located within a concrete, intellectual framework to which all can relate. That framework must in turn be embodied by consistent and predictable law. Organizations may well be merely perceptual, but their persistently common form does demand some consistency.

The individual *per se*, therefore, is discredited as the only determinant of organization. By definition, the individual's unpredictability and inconsistency makes him/her so. Maslow's hierarchy of need explains the individual but no more. It does not explain the individual within an organization other than by tautological reference. It is obvious that a person has different needs which are of different levels, but how do they come about and how do they affect other parts of the organization? It is no defence to say these are not theories of organization but theories of individual behaviour, since the two cannot be meaningfully separated.

What we seek, therefore, is a mechanism which brings these two aspects together. There are many models such as Leavitt's classic one which brings together both organization and people,[13] but their emphasis is upon people as a part of an organization and not in the psychological sense of being beyond the immediacy of their surroundings. In other words, we are returning to the argument that a model should emphasize both the perceptual and physical domains. This has been discouraged to some extent by the reductionist methodology used in many behavioural models or by the misuse of systems methodology in our structural/process models. This has created the dichotomy mentioned above by preventing, through conflicting and inconsistent methodology, the two sides from marrying.

In the following section it is intended to lay the foundations for a new integrating model. This is be done through identification of unifying mechanisms between the individual and their environment. In particular we look at interaction.

6.3   Interaction – a fundamental of organization

One of the major aspects in understanding organizations is the fact that human beings interact with one another and are thus influenced by that process. It is through this that groups are made possible. But it is also the lifeblood of any social cohesion and should thus be of extreme concern to management. Within systems theory, for example, interaction is viewed as a force which maintains solidarity between the various elements. It is also a dynamic mechanism by which management can control.

Labovitz saw the link between the individual and organizational objectives as being important.[14] He determined that link to be established through interactive processes. He and many others saw organization being expressed in terms of interpersonal activity or interaction. Indeed, within the psychologists' own backyard there was increasing recognition that interaction played an important role. For example, some twenty years ago, Secord and Backman aligned the importance of social-psychology to group interaction.[15] But once again the models, on both sides of the divide (behavioural or organizational), emphasize interaction between individuals or structural forces but not between individuals and structural forces.

6.3.1   A proposed analytical framework

The foregoing discussion is well documented in the literature. What I intend to show is that by understanding the interactional processes within an organization one can indeed understand the individual. In doing this I put forward four propositions:

1. Interaction is a function of individual perception.
2. Interaction is a function of organization structure.
3. Organization structure is a function of perception.
4. Individual action/behaviour and organization structure are closely interrelated.

The support for these propositions is to be found to a certain extent within the established literature. Udy's model highlights the relationship between individuals and structure.[16] The four proposals above take this a step further by suggesting firstly, a two-way interactive and dependency process. Secondly, that it is not the individual *per se* which is important but their perception; these are not always the same thing. The individual is seen in terms of a formal and conscious behavioural activity.

An individual's perception is not totally controllable and is open to forces at the subconscious level and thus not so easily predictable.

NBS research also lends limited support to these four propositions. In the main the propositions are the consequence of the distilling of the established literature. Their proof is in the logic of the relationship being expressed.

1. Interaction as a function of perception

A typical dictionary definition of interaction is to 'act reciprocally or on each other': the implication being that any element (individual) acted upon by another will respond in an appropriate manner within the framework of the system of which it is a part. For living beings such as ourselves, how they will react depends upon how they perceive a particular action. Thus perception plays an important role in the process of interaction.

For example, a gesture by one party could be construed as friendly or acrimonious by another. In many cases there are muddles in transmission of meaning (interaction) when one of the parties involved misunderstands.

The fact that the results of Research 6D may seem rather obvious tends to suggest the logic of the first proposition. It is also one which would be supported by the behaviourist school in that its perspective is upon the individual outwards. Needs, motivation, traits or whatever are seen to create the perception which in turn determines the interaction.

2. Interaction as a function of structure

The characteristics of an organization (essentially its structure) also determine the way we, as employees, interact. Woodward portrays a

---

RESEARCH 6D

NBS research found that, without exception, external forces changed employee perceptions and as a consequence changed their behaviour towards others. The example that we were particularly interested in was the influence that information technology had in this area. An examination of relevant firms (10 per cent of total) before and after computer implementation confirmed changing behaviour, particularly in terms of role relationships. One extreme case was between two managers who previously harboured no acrimony for one another. The computer installation brought them into direct competition for its use. Their perception of one another was changed by it and hence their interaction.

firm's structure being determined by its technology.[17] Thus a mass production technology would result in a firm like Ford Motor Company, and so on. But she also suggested that the human relationships within the organization are affected by its structure through the technological process.

There is a close causal relationship between structure and technology, especially if the latter is defined in its widest possible sense. As we have already discussed, individuals use their technology to interact with the environment, but it also governs the way they interact with each other. Structure is the vehicle for both human interaction and technology within the firm, and therefore a determinant of the way we act.

For example, the structure of a prison prevents its inmates from interacting. But people also interact differently in different organizational structures. This is not purely because each organization may be located in a separate environment, although this would obviously be a contribution. A mass production organization demands a formal relationship between manager and employee, whilst a small business requires a far less formal one. Individuals who do not enact their roles with others as set by the structure of their organization are seen to be deviant.

Pettigrew[18] or Mintzberg[19] provide interesting perspectives which support this proposition. They see organizations as interactive arenas which determine the organizational design. For Pettigrew it is determined by information control, whereas for Mintzberg it is manifest in the political processes.

Once again the outcome may seem obvious, thus supporting the logic of the proposition. The interesting aspect, which is discussed in the conclusions, is that we now have two propositions which represent either side of the analytical perspectives mentioned earlier (individual-centred, organization-centred) and yet supported by the same research.

RESEARCH 6E

In the small number of firms that the NBS researchers studied which allowed a before-and-after investigation of the impact of information technology, intuitive support was found for the proposition that the implementation of computer technology can change employee or user behaviour or interaction. The dispute, for example, between the two managers mentioned in Research 6D could also be interpreted in these terms. That is, the managers' departmental structure was changed by the installation of a computer which resulted in the change in their interaction.

RESEARCH 6F

NBS research discovered in many organizations the recognition that
training is important subsequent to a reorganization caused by
computer installation. Departmental boundaries, for example, can be
changed as part of the new regime. Without the training (indeed,
quite often after it too) it was felt by many managers that individuals
did not 'see' the new structure. In effect, the physical aspects were
the same, excepting new terminals and so forth here and there, but
they could not relate to the new ways because the established
structure maintained their focus on the old ways.

---

3.   Structure is a function of perception

Watson made the point that organizations exist ultimately in the minds
and actions of individuals.[12] Structure, therefore, must be an abstract
concept. As we have already discussed, it comprises both the physical
domain and the perceptual domain. Where individuals choose to
allocate boundaries around collections of physical and perceptual
resources depends upon their perception. One person may view the
extent of their firm's production system, for example, differently from
another. Consistency in their interpretation could be achieved through
training and formal identification (organization chart, etc.), so that how
employees see their organization depends to a great extent on how good
their management is in encouraging a consistent and desirable
perspective. If they are lacking in their instruction then contradiction
and confusion can set in.

For example, reorganization within businesses often occurs:
departments merge or are given new names and so on. This can be
purely a perceptual exercise. The employees may remain at the same
desk, perhaps using the same resources, but their perception has been
altered by retraining. Different relationships/interactions are built which
affect the structural characteristics of the firm. For instance, departmental boundaries may well change.

4.   Individual and structure are interrelated

The individual's perception is based upon the environment, and in turn
the characteristics we see of the environment mold our perception. This,
then, is the message of our final proposition, and if it does appear
tautological then it is no less a proposition for being so because it is
something which is regularly ignored by management.

Gross and Etzioni examined the different generic organization models available.[20] Part of their conclusion about those emphasizing the importance of structure was that although design choice existed at the time of set-up, beyond that point it would seem that the structure endures of its own accord and possesses a life of its own. Our perceptions are locked into it through culture and tasks which do not allow us easily to break free. The structure, as it were, steps beyond our direct means of control.

Individuals *per se* are merely elements within the structure. They come and go, bring in different qualities and abilities but the structure on the whole, with a few exceptions, continues unchanged. It is the interactive processes which individuals may be part of and indeed stimulate which are the worthy aspects to analyse in order to understand organization. This is true not only for the academic but also for the manager, since to understand the individual as an management exercise is not particularly productive. We are nothing more than transmitters and receivers of information; how we act and the roles that we play are a consequence of that. Structure and the individual are so entangled, therefore, that it is impractical to attempt to separate them.

6.3.2 Conclusions

The purpose of this section is to highlight the importance of interaction within organizations. It is the mechanism by which all other elements of organization such as technology and structure maintain their validity. Without interaction, for example, the structure of an organization is not sustainable because the message of what the structure should be would not be communicated. It is not sufficient to assume that organizational aspects such as structure can stand in their own right. They need to be perceived to have meaning, but they need to be perceived by everyone in generally the same way, and for that we need interaction. When there are dysfunctions within an organization this is because the message has been transmitted wrongly and we do not all perceive the same thing in the same way, thus our behaviour may contradict that of others.

The specific proposals stated in this section are not particularly innovative. The first two, especially, reflect the analytical dichotomy that was discussed earlier. But to date these propositions have been seen by conventional wisdom to be either/or statements: that is, only one can be supported at the expense of the other. What is suggested here is that all four propositions complement rather than contradict one another. The tentative evidence of NBS research tends to support this, although it must be conceded that the sample is not sufficient to be conclusive.

The implication of this is that organizations cannot be so easily defined in terms of a particular element, for example human behaviour or structure. The salient factor is no longer these but rather their links which can be described as their interaction. Thus using Leavitt's change model as an example,[13] what we should be interested in is not the boxes (structure, technology, people, tasks) but the arrows between them which define their interaction. This is because the elements or boxes are better understood in terms of their relationship with other elements or boxes (see previous chapter).

We have returned once more to the idea of organization definition through the location of its boundaries. Since boundaries are abstract concepts and are thus not easily identified, their limitations can be seen in terms of their restriction on interaction. In the following section we examine this further with particular reference to groupings within an organization. It is through these that boundaries and interaction are most manifest.

6.4 Group boundaries

The presence of any form of interaction between individuals tends to create a group, be it formal or informal. Robbins, for example, defines a group as comprising two or more persons interacting and interdependent with common purpose.[6] This is, perhaps, representative of the classical view: it suggests a spatial and temporal cohesion but ignores the possibility that a group may not be physically located in the same room. In many ways the main thrust of this approach is a pluralistic extension of the individual-driven models of the behaviourists.

Mayo's Hawthorne investigations, for example, recognized the strong link between individual and group. Others, such as Ivancevich *et al.*,[21] applied a definite structure and boundary to them for the purposes of further analysis. They saw this as comprising: (1) group composition; (2) norms; (3) status; (4) emergent leaders; (5) role definition; and (6) group cohesiveness. From this sort of framework, and there are many variations, group dynamics are assessed and then placed in the context of organization.

Once again this has a bearing on the management of organizations. The division of resources, whether human or not, is by finite grouping in terms of departments and so on. People are assessed, controlled and motivated by group-orientated action. Planning is seen as a group pursuit. Strategy arises from group interaction. This is not necessarily the wrong interpretation but the temptation that goes with this approach is to pack these groupings into tidy packages. Thus when something comes along which is not one-group related, such as information technology, it can be dysfunctional to the management control processes.

6.4.1 The nature of the group

The problem of dysfunction originates from the nature of the group itself. In the context of an organization it is very difficult to understand groups as isolated, discrete units – as if, indeed, they were locked away in a room. To begin with, their boundaries are not so easily identifiable. In most cases people are members of several groups, the experiences of which they carry with them into yet other groups.

For example, a finance department is a formal group charged with certain objectives under the control of a manager. But even here, the boundaries are not so straightforward. Individuals could be members of other groups such as management or staff, a particular steering committee, or the sales ledger division, some of which are more formal than others.

A grouping reflects also the structure of organization, not only physical but also perceptual. People find it more difficult to come together as a formal group if they are physically apart or perceptually misaligned. But there are many other groupings than those which you or I could readily identify. The objectives of individual members may not even be the same and in cases contradict one another. The division between the male and female employees is an example. Each group may not have a set of objectives, they may not even see themselves as being part of a group (a criterion which many models demand) but nevertheless they have an important influence upon the structure of the firm. This is contrary to established group theory, however, because groups are defined in terms of their conscious and physical domain commonality: that is, they must be aware of other group members and have some empathy with them, and as such they can only do that in the physical domain.

It would seem, however, that this is not entirely appropriate given the close relationship between individual and structure. This is because the necessary link which formulates a grouping can be determined by the qualities of the organization structure. Thus in our example, the two groups – male and female employees – are not interesting *per se*, as the usual group definition would lead us to believe, but rather in the ways they interact with structure. That does not mean they have to perceive themselves as a group, but have sets of perceptions and actions which interact with the structure as if they were a group.

The implications of this for organizational analysis are two-edged. Group dynamics cannot be understood without a detailed knowledge of the organizational structure within which each particular group is placed. Alternatively, no analysis of structure is complete without the accommodation of the groups operating within its framework. There needs to be identification of some transmission between these two concepts. This is not only an academic requirement but also essential for the manager. To manipulate individual/group behaviour is to affect the organization's structure and vice versa.

6.4.2 Power linkage

Thus far it has been argued that groupings are an essential part of an organization but they are not necessarily readily perceived. Since individuals rarely act on their own within organizations the group is important as an interactive interface. It will be further argued that the driving mechanism of such interaction is power. It is the source of all management and organizational control, but it is also the determinant of individual and group activity within the organization. This relationship between power and control has been identified by many authors and is nothing new. Handy, for example, used their interactive processes to develop his models on culture,[22] whilst the widely recognized work in this area by Tannenbaum placed control as an inevitable correlate of organization.[23]

Power, therefore, is a structural consequence just as much as it influences structure. The individual is very much part of that process: not as the sole contributor, but more as one of many actors,

---

RESEARCH 6G

Drastic structural change implemented in a small manufacturing firm altered detrimentally the relationship between two departments. The old system had established the purchasing function as a separate and independent department. The relationship between the finance department and the production department was, as a consequence, balanced, neither side being able to dominate the other. The new system, however, brought about an amalgamation of both the finance and purchasing functions. This subsequently led to a shift in the power relations between the now enlarged finance department and the production department. As a consequence the production output deteriorated.

manipulated and determined in action by the ebbs and flows of organization. Research 6G demonstrates this point.

6.4.3   The arena

NBS research at a particular company (see Research 6G) highlighted two important aspects of any organization. Firstly, that the structure is finely balanced and any change imposed upon it will compel a shift to a new equilibrium. Secondly, the relationship between groups or individuals changes if the balance of structure shifts. This is expressed in degrees of power between those groups, allocated to them, as it were, by the framework provided through a particular series of structural characteristics. This framework is often referred to as the arena to indicate its encompassing nature.

6.4.4   Transmission mechanism

In short, power is considered to be the transmission mechanism between group interaction and structure because it is the dynamic arising from both structural and group influence. Hinings *et al.* allude to this idea in a study they conducted.[24] Mintzberg identified what he termed as a political arena within certain organizations in which struggles for power took place.[25] The nature of this arena was governed by the interactive processes of the organization's groups, the structure of the firm and the environmental conditions. The consequential characteristics of the arena (of which he identified four) would in turn determine the structure of the organization itself, to the extent of its own extinction. Perrow is another contributor to the importance of power as a transmission mechanism in organization.[26]

Unfortunately, Mintzberg's valuable model is limited by his own perception of organization. He sees the political arena as a transitory process of adjustment arising from the structural rigidities of the firm. Such adjustment can bring about change in the structure or the eradication of the political arena. By implication, therefore, the process is limited, in time if not spatially, and thus its existence is dependent upon a combination of external variables. The consequence of this is that Mintzberg has denied it permanency and as such a subsystem status. This is an important point and not just polemics, because the transmission mechanism, to work, must not be intermittent.

In reality any organization is always a political arena. There are ebbs and flows to which contributors/actors come and go, but the

---

RESEARCH 6H

Out of seventy firms that the NBS studied, there was a strong
negative correlation (−0.95) between their structural rigidity and the
political awareness of employees. We defined political awareness as
being the knowledge of a political network within the firm and a
willingness to participate in it. Structural rigidity, on the other hand,
we defined as the functional division and control of the organization.
Thus the more departments, units and managers a firm had the more
likely it was that its structure was rigid. The brief explanation of our
findings is that in determining a negative correlation between these
two variables, political awareness increases as structural rigidity
decreases. In short, the less control there is in an organization, the
more the political activity.

---

essence of organization is found through political process, expressed in
terms of power relationships. To be without that is like trying to
understand organization without the people.

6.4.5 *Information and power*

For the average manager, however, models are all very abstract. What
they would want to know is how such political activity would manifest
itself in the organization. The short answer to that is: through the
information network. We have already discussed in detail the
characteristics of information. One of the major points brought out
then was the subversive nature of information, and indeed whoever had
information had power.

Pettigrew, in particular, pursued the relationship between power
and the control of information.[27] His political arena was organization-
wide and continuous, in which the struggle for power was, in reality,
about who controlled what information. Managers had power because
they were 'gatekeepers' for certain sets of information.

A classic example of such a concept is the managing director's
secretary. Depending on her style she can be a problem. In the many
organizations I have worked in, I have known senior managers to be
terrified of her. If they want to approach the m.d. it is through her they
must go. Any information to or from the m.d. must pass through her.
They even have to involve her in some decision processes in order to
gain her alliance and thus to allow the necessary information to pass.

More seriously, however, Pettigrew envisaged the firm's information network being controlled by managers and technologists and not a

corps of over-enthusiastic secretaries. And where there was a point of control there was as a consequence the location of a gate. He saw this being multi-dimensional, in that groups such as departments as well as individuals were controlling information and thus gaining power from doing so.

Perrow believed this aspect to be more important than what he termed as 'interpersonal power'.[26] Through his research into large manufacturing companies he sought to determine which group within the firm had the most power. He concluded that it was usually the sales department. It had developed as a company-wide gatekeeper and its members had achieved power and prestige as a consequence. In those firms we would say they were sales- or market-driven, their structural characteristics uniquely attributable to that. On the other hand, in production-driven organizations, Perrow proposed that they were so because the production function was dominant and therefore acted as the company-wide gatekeeper. His conclusion was that the most salient functions had the most power.

6.4.6 Power, information and structure

Perrow's model demonstrates the interrelationship amongst power, information and structure. The groupings of individuals are formed by the consequences of their relationship. Functionality (departments, etc.) is the consequence of structure and the information network. The dominance of one department over another arises from the positioning of the former in relation to the latter, and hence the gain of power from that. Within this context, some individuals are obviously more or less capable than others. But their ability to change the information–structural power relationship is at best incremental. In other words a sales-driven firm remains a sales-driven firm because the dominant department will attract the most capable managers. Those who do not perform are quickly sidetracked or disposed of.

Occasionally persons are recruited to an organization to act as implementors or agents of change, or perhaps they are already installed or are the owners of the organization. In either case their personalities dominate and form the character of the firm. This does not contradict the Perrow-type approach because their input is like a one-off, indelible shot into the structure and then they become subject to the forces of their own making.

To conclude, therefore, the behaviour characteristics of both individuals and groups are not important for the understanding of an organization because people's actions within their particular firms are a consequence of the forces within the organization, of which their behaviour is a fully integrated part.

6.4.7 The invisible organization

Much analysis of power is expressed through a reductionist or holistic methodology. That is, interaction is indeed discussed but it is either examined in detail or alluded to as part of a whole, and yet in neither case is it fully integrated into the organizational system in the ways discussed in Chapter 5.

If systems methodology is indeed used to express an organizational model encompassing groupings and their interactional processes in terms of power relations, then a different world comes into focus. The groups of employees, whether concrete (functional) or abstract (descriptive), become frameworks for a whole series of interactions which in turn express the organizational boundaries and hence the organizational structure. The group members *per se* are not interesting, as many models would suggest; in this new world they are vehicles for the perceptual transmission of interactive forces which bring the organization to life.

There are two problems with this. Firstly, in this fluid, almost arbitrary world, how is stability maintained? It is only when a firm is stable that development takes place. Secondly, how can we demonstrate the existence of such a world? In answering the first question we can go some way to answering the second, although to a great extent (as with all aspects of the mind) its identity must be an act of faith.

6.5 Seeking a balance

The discussion so far is based upon a contingency perspective in that certain variables have been identified which influence the composition of organization structure. However, it does in fact differ from the contingency perspective by the proposal that structure can itself be a determinant and not just a determined factor. This allows the adoption of a true systems perspective of an organization.

6.5.1 Balance

What separates us from the Perrow/Mintzberg models is a greater emphasis on balance. By implication, their models do seek some form of status quo. Perrow's model, for example, does not explicitly portray a need for balance, although the permanency of the 'critical function' within the organization does suggest that there is one. Within the Mintzberg hypothesis a balance between all the forces is emphasized.

Organizational balance means that there is a particular moment in time when all interactive forces are positioned in such a way as to produce an equilibrium. To remain stable a system must not only continually seek equilibrium but also intermittently achieve it (homeostasis).

6.5.2 Relationship of power to balance

The proposition to be made in this section is that if there is an adjustment to any element of the organization, for example the information network, through a shift in power, then by implication there is an ensuing shift in organizational balance, which may or may not regain status quo. This then suggests a 'best fit' situation (see Handy[22]) whereby all elements of organization are appropriate within the context of its balance. The organization is in equilibrium. Any change to elements or force will upset that and generate need for adjustment to a new balance.

It has already been proposed that information, especially through its network, is an integral part of an organization: it is the essence of any organization affecting the organizational structure through the political process. Thus when we examined the subversive nature of information, we did so in relation to the consequences of its use and manipulation upon the host firm. To change the way we collect, transform and use information within any firm is, in effect, to reorganize the relevant processes, and hence the structure of the firm. (See Case Study 6.1.)

CASE STUDY 6.1

The NBS research project observed over a period the consequences of changing the reporting structure within a particular firm. Its buying department was told to report to finance rather than to production as it had done for many years previously. By doing this managers had changed their information network. This was evidenced later in the different ways these groups transmitted and received their information. Managers found later still that this change had also had an impact upon the organizational structure. The changing relationships between the three departments led to the necessity to redefine tasks to accommodate different interactive processes.

6.5.3   An undocumented relationship

The relationship between information and structure is not particularly well documented, despite there being considerable discussion in the literature of information in terms of power and communication. Pettigrew refers to structural impediments to the flow of organizational information thus suggesting a dependency of information upon the design of the organization.[27] But in general the position of information within a business has been in keeping with the resource-driven paradigm discussed earlier, namely that information is a resource of a business. However, unlike any other resource it seems not to have been allowed the ability to affect structure. It seems instead to have been regarded as operating independently of the organization in many respects so that changes to it do not have much bearing upon the design of a firm.

Such a position is not good for assessing the impact of information technology. It is understood that information *per se* and computer technology are closely linked. But because there has not been much exploration of the link between information and structure there has also not been particularly meaningful discussion on the impact of a computer upon aspects of organization which have no direct link but are nevertheless part of the firm's structure. A classic example would be how the introduction of a computer may well affect the ability of a firm's management to control its environment.

6.5.4   So what's new?

There are two lines of thought to be drawn together. On the one hand, the modern organization is encouraged by conventional wisdom to treat information as a resource with all the ensuing consequences upon design. On the other hand, despite there being acceptance of power through information control, there is no perception of a direct causal relationship between information and structure. These two together have created what can only be described as a credibility gap between the prescriptive/management aspects of organizational analysis and the descriptive aspects.

In other words, to help managers in their jobs we propose information as a resource and give them prescriptive models to cope with that. For understanding how a firm works we develop other paradigms of power relationships and information control. But we do not seem to link the two, the consequence being that when we try to assess the impact of something like a computer network there is no link between information and structure. Further, because information is treated as a quantifiable, definitive resource, we see no causal link between information technology and the organization's power relationships and structure.

6.6   The technological interface

No matter where an organization is situated within the matrix identified in Chapter 2 (i.e. managerial or bureaucratic, etc.), information still maintains qualities firmly located in the perceptual domain of the organization. That is, it is to do with the thinking/perceiving aspects of organization rather than the division of resources, etc. Information treated as a resource still has to be understood in those terms rather than just possess value. How those perceptions are established in any particular organization arises from a complex relationship between the organizational design and its political process. In those firms where computer networks have been implemented the first stepping-stone to such understanding is what could be termed the technological interface, the point where people and computers come into contact.

Weizenbaum has paid particular attention to this area.[28] His concern, expressed through many research programmes such as Eliza, was how our perceptions would be changed by close liaison with the computer. He interestingly defined the computer as a metaphor for better understanding of our world.

For Weizenbaum, therefore, the computer is very much in the perceptual domain of an organization and not the physical. This has greater significance when it is applied to the proposal that organizational definition and its eventual design is achieved through the processes of interaction between the many elements. If the employee is the vehicle for these events then any metaphorical interpretation such as the computer (Weizenbaum's suggestion) could have a profound effect upon the nature of those interactions and hence upon the nature of the organizational design.

6.6.1   Determinism?

Earlier in this chapter it was argued that there is a strong link between the individual and the organization structure, to the extent that neither can be regarded properly without input from the other. This position is enhanced considerably by the introduction into a firm of a computer network. The individual is then 'locked in' (and far more securely than any manual system could lock them in) to the organization structure through the information network.

Weizenbaum continually pointed out that individual perceptions are changed by computer networks. His argument is based upon the idea that individuals act in their environment through the perceptual models they have developed and which may or may not reflect reality. The computer can change those perceptions thus enabling an individual to act differently, an example being that the greater allocation of information to individuals through computerization can widen their perception of their environment. This in turn can weaken management control because a greater dissemination of information can lessen the departmental manager's role as gatekeeper.

6.6.2 The importance of time

Temporalists such as Flaherty have opened up another dimension in this debate – time.[29] In brief, they utilized Einstein's famous proposition that time is relative. Because we have clocks does not mean that we all perceive time in the same way; for example, time seems to pass more slowly when we are bored. Different emotions and perceptions bring forth different perceptions of time.

This theory can then be applied to the organizational environment. If a computer changes our perception of the environment in which we work, it may also change our perception of the time frame of the organization.

Organizations are structured in our minds both spatially and temporally. Our relationship with other departments, for example, is governed by where they are physically and the time it takes to get to them. Thus if we need a piece of information from another department then our relationship is governed in part by the time it takes for us to interact. We may pick up the telephone or we may go there personally or we may have to wait several days for it to arrive through the internal mail. These temporal and spatial perceptions are ingrained upon the organizational map and form part of the structure through the information network.

6.6.3 Information and balance

Computer implementation creates short-cuts to existing information paths and generates new interactive processes. As we have seen, the link

RESEARCH 6I

As many as 60 per cent of firms studied experienced structural problems within two years of a change in systems design, usually post computer network implementation. Typical manifestations were political conflicts, production rigidities, and falling efficiency and effectiveness criteria.

between the structure of the organization and its information network is strong. Thus changes in the information network will bring about changes in structure, so that once again we can see a disturbance in the balance or equilibrium of the firm.

To put it simply, at the point of computer implementation an organization can experience structural changes which go beyond what is obvious physically. The new information network which it generates is, to a great extent, out of balance with the established structure of the firm. People are forced to operate in ways which do not complement existing formations (departmental, managerial, resource allocations and so on). As a result dysfunctional pressures arise which force the firm, at best, to find a new equilibrium and at worst to continue in imbalance. The NBS research described in Research 6I supports this view. The consequences of these dysfunctional pressures are explored in subsequent chapters.

6.6.4   A new approach for the practitioner

Chapter 2 presented a matrix which identified a functional relationship between information and structure of the firm. To emphasize again, these two must be in balance for the firm to be in equilibrium, thus functioning properly. If the firm has a managerial-type structure then achievement of this balance is through information being resource-centred. If the firm is small and entrepreneurial then information should be perception-centred. These are the two extremes of a continuum; there are also varying combinations between them.

The practitioner must, therefore, identify the nature of his/her organizational structure and develop and design an information network in accord with that. Unfortunately, it may not always be that simple, especially for larger firms. There are two reasons for this:

1.   The division of a typical firm is multi-dimensional. That is, the overall organizational structure may be managerial in type, but

specific departments may reflect that or they may be tending towards bureaucratic/entrepreneurial characteristics. Design of any systems application would have to take that into account.

2. It is not often that we are given a clean sheet on which to draw new systems. More likely a system is already in place, probably manual, but certainly attuned to forces different from those that the new system will create. There is, therefore, a transformation process which has to be handled carefully for the project to succeed.

What in reality happens is that managers either leave information network design to develop as it will and tinker with the organization's structure, or they implement computer systems and thus alter the information system so that it is in keeping with the needs of, say, data processing. In any event they ignore the interactive processes between all these aspects which is the fundamental driving mechanism of the organization. As a consequence they do not ensure that the information network remains in tune with the structure by either redesigning the structure or the information network or both.

6.7 Summary

A great deal of emphasis has been placed upon the individual as the main factor in an explanation of organization, particularly when the behaviourist's perspective is examined. It is reasonable to suggest that organizations have meaning only within our minds and that therefore how we behave and perceive describes the eventual characteristics of organization. The problem with this is that organizations are considerably more complex than the consequence of our collective minds. There are many activities and forces going on around us and beyond us that we cannot possibly know about, so in many cases when we examine individuals to determine their behaviour we do not highlight these other forces. In other words, there are forces within our minds appertaining to organization which are beyond our control, they are stimulated by external factors such as culture and structure. These cannot be treated as a context for the individual to operate in, an environment, because the organization and individual are so closely integrated.

On the other hand, the functionalist's perspective of the structure being the organization's reality also ignores the importance of cognitive aspects. What these and many paradigms ignore are the interactions which occur between organizational elements. They are the links which give a firm its form. They are our perceptions expressed in terms of structure, culture or technology, and as such turn the organizational entity from an abstract concept of mind into a real activity.

In doing this, however, the two domains (physical and perceptual) of an organization should not be ignored. One cannot be highlighted at the expense of the other: they are both inexorably linked. This means that organizational boundaries are not purely physical, indeed their full meaning must be seen in terms of a perceptual phenomenon. They are the expression of what is or is not an organization, and therefore reflect the characteristics and limitations of our interactions within a framework perceived by us to be the organization. This relationship is important because through it, manifest upon a firm's information network and expressed in terms of power, we can gain a better understanding of the true organization: that is, one which is dynamic and changing, depending not upon physical resource as much as perceptual interpretation of that resource, and one which is sometimes in equilibrium but at other times in disequilibrium. It is a world where nothing can be guaranteed or indeed predicted to any great extent.

This chapter has also implied that the analytical methodology used in understanding organizations can determine the outcome. It is suggested that the reductionist and holistic methodologies adopted by many models of organization have not encouraged the inter-systems perspective required to understand fully an organization. A reductionist methodology propelled consequent models to highlight minutiae in terms of one element linking into other elements in a controlled way. A holistic approach, on the other hand, determined concentration on wholes but not always the interactive processes or relationship with the analytical hierarchy. A systems methodology is the only one which can highlight the aspects which this chapter has examined.

Redefining the perception of organization with a greater emphasis on the perceptual domain than it has yet enjoyed has implications for the assessment of the impact of information technology. Much has been alluded to in this respect within the content of this chapter, in particular with reference to the information network which creates the channels for interaction to take place. As we have already seen, information technology and the corresponding information network which it serves are closely linked in that one affects the other. Therefore to see an organization as a series of interactions rather than as a collection of resources places perceptual forces such as information technology in a central position. The implications of this for its management are discussed in the following chapter.

REFERENCES

1. Morgan, Gareth. *Images of Organization.* Sage, 1986.
2. Pugh, D.S., Hickson, D. and Hinings, C.R. *Writers on Organizations.* Penguin, 1986.
3. Trist, Eric, Higgin, G.W., Murray, H. and Pollock, A. *Organizational Choice.* Tavistock, 1963.
4. Mayo, E. *The Human Problems of an Industrial Civilization.* Macmillan, 1933.
5. Maslow, Abraham. *Motivation and Personality.* Harper & Row, 1954.
6. Robbins, Stephen. *Management.* Prentice Hall, 1988.
7. Herzberg, Frederick, Mausner, B. and Synderman, B. *The Motivation to Work.* Wiley, 1959.
8. McGregor, Douglas. *The Human Side of Enterprise.* McGraw-Hill, 1960.
9. Vroom, Victor. *Work and Motivation.* Wiley, 1964.
10. Alderfer, C.P. 'An empirical test of a new theory of human needs', *Organizational Behaviour and Human Performance*, May 1969.
11. Hersey, P. and Blanchard, K. 'So you want to know your leadership style?', *Training and Development Journal*, Feb. 1974.
12. Watson, Tony. *Management, Organization and Employment Strategy.* Routledge & Kegan Paul, 1986.
13. Leavitt, Harold. 'Applied organizational change in industry: structural, technological and humanistic approaches', *Handbook of Organizations*, James March (ed.). Rand McNally, 1965.
14. Labovitz, George. 'The individual versus the organization', *Advanced Management Journal*, Jan. 1970.
15. Secord, Paul and Backman, Carl. *Social Psychology.* McGraw-Hill, 1964.
16. Udy, Stanley. *Organization of Work.* Human Relations Area Files Press, 1959.
17. Woodward, Joan. *Management and Technology.* HMSO, 1958.
18. Pettigrew, Andrew. *The Politics of Organizational Decision Making.* Tavistock, 1973.
19. Mintzberg, Henry. *Structure in Fives.* Prentice Hall, 1987.
20. Gross, Edward and Etzioni, Amitai. *Organizations in Society.* Prentice Hall, 1985.
21. Ivancevich, John, Szilagyi, A. and Wallace, M. *Organizational Behaviour and Performance.* Goodyear, 1977.
22. Handy, Charles. *Understanding Organizations.* Penguin, 1968.
23. Tannenbaum, Arnold. *Control in Organizations.* McGraw-Hill, 1968.
24. Hinings, C.R., Hickson, D.J., Pennings, J.M. and Schneck, R.E. 'Structural conditions of intraorganizational power', *Administrative Science Quarterly*, vol. 19, issue 1, 1974.
25. Mintzberg, Henry. 'The organization as a political arena', *Journal of Management Studies*, vol. 22, no. 2, 1985.
26. Perrow, Charles. 'Departmental power and perspective in industrial firms', in *Power in Organizations*, M. Zald (ed.), Vanderbilt University Press, 1970.

27. Pettigrew, Andrew. 'Information control as a power resource', *Sociology*, vol. 6, issue 2, 1972.
28. Weizenbaum, Joseph. *Computer Power and Human Reason*. Penguin, 1984.
29. Flaherty, Michael. 'Multiple realities and experience of duration', *The Sociological Quarterly*, no. 3, 1987.

FURTHER READING

Gross, Edward and Etzioni, Amitai. *Organizations in Society*. Prentice Hall, 1985.
Robbins, Stephen. *Management*. Prentice Hall, 1988.

CHAPTER 7

Information management

7.1 Introduction

'Was it the same for you?', one demanded.

'Yes', the other replied. 'We were given two days' notice that we were to be computerized.'

'I've never had anything to do with a computer in my life', the first member of staff said, more than a little worried. 'Now they expect me to run one!'

'I've had a bit of experience on terminals and the like,' the other retorted with not much more confidence, 'but I'm also expected to understand how the thing works. I'm not even sure that it will make my job easier!'

'Typical of this place.'

'Yes, no one even bothered to consult us.'

These few words, seemingly a frivolous conversation between two employees, reflect a growing problem in business. As we increasingly complicate our information systems with computer technology, a gap develops between those who implement them and those who are expected to use them. But there is also a definite perceptual gap between those who manage these systems and the staff who must use them. What the above conversation suggests is that the great debate about who should drive the system – user or technologist – is a somewhat simplified synopsis of what is a multi-dimensional problem.

As discussed in the previous chapter, identifiable groups are much more than a collection of individuals: they are an amalgam of perceptual and structural interactions. When we talk of the user we should be referring to something more than just the client (the person, generally a manager, requiring a service), thus any analysis of the user group must include all its members, i.e. not just the management but also its cultural aspects which are a consequence of its interaction with the organization's structure and so on. It is only by doing this that we can understand how to restructure business environments after the implementation of change factors such as information technology.

7.1.1 Relational framework

The starting point for any organizational redesign should be its relational framework encompassing the information network, the political process and the structure. These will be affected by change which could in turn throw them out of balance. The introduction of a computerized system, then, will not only affect the information network of the firm but it will also have knock-on effects for the other two (see Case Study 7.1).

The literature discussing this area is contradictory. For example, Udy determined that the more complex a technology is, the greater is the emphasis on its administration.[1] Hage supported a similar conclusion in his meso-structural model of an organization.[2] On the other hand, there is a common belief in much of the 'management' literature that computerized systems reduce complexity not increase it by reducing the layers of administrators. Typical of this genus is the work of Stewart,[3] who sees the implications of computer technology as a challenge for change management presenting the possibilities of reduced administration.

7.1.2 Change and balance

There are many changes which managers can implement which would upset the balance of their organization. Generally, each has an obvious

---

CASE STUDY 7.1

A computerized system introduced to a small marketing organization fractionalized a highly integrated information network. Before computerization, employees were operating within an informal network of contacts and so on. Post computerization such links, although surviving, were reduced by the greater formality. The structure changed to reflect the greater formality by becoming more hierarchical. There are posts (and gatekeepers) where there were previously none, and as a consequence a complex network of perceptual barriers. This, in turn, affected the political process by developing a more power-orientated culture.

impact which is immediately addressed. A new work procedure should bring about new management procedures and hence new power relationships. The adjustment is immediate because its effect is obvious.

There are, however, other, less obvious implications of those actions which are rarely addressed. Unfortunately they fester and sometimes grow within the body of the organization, both perceptual and physical, preventing it from achieving a healthy equilibrium.

The introduction of information technology is one such change, or, indeed the redesign of a system which is already supported by such technology is another. It is the contention of this chapter that personnel responsible for information technology's control or implementation do not act in accord with the overall needs of the organization, and that consequently the traditional methods of information control and organization are not appropriate. In particular, traditional strategies are unable to recognize or manage the fundamental issues because they are based in the physical domain alone and do not recognize the interactive channels in the perceptual domain through which most of the computer technology impact is transmitted.

7.2 Conventional application

Every organization possessing a computer system large enough to have a substantial impact is faced with a split in its task structure. This split is between the technicians (people knowledgeable about computing and information technology) and the user (people who use the facilities but generally do not fully understand them).

Such a dichotomy, which is both perceptual and physical, has caused considerable problems for organizations because computer systems subvert the organizational structure by creating centres of power not in keeping with established control (see Chapter 6).

A particular firm is seen to be in disequilibrium because its three elements (structure, information network and political process) are not

---

RESEARCH 7A

NBS research confirmed the existence of the black box in many firms (30 per cent of those visited). We found that the firms most affected tended to be the larger manufacturing firms with an inclination toward formality. In the smaller firms we also found evidence particularly in those experiencing considerable growth (more than 20 per cent per annum).

in balance. The consequences of this are often manifest in what has been termed the black box syndrome. Its symptoms, if not its nature, are well known throughout the business world. These are, briefly: the lack of management control over what is perhaps its most important technology; the creation of a three-way power dichotomy between management, user and technician, and an increasing alienation between employee and the work process.

7.2.1 The black box

An example of this syndrome can usually be found in every firm with some form of data processing function. The black box represents the point where the information is processed (normally in the data processing department). How it is done and the operation behind it is, in most cases, beyond the perception and control of management and user, hence the name. At one end of the overall process, of which the black box is a part, data are prepared for input to the black box and are generally understood by the user. At the other end, the output from the black box is received and, it is to be hoped, understood by the user. The middle area is, to both user and management, an unknown – a black box. For management there may be some political/line control but no understanding. For the non-management user there may be some understanding but no political/line control.

Any user audit trail tends to follow input data to the point of entry into the black box, stop there and then to pick it up as output at the other end. The black box itself is very much under the control of a specific set of personnel, the technicians. They are, in effect, gatekeepers to all information which passes through their domain. Thus the more an organization computerizes its information network the greater their control as gatekeepers and the greater their power.

For example, financial data are produced by the finance department for processing. At that point the data are in control and possession of the originating department (finance). However, once they are received by the data processing department it is that department, acting as an agent, that gains temporary ownership of the data. This is because the originating department is not able to maintain control of it whilst it is in the DP department's domain. As such, the latter can process it in the way it thinks best, which may or may not coincide with the finance department's needs.

Within this part of the process the data are, in effect, in a black box. When they reappear at the other end they have been transformed into financial information and once again pass back into the ownership of the finance department. But more than this the DP department, through its ability to change data to suit its perception of the environment, can influence the actions of its client departments.

7.2.2 The role of history

The black box is a product of technological history. The way we organize information processes, even in a modern day micro-orientated business, has been determined by the mainframe applications of the late 1950s and early 1960s. These were not user friendly, requiring highly qualified specialists to run them, and very complex, almost indecipherable, programs to make them work. Neither of these allowed for much interaction with the user. Indeed, it was debatable whether there were such things as users in those days. They just seemed to be at the end of a complicated process and not considered at all.

The machines themselves were bulky and their operation did not allow for flexible workflow. They were locked away in contamination-free, air conditioned rooms with restricted access so that any integration was negligible. Input was thus introduced in batches and returned to the user as output in batches. This was not a work methodology adopted out of choice. The computers themselves could generally only run one program at a time and therefore processing work had to be queued. Input devices were slow and cumbersome, more often than not comprising card readers which aggravated the batch nature of the system. Output devices were generally printers, chain driven and very slow. These were widely recognized as the bottlenecks in the system even though the computer itself (the central processing unit) was not particularly fast.

As an example, work such as purchase or sales ledger control which would have been more advantageously conducted as a continuous process was being forced into a batch process by the limitations of the new technology. Many a firm's cashflow was disturbed as a result.

7.2.3 A solution applied

Managers' response to this new technology was to create a shell around it, almost to protect themselves from its impact. Data processing departments sprang up to house the technicians and the new technology and they quickly became something apart. Their jargon was not easily understood by outsiders; their culture was also not fully integrated into the rest of the company. In effect the manager of such a department had no immediate superior because none was able to understand its needs and objectives. As a consequence the data processing manager was placed in a powerful position because he/she became a gatekeeper to vital information sets.

Leonard-Barton and Kraus highlight this point by stressing that the relationship between user and technician has to be developed if its computer implementations are to be a success.[4] This paper was written with latter-day information technology in mind, and more importantly with latter-day expertise in mind. During the early 1960s there was no user available who could act as implementor or developer alongside the technicians. Those in charge of the technology did not themselves see the need to develop such skills in the user, and spent most of their energies in jealously guarding their newly founded domains. The responsibility for innovation, implementation and day-to-day running was given to them alone.

7.2.4 Why look back?

The purpose of presenting this potted history of computer development is to demonstrate that the present organizational structures controlling information are derived from those of the early days. Despite advancing beyond batch processing into real time processing we still quite often organize information as if it is to be batch processed. And despite the rise of the microcomputer and demise of the mainframe, we still have data processing departments attempting to control the work. Examples of such may not always be identifiable in the physical sense but rather in the perceptual sense. Recall of the discussion in Chapter 6 will bring to mind the concept of a perceptual, as opposed to a physical, grouping. In the same way, modern-day DP departments may not formally exist, but the perceptual grouping of those who control its technology is still there (see Case Study 7.2).

To look at the computer magazines and management literature a casual observer could be forgiven in thinking that all our firms have reached fourth generation computing and possess nothing out of date. The reality is rather different.

Even in those cases where this is so, such as in the example of Case Study 7.2, it is quite often negated by staff attitudes. In many cases senior managers are not comfortable with the computer, let alone a networked system. Their learning experiences took place when the computer was still young, and they are now unwilling to learn anything new. On the other hand, those technicians who are now themselves managers learnt their trade on the older style, batch processing

---

CASE STUDY 7.2

A typical example of the carry-over of DP departments is to be found in a local firm in north-east England. It is a medium-sized division of a large multinational and regards itself as being at the leading edge of its particular industry. Its information technology comprises a mainframe networked into a number of microcomputers. Despite the increasing expertise of the user, they are not allowed control over their own programs: everything has to be downloaded from the mainframe, no separate stand alone packages are allowed.

This has created a batch type environment for the information flow of the firm. To save computer time, personnel are required to batch their work, even though they can operate in real time. They are not allowed to access other microcomputers without going via the mainframe. Thus procedures develop which are time-consuming and cumbersome.

---

computers, and although they are undoubtedly competent in the newer technologies their perceptions of the user and how their technology should be applied are based upon their early experiences. The net effect is that even today senior managers are willing to give up their control of what is an important resource, and the technicians/specialists managers are willing to accept such a responsibility.

The following section examines how this shift in power can affect the equilibrium of an organization. We have already discussed that there is an inexorable link between the information network of a firm, its political process and the organizational structure. It has also been stated that computerized information systems are implemented without regard to the upset that they will cause to this status quo. What, then, are the possible effects?

7.3   The inherent weakness of black box

Socialization is the transmission of values and norms to individuals so that they develop an acceptable and standardized fit within their particular society. Children, for example, are socialized into being adults. It is a perceptual process rather than a physical one. Stories abound of where the mechanisms have gone wrong, for example the 'wolf children of Midnapore' where two children had been found in India in 1920 apparently brought up by wolves. They walked on all fours and preferred the diet of the wolf. They were in effect perceptual wolves, if not actually so physically.[5]

This example highlights an interesting learning experience permanently colouring an individual's perception and hence his/her actions. It is an extremely powerful process: the laying down of a perceptual veneer continuously updated by different experiences and social forces. However, it is not easily changed. Individuals as they get older, for example, tend to be increasingly reluctant to revise their established behaviour. Despite the aging influence it is a continual process that is with us all our lives. It is also a multi-dimensional process in that it relates to the different facets of our experiential framework. Thus we are socialized into roles within our family, gender, work and so on.

7.3.1   The dimensions of socialization

Individuals are, therefore, socialized into their places of work in just the same way as any other aspect of society. In so doing we develop a range of norms and values necessary to be accepted into a business organization. Neither is it a one-off experience when we enter work for the first time. As our experience grows we may be able to develop techniques which can short-cut the process but when we change our jobs there will be new things to learn. Cultures and norms vary from firm to firm so that during the first few weeks of any new job we have to modify our established perceptions accordingly. Schein, for example, is particularly keen to analyze organizations in terms of their differing cultures.[6]

I believe, however, that this process is far more complex than many have described. There seem to be three relevant dimensions.

Firstly, there are societal norms and values. For example, it is the norm within our society not to steal. Any deviancy is not tolerated and formally punished. Being a member of a subgroup is generally not accepted as an argument for not complying.

Secondly, there are subset societal norms and values. These relate to specific groups or organizations within our society. The dos and don'ts of a business organization are an example, or the codes of conduct of the legal or medical professions. They have been developed as a consequence of the wider societal norms and, although aimed at a specific body, are embraced by them.

Lastly, there are what I have termed conventional perceptions. These straddle the structures of society and its subsets and tend to be more abstract than the other two. They are ideas or general perceptions which cannot be regarded as societal or subset norms, which indeed possess their own socialization process and thus their own particular norms and values. An example would be the general idea that firms are in business to make a profit. This is a convention arising from the 'Protestant ethic'[7] of our culture. It is not a societal norm since many may not even be aware of it, and yet it is not solely a norm or value of a specific subset, such as management. It is, and can be adopted by many subsets, and this is what makes it different from norms themselves: consequential norms or values are transferred to those adopting it. In other words, by adopting such a conventional perception an individual is determined by acceptance of the associated norms to act in a certain way, to strive for a profit within a business organization and so on.

7.4 Conventional perception

Once accepted, conventional perceptions become embodied within the accepted wisdom of many subsets. Ideas about information technology and its use are prone to becoming conventional perceptions. One such example is the idea that there is a need for a data processing department because of the technology's complexity. To be competitive, firms must computerize, is another; manual systems cannot be as good as a computerized system is yet another. The management literature is full of conventional perceptions about information technology.

Neither are conventional perceptions easily changed. Societal norms can be changed by enactment of law or social pressure to alienate deviants. In a similar manner, subset norms are enforced by codes of conduct or peer action. Conventional perceptions, on the other hand, possess no such social framework through which to produce change. They come into being and change through a complex process of social historicism and thus cannot be easily altered by management decree for example.

RESEARCH 7B

NBS research project found the idea that business organizations should make a profit firmly entrenched within the senior management of firms visited. We also found a range of perceptions on information technology. In summary, they tend to support the idea of senior managers distancing themselves from the technology's strategy as well as operation. One common manifestation of this was in the use of outside consultants. Interestingly, we also found that these ideas were also built into many of their management training programmes. Some managers have reported being ostracized for attempting to change such perceptions, and we had heard of at least one being dismissed.

The implication is that we cannot always directly control our technological environment because our perception of it is obscured by established ideas. We accept these ideas as being sound because we are comfortable with their familiarity. We justify them in terms of their historical continuity. That is, their persistence within the minds of people over the years ensures their increasing acceptance: the easy option is to do just that, accept them, and not to question them. In so doing we establish norms to enforce them into which newcomers have to be socialized.

If we then link this back to the ideas developed in Chapter 6 we can see that such perceptions also have an important role in the development of the design of the organization. We saw there that they are the consequence of our perceptions and the way we interact through the political process. These conventional perceptions form an important part of that, which ones we decide to adopt or reject have consequences which reach far beyond our attitudinal stance.

7.4.1 The bottom line

The net effect is that our information technology systems are the way they are not because that is their most efficient but because we are more comfortable with them that way.

There is support for this throughout a broad range of literature. For example, a paper by Stangor in a social psychology journal stated that the establishing of conventional thought is based upon prior expectations.[8] For their part, conventional perceptions formulate expectations and enable an individual to develop a comfortable pattern or map for future reference (stereotyping).

7.4.2 Back to history

Computer systems are implemented within a certain perceptual framework. At that time they are themselves constrained by conventional perceptions, so that ideas established to that date influence the way the system is organized. In addition, however, the logic of the system itself, based upon those conventional perceptions, constrains future actions to within and around them.

For example, a computerized information system controlled by a data processing department is implemented within a business organization. The characteristics of that system are the consequence of the perception of its implementors. In other words, a conventional perception is that there must be a DP department, or that computer systems are better than manual ones, and so on. Once installed, then over a period of time the demands that the system makes upon individuals will itself alter their perceptions and generate new ones. There is thus an interactive process which operates historically as well as in real time. That is the organizational framework for many of our activities has been inherited from the past. Organizations, therefore, are better seen as being time-independent, driven by interactions from the past and present, and creating the framework for future interaction.

Tranfield thought this aspect vital in understanding new systems implementation.[9] Individuals setting up systems brought with them a personal history of experience and conventional perceptions, which Tranfield described as their historicity. These then are built into the system.

7.4.3 Conclusions

Tranfield is, in effect, arguing against a conventional perception guiding the way we implement business systems, in particular management information systems. It is in fact a methodology, but then most conventional perceptions are, in their way, methodologies. The way we construct our present computerized information systems have been constrained by our past experiences and perceptions. This is in terms not only of systems having been implemented in those early days and subsequently updated, but also of new systems being coloured by the same perceptions. The black box syndrome is not a natural consequence of organizational equilibrium but artificially induced by external forces.

The next three sections comprise a discussion on the implication of the existence of this phenomenon for the three major elements of organization. These are:

1. The information network.
2. The political process.
3. The structure.

It must be remembered that for any organization to be effective in the long term it has to be in equilibrium. To be in equilibrium these three factors must be in balance with one another.

7.5 The information network

The development of a black box within any organization encourages information to be used as a resource. If we recall the matrix developed

---

RESEARCH 7C

During the NBS project in the north-east of England we found that amongst firms displaying black box characteristics, the bureaucratic structures tended to suffer from its presence more than the managerial or professional structures. Rigidities of information flow were evidenced in the bureaucratic structures; political activity was greater; management control had diminished. In bureaucracies not displaying black box characteristics, the dysfunctional aspects were not so profound. There was not such a marked difference between managerial structures with or without black box characteristics.

---

in Chapter 2, whereby the necessity of a balance within a firm is identified between how its information is treated (thus determining the characteristic of its network) and the corresponding organizational structure. If the two are not in sympathy then problems could arise and the host firm may not be effective. The implication of this is that the maintenance of a black box control mechanism could force an imbalance between the information network and its organizational structure.

7.5.1 Down to luck

Whether an information network and its organizational structure match and are balanced depends quite often on something akin to a managerial lottery. Before computerization the information network is in many cases in harmony with its host firm. Subsequent to computerization, whether the information network remains in harmony will depend upon two factors:

1. The nature of information control implemented. According to Mowshowitz managers have high expectations when deciding for the first time to implement a computerized information network.[10] However, such expectations are fuelled by more than hope: they are developed within the culture of management itself and linked to the established ideas on control which are themselves based upon experiential assessment from the existing environment.

   NBS research (7D) seems to suggest that managers do not link, in policy formulation or perception, the nature of their information network with the implementation of computer technology. The existence of the black box within organizations is encouraging this misconception.

> RESEARCH 7D
> NBS research showed that 75 per cent of managers interviewed saw central control of their firm's information technology as essential in achieving lower costs and increased efficiency. On the other hand, 80 per cent felt that due to this centralization they were personally losing control of their departments.

2. The nature of the organizational structure already in place. This aspect is the outcome of a historical process. Managers can at times set out to change their structures, but generally the timescale of computer implementation does not permit considerable change (see Chapter 4). When computer systems are installed management do not therefore consider the needs of their organization structure. Indeed, in parallel with the upgrading of their information network they generally, and artificially, implement totally inappropriate mechanisms of control.

This section has concentrated upon the relationship between the information network and its corresponding organizational structure, the implication being that the black box can be accommodated providing the relationship between the information network and the organizational structure is correct. However, such central control of information may be detrimental: to what extent is discussed in the next section.

7.6 The political process

It is essential to differentiate between efficiency and effectiveness. Efficiency is a physical domain based concept in that it refers to a productive entity's (firm, department, individual's) capability of meeting pre-set targets. Effectiveness, on the other hand, is more perceptual domain based and relates to the productive entity's capability to fit into its environment. Thus a firm may produce widgets efficiently but it is not effective in its market because the widget has no demand.

The contention of this section is that, in the final analysis, computer technology is not very suitable for the information networks of our organizations because of the way management is currently implementing it. There can be no doubt that such technology increases efficiency, but it is doubtful whether it increases effectiveness. This is because the black box creates anomalies within the organizational structure which makes it difficult to achieve a balance between the political process of the organization and its information network, and hence could threaten long-term effectiveness.

Mowshowitz hinted at such wider implications when he linked politics and information technology.[10] He is alluding to the use of such technology as a political weapon. It is new and powerful and not well understood, and the person who masters it will gain power from it. The black box approach creates company 'sorcerers' in data processing departments, or their equivalent, with power beyond their status. This, of course, has considerable impact upon the organization's political process. There is, however, an aspect more profound.

7.6.1 Close and inseparable

The balance between the political process of an organization and its information network is a functional relationship which includes the organization's structure as well. The information network and the structure together create the inherent characteristics of an organization. One or the other could be the dominant determinant depending upon circumstance; and one or the other could be affected by variables, such as technology affecting the structure of the organization. The political process molds itself to the needs of that relationship acting as a transmission mechanism between the two.

The relationship between the information network and the political process is particularly close. Within this context the structure merely provides a framework or an arena. The way that individuals are allowed to control information and how much it belongs to them will determine to a great extent how much they will act politically. Conversely, how politically aware the individuals are within any organization will also determine the nature of the information network (see Chapter 6). The two cannot be separate.

For example, if an individual has knowledge which others do not have or do not understand then that person is more likely to use it to his/her benefit, to promote themselves within the organization or to resist the action of others detrimental to their aims and aspirations. They have this power through the nature of the information network and thus have the ability to express such power through the political process. Both are therefore affected by the characteristics of the other.

7.6.2 A natural balance

Before the computerization of information networks the balance between them and the political process was one which often occurred quite naturally. The information needs of an organization were matched by its political needs; it was an automatic, determined consequence which was to a great extent not interfered with by management. Indeed, the information network itself was probably seen as not being controllable, it was merely the result of functional (departmental, etc.) arrangement. This assumption was no doubt erroneous but it did not matter since no part of it was generally tampered with and it was, therefore, left to its own devices. NBS research has shown a greater awareness of information control in post-computerized companies, which tends to suggest a greater interference in the information network.

7.6.3 Interference creates problems

It is when interference happens that problems arise because changes could well be implemented the consequences of which are not readily understood. As such, no corrective action will be taken to offset any imbalance. A classic example of this is a post-computer environment: the relationship between the particular information network and the political process can be affected in two ways.

Firstly, the computer technology itself drives the information network out of balance with the political process destroying the established mechanisms within the network (see previous discussions), thus making established political relationships inappropriate. One obvious example is the relationship between a department manager and his/her employees. As already discussed the manager maintains power by being the department's gatekeeper. The installation of a computer network could short-cut such a functional framework. No longer in control of the department's information the manager's relationship with the employees could change. For instance, power could go to that member who understands the new information system or who can access the most valuable information.

Secondly, the management response to computer installation by creating a black box splits the company into a power dichotomy. The forces of change which this can produce are more easily accommodated by a managerially structured organization (see Chapter 2) since the political processes of such a structure are more akin to this type of impact. Nevertheless this may be more theoretical than actual. The tearing apart of the information network and the political process in this manner can do no firm any good, and if its structures are not in any way prepared, such an impact could prove disastrous.

Pettigrew's[11] model of an organizational network emphasizes the

---

RESEARCH 7E

The NBS project visited one firm where computerization has caused a shift in power from the department manager and her employees. The political processes created through the department's structure and manual information network were no longer appropriate. Political interaction arose on the basis that the information network in and out of the department was ultimately in the hands of its manager. The structure of the department corresponded to that by positioning employees to accommodate such a flow and forced a dependency upon their manager. After computerization, those forces of control were no longer effective. Other links were informally created which short-cut the old ones and thus rendered the department manager ineffective by destroying her gatekeeper role and placing reliance upon others outside the department, such as the DP manager.

---

political aspects and impacts which NBS research identified. Within the political process all information is a resource. How an individual obtains information is dependent upon the information network; how it is then manipulated depends upon the political process. The expression or manifestation of this is in terms of power relationships. These are natural to an organization.

Thus A's relationship to B is formulated by his position within the information network. If A has a strong position in that he is a gatekeeper to information important to B, then his power over B is greater. His ability to be a gatekeeper is defined by the characteristics of either the political process, the information network itself or indeed the firm's structure. He could be a gatekeeper because the information that he controlled is necessary in the political machinations of the firm (political process induced). He could, on the other hand, be placed at an important juncture within the information network (information network induced). Or, lastly, the way that the organization has been departmentally organized has placed him in a strong position (structure induced).

It would thus be naive to believe that organizations should, and indeed could, be effective without such relationships. They are an important dynamic to change within any organization and as such should be encouraged. At the same time they should be treated with caution, the balance between them all is precarious, and major impacts could quite easily upset it without management really understanding why.

7.7   The structure

In the previous two sections organizational structure has been discussed quite often. This is hardly surprising since the structure of a firm, both physically and perceptually, is the framework in which the other two aspects – the information network and the political process – operate. They are dependent upon it just as much as it is dependent upon them. And yet we find once again that management policy after computer installation is tending to indeed drive them apart.

Simon defined an organization as a complex pattern of communications and relationships between groupings.[12] His model emphasizes how delicate an organizational structure is. How sensitive it is to the perceptions and actions of those within it. How in many instances, therefore, it is very much an abstract concept. The actions of managers, then, after computer installation may have a bigger impact upon their firm's structure than they perhaps realize.

7.7.1   Structure and change

The methods of work, control and interaction are in place because the previous way of doing things has determined them to be so. Thus any form of quantum, as opposed to incremental, change brings forth structural problems simply because the balance between the three forces is upset and not given time to adjust and reassert itself. In many cases, after a short period equilibrium is established and the firm is once again on an even keel.

The problem, however, with the existence of a black box within a firm is that the new equilibrium is rarely achieved. The black box is not a natural development but has been artificially implemented by conventional wisdom. The rigid dichotomy created by such an approach therefore may not suit or be in sympathy with the existing structure.

For example, using Mintzberg's methodology we can identify a particular form of organization which he has termed adhocracy.[13] He sees such an organization as being innovative. Its structure is supportive of that role being 'highly organic with little formalization of behaviour'. He has identified what he terms the co-ordinating function of this structure as being by mutual adjustment. In other words, the firm relies upon flexibility in its management and control processes. Employees can approach other employees directly and without too many gatekeepers blocking their way. This allows for an entrepreneurial and

> *RESEARCH 7F*
>
> The NBS project had the opportunity to compare two adhocracies, both marketing firms. Both are the same size, about thirty people – fairly large for such organizations. One did not have any computer system; the other had a network of micros with a small team of experts to run them.
>
> We found in the firm with a traditional information network that communications were similar to those anticipated by Mintzberg's model. That is, a lack of formality and few rigidities. In the firm with computers we observed over a period of a few months increasing complexities and a more obvious hierarchy. Communication had become more formal. The employees themselves were able to identify differences in the work environment and atmosphere as compared with before computer installation.

innovative drive within the organization. It has developed naturally and thus the structure, along with the other two major components of information network and political process, is in harmony with it.

The implementation of a computer system into this firm would create unnatural barriers and thus force it out of equilibrium. The information network would be treating information as if it were a resource, whilst the structure of the firm was developed to treat information as a perceptual phenomenon. The consequence is a confused political process which no longer aids the organization but acts as a hindrance, almost a catalyst to dysfunctional change.

In the situation described in Research 7F managers are presented with the problem of how to respond. Their dilemma would seem to be that if they do not computerize they will lose a potential or actual competitive edge. On the other hand, if they do computerize they could become less effective and then again lose their competitive edge. There would seem no way out.

7.8 Summary

This chapter has shown how integrated the three major components of organization are. That is, the organization structure, its information network and the corresponding political process are so tied into one another that it is unrealistic to consider change in one without considering the effects in the others. Yet this is precisely what managers are doing, especially in connection with computer systems installation.

Such action is not only through ignorance of the existence of these components of organization and their close relationship but also as a consequence of a conventional perception based upon early experience with the old computer systems.

The effect of this upon many of our organizations has been disastrous. Artificial barriers have been created within the information network (black boxes) which sit unnaturally between the structure and its information system causing dysfunctional forces for change in all three components but in particular within the political process. In the short run, a firm's efficiency may well be improved by computer installation, but in the long run, as a consequence of an ensuing disequilibrium, that same organization may well lose its effectiveness. At best this could mean a loss in competitive edge, at worst it could result in stagnation and decline.

REFERENCES

1. Udy, Stanley. *Organization of Work*. Human Relations Area Files Press, 1959.
2. Hage, Jerald. *Theories of Organization*. Wiley, 1980.
3. Stewart, V. *Change: The challenge for management*. McGraw-Hill, 1983.
4. Leonard-Barton, Dorothy and Kraus, William. 'Implementing new technology', *Harvard Business Review*, Nov./Dec. 1985.
5. Haralambos, M. *Sociology*. University Tutorial Press, 1985.
6. Schein, Edgar. 'Coming to a new awareness of organizational culture', *Sloan Management Review*, vol. 25, issue 2, 1984.
7. Weber, Max. *The Protestant Ethic and the Spirit of Capitalism*. Scribner, 1958.
8. Stangor, Charles. 'Strength of expectancies and memory for social information: What we remember depends on how much we know', *Journal of Experiential Social Psychology*, vol. 25, 1989.
9. Tranfield, David. 'Management information systems: an exploration of core philosophies', *Journal of Applied Systems Analysis*, vol. 10, 1983.
10. Mowshowitz, Abbe. 'Social dimensions of office automation', *Advances in Computers*, vol. 25. Academic Press, 1986.
11. Pettigrew, Andrew. *The Politics of Organizational Decision Making*. Tavistock, 1973.
12. Simon, Herbert. *Administrative Behaviour*. Collier Macmillan, 1976.
13. Mintzberg, Henry. *Structure in Fives*. Prentice Hall, 1983.

FURTHER READING

Mintzberg, Henry. *Structure in Fives*. Prentice Hall, 1983.

Tranfield, David. 'Management information systems: an exploration of core philosophies', *Journal of Applied Systems Analysis*, vol. 10, 1983.

Woodward, Kathleen (ed.). *The Myths of Information*. Routledge & Kegan Paul, 1980.

CHAPTER 8
Decisions, decisions!

8.1 Introduction

We have so far developed and discussed the major aspects of an organization: the information network, the structure and the political process. These aspects have always been present but because of the complexities of modern business we have determined that they need to be understood in new ways. Another important component of the model is the decision. It is the mechanism through which the organization becomes more than just an abstract concept. Whether taken by manager or minion, whether far-reaching or not, whether group-driven or not, the decision is both the catalyst and the manifestation of human action through the political process.

There is, therefore, a close relationship between the political and decision processes. The two are fully integrated in that political activity stimulates, and is the consequence of, decisional activity. The other two elements of an organization, structure and information network, are also important. The structure establishes a framework (an arena) for a decision, either constraining its outcome or aiding it. The information network can affect the quality or the style of the decision (see Simon[1]).

Our perception of decisions, therefore, affects the way we understand business organizations. But more than this it has a great bearing upon how we understand change and its effect upon firms. In particular, when we introduce new systems and technology, such as information technology, whether we are able to understand its implications for change will depend, in part at least, on our interpretation of the decision-making process.

This chapter devotes itself to firstly determining what is a decision. Then it will examine the three major paradigms which seek to explain the decision and its process. Lastly, we determine how a decision is affected by the introduction of information technology.

8.2 What is a decision?

Ofstad defines a decision in terms of three possibilities.[2] Firstly, an individual has initiated a process of behavioural activity. Secondly, an individual has made up their mind to act in a particular way. Thirdly, the individual has made a judgement. Two analytical dimensions are implied, one portrays the decision as a unique action occurring once only, the other suggests the decision to be a behavioural or social process. The problem we have is to determine which is more appropriate in the analysis of an organization.

8.2.1 A decision is subjective

The difficulty in understanding a decision is the subjectivity attached to it. In general we tend to attach some sort of value judgement to it. Good managers make good decisions, we seem to think, in the same way that a good speaker makes good speeches. But how can we judge objectively what is good and what is bad? Indeed in the case of a decision, is it actually the decision we are judging or its outcome? In other words, I may be a bad manager who habitually makes bad decisions, but fortuitously I often achieve a good outcome.

Time can also play an important role in determining a good or bad decision. At one time I may think a particular decision to be good, whilst at another time I may not. A decision may be a good in the short term but not in the longer term. Time shapes an individual's perception so that the decisions they take change and thus their view about their quality also changes.

8.2.2 Cultural aspects

It is difficult, therefore, to establish what is and is not a good decision process. For example, different cultures have their own ways of making decisions. Drucker cites a comparison between a typical Japanese process and a typical western process.[3]

Briefly, Drucker sees the Japanese way through debate and involving all levels of the firm, arriving at an acceptable definition of the question, with continual reiteration taking months if not years to process. (In the national news it was reported that Toyota took ten years to decide where to locate their first UK factory.)

For the majority of western firms this length of time is unacceptable. Their decision-making process is hierarchical and autocratic. They want answers rather than definitions of the questions. And above all they want speed.

When organizations from different cultures meet to do trade or negotiate, problems can, and often do, arise. Neither side seems able to appreciate that the other party has different perceptions and ways of conduct. The western businessperson sees Japanese thoroughness as a reluctance to do business, almost deceitfulness, whereas the Japanese are extremely worried by the speed with which their western colleagues want to make a contract.

This is a macro example of what can occur within organizations. They all have their own ways of taking decisions which are dependent, amongst other aspects, upon their particular cultures. This has important implications for the implementation of computer technology, which can be seen on two levels.

Firstly, such technology, both in-house and off-the-shelf, is developed as a culture-independent technology. That is, its design (software and hardware) is produced in accordance with broad principles which have themselves been created by others who may not have had any contact with current users. At best this means that the technology does not fit in with a specific firm's culture. At worst it may mean that the implemented technology becomes a transmission mechanism for the culture of the organization which has developed the technology into the user organization. For example, a firm may develop a software package which it sells to another firm. Inherent in that product is a technological process which is in tune with the seller and not the buyer. This problem is particularly acute in information technology because of its impact upon a firm's social mechanisms.

Secondly, since the decision processes of each firm are different, the technology they use should also be different. In most established

---

RESEARCH 8A

NBS research identified firms which suffered clashes between their cultures and the demands of information technology. Computer software manufacture in particular was demanding decisions to be made in ways which contradicted the established culture. One in particular informed us of how prior to computer implementation they prided themselves on shopfloor involvement in many decisions. Subsequent to installation, though, they found that the strict deadlines of the new regime now made shopfloor involvement impossible; despite the fact that theirs was a networked micro system.

manual systems this is, in fact, what occurs. Technological processes are developed over time and survive if they best fit the social processes of their particular firm. The impact of computer technology is such that, for whatever reason, management processes are forced to comply with it rather than the other way around. Decision processes are particularly vulnerable in that they are forced to the pace of the technology.

8.2.3 Is there a common standard?

A problem occurs when, for analytical purposes (academic or practical), an attempt is made to set a standard. Simply, which standard should be set? Whichever it is, someone somewhere is bound either to disagree with it or to fail to understand it. And in trying to understand a decision and how it affects business organizations, we have a similar problem in determining what is good or bad.

For example, a good decision is commonly regarded as one which is:

1. Arrived at by consensus.
2. Not eliciting an unfavourable reaction.
3. With the highest payoff.

At first glance this seems quite reasonable. There appears to be no emotive or evaluative terminology. But when this pattern of a 'good decision' is applied to the different environments its absurdity can become quite apparent. In war, for example, a decision to attack an enemy at a particular time may be a good decision. But it certainly will not be arrived at by consensus, nor will it elicit a favourable reaction. It may not even produce the highest payoff.

This problem is particularly acute when considering information technology. Its characteristics based upon general norms require an adherence to standards, that is in application and in use. For example, Simon identified particular decisions which are suitable for computer processing and which he terms programmable decisions; others, which are not, he terms non-programmable decisions.[1] The temptation of many firms, post computer installation, is to convert as many non-programmable decisions processes into programmable ones as they can, particularly through the usage of management information and decision support systems.

Case Study 8.1 cites one example; there are many more on a larger scale. When the London Stock Exchange was computerized (the 'Big Bang') it was found that the computer systems were working too fast for their users to make appropriate decisions. Indeed, the suggestion

---

CASE STUDY 8.1

NBS research highlighted one medium-sized manufacturing firm suffering particularly badly from this anxiety to computerize all decision-making. They have attempted to transfer what were strategic decision processes taken by senior management, and thus non-programmable, into programmable decisions embodied by their decision support system. In one case the firm had computerized the weekly production decisions taken by the board.

The firm was a batch producer of engineering products. Prior to computer installation the board had to decide at the end of each week which batches had priority for the following week, based on length of order, customer importance and so on. When these facts were transferred to a computer database the weekly board meetings were then terminated in favour of a printout which took their place. Managers quickly found, however, that the quality of the action which ensued was declining. The computer program failed to capture the essence of human sensitivity and judgement.

---

seems to be that the technology itself began to drive the market and decisions that were once with the dealers were taken over by the information technology systems, not by deliberate design but because of the intrinsic and subversive nature of the technology.

8.2.4 Why analyse decisions to understand IT?

The quality of a decision and its characteristics are often shaped by the nature of the technology in place. More specifically, information technology is implemented to improve not only output but also the organizational decision processes. Partly at least, the reasons for implementation have to be seen in terms of the decisions that the particular information technology is going to support. However, whether or not decision support is the purpose for computer installation, in a structural sense the linkage between decisions and information technology is important.

The three major elements of an organization discussed above interact with one another to produce the manifest organizational characteristics. We have seen that their interaction is governed by the perception and ultimately the behaviour of the employees. This behaviour can only be analysed in terms of outcomes; one such outcome is the decision. A person decides to behave in a particular way. The decision is seen as a stimulus to action and therefore regarded as a dynamic of any organization. In other words, it is a major change factor.

Through these processes the links are made with information technology. Both are agents of change and both have important implications for the perceptual and physical domains of the firm. A question, however, seems to hang over the adequacy of our existing decision models to highlight such aspects. In the next section we briefly review the major areas and determine their capability to assess the impact of information technology.

8.3 An overview of decision theory

From a theoretical perspective the analysis of decisions implies three dimensions:

1. Decision as an action.
2. Decision as a process.
3. Decision as an organizational dynamic.

The last of these is discussed in Chapter 9. The other two are presented below very much in general form, highlighting a perceptual framework rather than a detailed analysis of work available.

8.3.1 Decision as an action

The decision within this view is a unique action resulting from several options. Its ownership is with the decision-maker and is the consequence of a perceptual and behavioural process which is unique to the particular individual. The implications are that: firstly, only important people make decisions because the activity is related only to a management function; secondly, that it is instinctive and not programmable (see Simon[1]) in some way, a talent which very few people have. A book by Sir Geoffrey Vickers[4] is a classic example of this perspective in which he portrays the senior manager as being a proactive (rather than responsive) and self-determining individual who makes decisions by judgement. This is a viewpoint for which the practitioner has the most sympathy. It gives the manager control over his/her own actions and it is simple to prescribe through a series of management training programmes, although Vickers himself probably did not see it in quite the same way.

Such an approach is the basis of many quantitative decision models. When we talk of probability theory or critical path and PERT, we are viewing the decision as an action in its own right. The decision is a focal point of a specific set of options from which other paths lead to yet more focal points and more options. In each case the decision is unique and independent, although quite obviously established within an overall analytical framework.

Vroom[5] provides a typical example of this with his model of decision tree analysis which is widely adopted by practitioners. It predicts a critical path which leads from one decision to another, each being the natural consequence of the other and indelibly tied to one another through a network. There is no recognition of processes behind each of these decisions. They stand alone. But their outcomes or consequences lead to other decisions. The manager therefore has maintained his independence in the act of making a decision but has been linked into an activity-based network. In other words, any decision he happens to take will be his own but it will affect other decisions though not other people.

This perspective forms part of the scientific management viewpoint in that the behavioural processes behind any management action are not considered to be important because managers are fully in control of their environments. This has implications for the analysis of information technology.

The computer in these terms is seen as a management support tool. The management decision is not programmable but can be supported by computer technology to improve its quality. Hence, within our organizations there is a rash of management information systems and decision support systems. Output from these is not seen as competing with managers but subservient to them. Productive output from other computer systems (e.g. CIM) is not interpreted as taking over the management decision role since choices made within it are not seen as decisions because they are not made by managers.

The decision and the computer are therefore not linked in an analytical sense. Both are seen to be controllable by management. The decision forms part of the manager's own ability to judge and is therefore not automatically open to external forces. The computer is technology and merely a tool of management. It is this gap between the two which has generated much complacency within management teams about the impact of the computer.

8.3.2 Decision as a process

To determine a decision as a process, or indeed as part of a process, is to accept the influence of structural or behavioural factors upon the individual decision-maker. There is by no means agreement on the impact of such forces, and there are several schools of thought relating to how the decision process fits into an organization. These are as follows:

1. The classical paradigm.
2. The contextual paradigm.
3. The political paradigm.

The classical paradigm

The title of this group of models should not necessarily link them to scientific management principles although their characteristics do attempt to make them prescriptive. They are concerned with the decision as a process rather than as a one-off action. In particular, they tend to portray the process as having easily identifiable stages. The specific number varies from model to model: for example, Lang *et al.*[6] provide ten stages, whilst Robbins[7] identifies eight. Simon[1] defines a much simpler framework with only three: firstly, finding occasion to make decisions; secondly, identifying courses of action, and thirdly, choosing amongst these.

The decision is once again seen as a management function in that only important management decisions are worth analysing. But there is a strong recognition not only that decisions are affected by individual ability but also that the decision itself is the consequence of a behavioural process. This presumption is critical in the social psychologist's view of organization. Maslow's needs hierarchy implies continual environmental scanning by the individual and a continual decision process readjusting to and equating with their particular needs.[9] Others such as Alderfer[10] emphasized political needs, or McCelland[11] highlighted our need for achievement. They all saw our behaviour, in particular the needs we have, as the overriding determinant in our decisions.

The prescriptive nature of these models implies that decisions are determinable against a standard of good or bad. Clearly, if a manager continually makes decisions which have beneficial outcomes, it would be reasonable to attach some sort of significance to that. However, it may say more about the person than the process. These models suggest that a good outcome (decision) is guaranteed by following prescribed action. They do not really tell us anything particularly interesting about the organization, since it is not their intention to be descriptive.

More importantly such models lead us into a misguided sense of calm about the effects of computer technology. They suggest that all decisions are programmable: after all, the stages are uniquely identifiable and thus transferable to a computerized process. In this world the decision is still not fully integrated with its environment in that it is the consequence of interaction but never a part of it. Therefore the computer is not seen as affecting the decision process in any fundamental way. It can take the place of humans but the process will be the same, only perhaps quicker.

It is my contention, therefore, that the classical approach to decision analysis is not appropriate. It tends to separate the decision process from its environment, and in so doing enables appraisal to be made of it which cannot possibly be realistic. By establishing an identifiable process such models are actively encouraging a mechanistic rather than an interactive approach to management. In other words, managers respond by prescribed method rather than what is actually needed. This is not desirable for a firm at any time because it tends to make them rigid and inappropriately responsive, though not necessarily unresponsive. In times of change such rigidity could prove disastrous. The implementation of information technology is especially one such time.

The contextual paradigm

This collection of models proposes that a decision, or its process, cannot be successfully analysed without it being considered in relation to its environment. The contributors are numerous and by no means in agreement or cohesive. The major identifying feature, however, is the importance placed upon the particular environment surrounding the decision.

An example of this perspective is provided by Simon and his extensive work on decision analysis.[1] Although, like the majority in this school, he is concerned with the decision and its process, Simon has placed it squarely into the organization by attempting to understand the force-field relationship between the process and the surrounding environment. How does the work environment of an employee affect his/her decisions? In what ways do such decisions then act as agents for change? These are examples of the questions he asks. Unlike the previous approach which regarded the decision (and/or its process) as being central to the model, Simon views it as being only part of the model. The decision process is still identifiable but is a fully integrated part of its environment.

This is conceptually different from the classical paradigm which treats environmental variables as inputs. In the latter case the decision process remains intact, it is only its outcome which is changed by the variable. In the contextual paradigm, however, the very nature of the decision process itself can be changed by the environment. An example can demonstrate this point.

EXAMPLE

A manager has to decide to make one of her employees redundant. She has limited time in which to do it and then to report to her superior.

1. The Classical Approach. Here, the decision process is given. It would be something like the following:

1. What am I required to do and with what objective?
2. What are the details of the members of my department?
3. Who fits the needs of the identified objectives?
4. Of those identified which person is most appropriate?
5. Do I have enough time to reassess before submission?
6. Submit proposal.

Whether individual abilities and constraints are allowed for depends upon the particular stance of the theorist. The psychologists such as Maslow and Hertzberg, for example, would believe that individual perceptions are important.

2. The Contextual Approach. Although there is a decision process to be identified, it is in no way as precise as the above. An example of this could be as follows:

1. Now is my chance to get rid of a potential threat.
2. Although I am sure it is for the firm's good, how can I justify sacking him?

The decision process is still present and identifiable, but unlike the previous one it does not give us the complete picture. We would have to know the story behind that rather extreme initial statement.

8.3.3 Bounded rationality

Simon's argument is that the classical paradigm in ignoring the environment is giving the decision-maker omnipotent knowledge. This, he proposes, is not realistic in that any individual or group cannot possibly know everything there is to know about their environment. In other words, their knowledge and perception are bounded by many aspects of the environment itself and their own inabilities. This means that decisions cannot be as perfect as the classical approach suggests. At best they are satisficing rather than maximizing.

The implication of bounded rationality

To a great extent the justification of the importance of the relationship between the decision and its environment is no longer an issue within the context paradigm, its members believing that it has long since been demonstrated. What is discussed now is the nature of that relationship and the ability of one to mold the other. Perceptions of these are generally divided into two categories. The first category states that the complexity of the environment makes it the determining factor in the analysis. Quinn[12] or Lindblom[13] determine the decision environment to be so complex that easy analysis is almost impossible. Equally, the decision process itself cannot be clear-cut because everyone is uncertain about what is going on.

Their particular concern is with how a manager makes decisions in such a complex environment. Lindblom sees that most models to date do not provide an adequate answer because they are based upon what he terms 'the rational deductive ideal'.[14] This he determines is an overriding assumption that in all things people/managers act rationally. He wonders whether such an approach is realistic and whether a decision-maker's perceptions are so unbounded. Lindblom's vision, and to a lesser extent Quinn's, is of an organization where decisions are taken incrementally to move away from the ills of the day rather than to make quantum leaps.

The second category states that the complexity of the decision process makes it the determining factor in the analysis. Lindblom saw the environmental complexity as the major determinant in the decision process. Others view the decision process itself, irrespective of the environment, as being too fragmented to be regarded as a process. One such group is Cohen, March and Olsen who published a paper and model entitled 'A garbage can model of organizational choice'.[15]

Cohen *et al.* propose a disjointed decision process. The environment is so complex that it is beyond meaningful interpretation other than as a framework for opportunity. Problems and solutions are quite often identified and presented by different sets of individuals working in isolation from one another. Problems are perceived by one department and documented; solutions, to perhaps entirely different problems, are generated by yet another department; and then perhaps a third party brings the two together as a package for action.

This is underpinned by the previous discussion in Chapter 6 in which it was argued that organizations present two dimensions to be managed: the structural dimension and the people dimension. The two are generally dichotomous in that they are managed separately. These two dimensions also produce problems and solutions on a separate basis, which on many occasions can cover the same aspects of the firm.

CASE STUDY 8.2

A management services department at some time initiated its own project in an attempt to increase efficiency on the production line.

At another point in time the production manager identified problems in the production line. The root cause may or may not have anything to do with efficiency.

The production director is under pressure to find a remedy for the latter problem. He becomes aware of the management services report and discovers he can justify the implementation of its recommendations in this particular case and thus quickly ease the pressure on him. Once again he may or may not be interested in whether the action is really appropriate. Provided it looks appropriate, that will be his prime concern.

Change in market demand, for example, can produce problems which need solutions for the line as well as the technostructure. What the Cohen *et al.* model provides is a dynamic mechanism by which both these dimensions can feed off one another to make decisions. Case Study 8.2 demonstrates the point.

The classical *post hoc* analysis of the situation described in the case study would more than likely interpret, through a step by step decision model, a logical flow which is simply not there. But even within the framework of the contextual paradigm, Cohen *et al.* would argue, wrong interpretations of decision processes would be made, based upon the assumption that once a problem is identified its solution is the consequence of one continuous process. The garbage can is like some perceptual black hole into which inputs are fed, and the outputs are by no means the consequence of an easily definable process.

Implications for the computer

Upon implementation of any computer system the implied assumption of those driving the particular project is that the decision processes are within the control of management. That is, the employees are making decisions more or less effectively in the way management would want them to. The purpose of introducing a computer system, therefore, is to in some way make that existing process more efficient by increasing quality or quantity of information and production.

NBS research has told us that this is a dangerous assumption to make; the Cohen *et al.* model also tells us this. There are two major reasons. Firstly, the computer system itself behaves in a similar way to the decision process predicted in the Cohen *et al.* model. That is, problems and solutions are fed into the system, pooled in a database and extracted as solutions for decisions at the other end. More research would have to be done to determine just how similar they are, but if this is the case then the unpredictability of an organization's decision process is being exacerbated, not reduced, by computer installation. This is not good for managers because their line and operational control will diminish.

The second reason is that such assumptions ignore the intra-organizational forces which have a strong influence on the decision process. The presence of computer technology tends once again to exacerbate the influence of these forces by tapping the information network over and above the functional boundaries laid down by management. This then acts as a direct communication channel between one part of the organization and another. One such force is the political process, a major element in any organization, but also profoundly integrated with the decision process. It is indeed the aspect most emphasized in the final paradigm.

The political paradigm

In many respects the garbage can and incremental models provide the link between the previous paradigm and this one. Its exponents see decisions and their processes as the consequence of power relationships within an organization. To them the understanding of either decision or its process for their own sake is irrelevant or of little importance. The decision is seen, therefore, as a mirror reflecting much more interesting underlying currents of human and organizational interaction.

Pettigrew viewed decision-making as a set of interactions through which organizational demands are processed.[16] These do not occur by chance but are directed from power sources within the organization. He terms the individuals at these loci of power 'gatekeepers' because they sit at the junction of a number of communication channels and thus are able to regulate the flow of information. In other words, when a decision is about to be made, it does not mark the beginning of a process but rather the end. How the decision is made will tell us nothing particularly useful about the environment or the decision-maker. But finding out why it was made, determining the interactive processes before the decision, will reveal the essence of the organization.

8.3.4 *The real decision-maker*

Pettigrew's gatekeepers will no doubt make decisions in much the same way as everyone else. Whether they gather all their information or not, make their decisions incrementally or by quantum leaps, can be identified in a logical decision process or not, does not dilute the impact of the model.

However, this view is not new. Indeed, the discussion of power and its effects in society have been debated a considerable time before management science began to develop the notion of a decision. Sociologists such as Pareto[17] and Mosca[18] had been developing ideas about power relationships between different sets of people. Marx himself pursued this many years earlier as his main theme in much of his work. In particular, a school of sociological thought was established known as elitist theory.

8.3.5   Gatekeeper or elite?

An elite and a gatekeeper appear in many ways to be one and the same thing. Both have power through their control of information. Both are thus able to make decisions which will affect other people in measurable ways. Parry highlighted this by stating that the main theme of elitist doctrine is that there exists in any society a minority which takes the major decisions.[19]

However, there is a fundamental difference between the two. Pettigrew's gatekeeper, unlike a member of an elite, has not been placed in a political context. He has power from control of information, but does he choose to use it and in what ways?

The boss's secretary could be a gatekeeper but she is probably not a member of an elite. The boss herself is also a gatekeeper, she is in control of information appertaining to her division or department, but she could also be a member of the elite group within her firm. So what is the mechanism which allows one gatekeeper membership and another exclusion?

In a complex organization it would be too simplistic to discuss such a mechanism in terms of class division: the ruled and the rulers, the workers and the managers. There is, of course, a broad division along those lines, but to be a manager does not necessarily make you a member of an elite.

To my mind, elite membership comprises three elements:

1. Quality of information controlled.
2. The degree of authority perceived by others.
3. The political orientation of the individual.

To possess quality information is not sufficient to gain access to an elite, although it may make an individual more effective in the political arena. It is through this greater effectiveness that elite memberships can change. The computer can increase an individual's power through repositioning on the information network and thus affect that person's political orientation. If, then, the role which an individual has within the organization is in keeping with the requirements of a new elite membership then by indirect means a computer may not only affect the power distribution within an organization (NBS research) but also the composition of elite membership (conjecture).

For example, the boss's secretary may be powerful because she is a gatekeeper but she will never be a member of the organizational elite because conventional wisdom determines that secretaries do not form organizational elites. Therefore she fails on the second condition above. A data processing manager on the other hand frequently fulfils all three conditions and is often a member of the organizational elite. In short, the computer could be indirectly creating new elites and new members of established elites.

Similarities between old and new

This modern organizational perspective differs somewhat from classical elitist theory in that membership of an elite does not usually come about through arbitrary occurrence such as birth, education, wealth, etc. But once established, in whatever way, the capacity of the elite to control is still much the same. Parry interpreted Mosca making the point that elite power derives from two factors. Firstly, the elite possess some attribute which is valued by society, the ability to manage for example. Secondly, because they are a minority they are able to weld themselves into a cohesive force which gives them power over the unorganized masses.

For a business organization with its particular social hierarchy, the control and manipulation of information is vital to both elite positioning and control. Business elites have to be gatekeepers, as we have already discussed, but that information must also be of such quality that they are capable of making high-grade decisions. Not only that, they must ensure, through their gatekeeper functions, that others are not allowed complete access to the same information and are thus able to make the same decisions.

This, then, is the link between decisions and the political process. The degree of power, through whatever process, is seen as the key because the nature and importance of the decision taken will depend upon it. To be powerful is to get your own way and thus the decisions you make will influence the organization. Wright Mills once stated that the power elite were those who took the important decisions.[20]

Thus the essence of this approach through its power relationships tends to render the understanding of the stages of a decision for analysis as almost perfunctory in its neglect of all that goes on behind it.

Implications for the computer

Pettigrew's gatekeepers were introduced in Chapters 2 and 3 in which it was suggested that they were important players on an organization's information network. It was also suggested that all firms have information networks whether they have computers or not. In the traditional firms without significant computer technology the information network would match the traditional hierarchy developed by management. There was a balance between information usage and control. It was also argued, however, that the introduction of a significant information technology system would tend to upset this balance because amongst many reasons, it tended to redistribute power sources on the information network by creating new gatekeepers and eliminating the old ones.

Central to this argument is the effect such redistribution would have on the firm's decision process. Individuals have power from positioning on the information network because it affords them good quality information which enables them to make appropriate decisions. The implementation of information technology through the information network changes the nature of information access by individuals and hence ultimately changes who can make the decisions. For example, a manager in a traditional organization controlling an important information junction, perhaps through a head of department role, may well be by-passed in a computer system and thus his decisions are no longer supported by quality information. NBS research found many instances of managers who claimed that their power had diminished subsequent to computer installation.

The organizational elite itself may well find itself transformed into something different by the implementation of computer technology. As discussed above, the shift in power on the information network may create new elite membership. The way that a firm makes decisions will then be changed not only by the technology itself but also by these new members wanting to manage and hence make decisions differently. There will pressures to change, therefore, transmitted through the decision process from all three elements of organization.

8.3.6 Conclusions

Most managers, if asked, would prefer the more prescriptive approach of the classical paradigm simply because it affords an easily identifiable menu for possible action. It is all very well, many of them would no doubt say, knowing how complex it all is and being told that at the end of the day it is all so complex that nothing can be done about it. Managers, they would go on to say, are paid to make decisions which means they must act, and not to do so is no excuse!

There can be no denying this. However, none of the paradigms has ever seriously suggested that because of environmental complexity organizations are better off doing nothing. On the other hand, to ignore something because it is complex is no answer either. Lindblom did however claim that a contextual approach for all its faults did at least deny the decision-maker god-like qualities and place him in the true world.[13]

Ultimately we have to decide the purpose of our analysis. Are we trying to understand an environment, and from that be able to operate more effectively? Or are we wishing to supply models for action against some predetermined norm and despite the environment, to achieve consistency in our businesses? The latter is addressed by the classical paradigm, the former by both the contextual and to a greater extent the political paradigms. But to act without knowing what it is one is acting in is not a wise course to take.

8.4 The two dimensions of a decision

Returning to Simon's[1] identification of decisions according to those which are programmable and those which are not, it would be tempting to suggest that the programmable decisions are easily computerized and the non-programmable ones are not. A computerized system is then built around the programmable functions and avoids, or permits access to, the non-programmable areas. This is indeed the premise upon which many installations are based, which is manifest on two levels:

1. As a substitute. If the decision elements are programmable then they can be replaced by a formalized system such as a computer system. For example, repetitive work can be readily taken over by a computer.
2. As an aid. If the decision elements are non-programmable then they can only be aided by a formalized system. For example, one-off decisions cannot be programmed but their quality can be increased with the aid of a decision support system.

Even if we ignore the wider aspects of decision processes however, by Simon's own admission the analytical framework of a decision cannot be defined realistically in terms of the two extremes: most, if not

CASE STUDY 8.3

The regional division of a large manufacturing multinational was observed over a period of three years as it combined islands of computer technology into one integrated manufacturing system. NBS researchers interviewed and observed key personnel over this period, gaining a profile on how they made decisions at a time when the computer technology, though present, was not significant, and subsequent to full integration when these individuals were members of a network.

We found that their functional responsibilities remained unchanged in that they were still formally required to report to the same people and were responsible for the same operational areas. Their decision processes, however, had become disjointed. There was no longer a match between their roles as defined by the elements of organization and the decisions they were compelled to take by interfacing with the new computer system. For example, one individual responsible for the interpretation of certain costing information was required to make judgements (non-program decisions) on information defined as appropriate by the computer system (program decision). She found that her role needs were not always satisfied by the data supplied to her. Manifest control problems ensued.

all, decisions probably fall somewhere along a continuum between programmability and non-programmability. These two dimensions exist within a decision whether it is part of a computerized system or not. The point is, however, that in a manual system the differentiation between them is not critical. The decision processes have evolved to best fit the interaction of the organization's elements (structure, information network and political process). With the implementation of a computer system, on the other hand, the situation becomes considerably more forced.

The requirements of its implementation tend to force identification of the programmable and non-programmable decision elements. It is only by doing this that systems can then be designed either in a substitutive capacity or as an aid. The effect this has is to destroy the natural balance between the decision process and its organization. Elements have been extracted and attached to other elements in order to create entirely unnatural decision processes for the convenience of the computer. Case Study 8.3 from the NBS project demonstrates the argument.

The problem described in the case study is more than the wrong data at the wrong time. The decision process which once belonged in its entirety to the costing function in the example is now split between two or even more functions, all, excepting one, being immersed in the computer system. What creates the imbalance is that the traditional hierarchy is still intact, more or less, and therefore the decision processes have not been formally re-established on the information network to match the new computer system. In short, employees, particularly managers, have decision responsibilities which are not in keeping with the new system.

Such a veneer of interaction adds complexity to an already complex force-field. The effects of a computer on decision processes (as with other aspects) are not easy to predict or assess. In the next section we condense all these variant forces into two major impact frameworks for the decision process. This section also serves to act as a collecting point for all the ideas on decisions and information technology scattered through the chapter.

8.5 The force-field of information technology

The two dimensions of interest are firstly, the decision process itself and how it is changed, if at all, by computer implementation. Secondly, the positioning within the organization of the decision. In other words, does the point of decision change within the process after a computer is installed?

For ease of analysis I have labelled these two dimensions as:

1. The concertina effect – to reflect the decision process change.
2. The positioning effect – to reflect the potential displacement of the decision within its organization.

8.5.1 The concertina effect

NBS research has shown that many managers and employees are finding that the way they make decisions is being changed by the information technology they are using. There is considerably less time to make a decision. What may have satisfactorily taken days in the old, manual systems now demands only hours so that deadlines are met. This may not always result in superior outcomes. Employees are often rushed into a decision which they may subsequently regret. The effect appears to be similar to a concertina, the compressing of an original decision process into a much smaller temporal space.

As such, the decision-maker's objective seems to turn into meeting computer deadlines rather than making the best decision. This can also

---

RESEARCH 8B

NBS research found that over sixty per cent of managers from a cross-section of business organizations within the north-east of England think that the decisions they make are for the convenience of the computer process: it is that which sets the deadline. In many cases it is also that which sets the parameters for possible decision outcomes.

---

be seen as a manifestation of the split decision process discussed above. The one-time strategic decision, for example, divided into both programmable and non-programmable events, and because the programmable event is computerized and thus must meet deadlines it tends to take priority over the non-programmable event.

There is increasing acceptance that decline in quality is a necessary consequence of this pressure upon people to make speedier decisions. The logic of the decision process is transformed from one of choice focus into one of an agency role for computer organization. You make a decision in order to complete the link in a computer process. Therefore the reasons and the logic behind such a decision are very much governed by how the computer system interfaces with your function.

Employees often feel that they must 'suffer' a computer system: that since its implementation they feel like cogs in a large machine. It does not seem to matter what decision they make, providing they make one which is acceptable to the computer. The decision then becomes an action predetermined by the characteristics of the system employed. Decisions are no longer dynamic in that they do not provide crossroads for organizational development, they are just links in a processing chain with its own internal logic which may be totally divorced from the needs of the organization.

Case Study 8.4 and others like it demonstrate that many decisions from within user departments have been transferred out into the computer system itself. Generally what is left for the departments is very dependent upon the other part within the computer system. Employees are then required to go through a process which is judged by its ability to meet computer processing requirements and not by its ability to produce the right thing. As a consequence people become confused and demoralized. They see the quality of their jobs deteriorating because of something (the computer) which they cannot fight because no-one will listen. More importantly they eventually realize that they must live with this thing and therefore they try to force their confused perceptions into a mismatch with the computer system.

CASE STUDY 8.4

In one NBS 'before and after' study of a manufacturing firm we observed a production manager, one of whose tasks was to decide whether to reorganize his line in order to meet specified targets.

In the manually-driven system. He was presented with a report on a periodic basis. This was generated by his own staff, or certainly by staff tuned into the needs of his department. From this he compared actual production with targeted production and any shortfall or over-production would be highlighted. Then, given the political and operational realities of that time, he would be able to come to a decision. He felt ownership for the decision and considered himself more committed to it.

In the subsequent computer-driven system. He is presented with an exception report generated by the data processing department from figures his staff have supplied. It often does not arrive at a suitable time in the period and in any event is often late. The figures are not quite synchronized to his needs. He must then take decisions based upon information generated by foreign departments (his staff only supplied the data) and must act to meet the computer shut-off date for the next month. His decision is then part of an organizational process controlled by others and about which he feels no ownership and therefore no commitment. He believes the quality of his department's output has declined.

Their actions and behaviour become pathological as a consequence. And since firms exist within the minds of those people the elements of organization also suffer and the firm is likely to become unbalanced.

8.5.2 The positioning effect

The second aspect is the effect a computerized system will have upon the positioning of many decisions. By positioning I mean the location of a decision, or its elements, within the interactional flows of an organization. As Case Study 8.4 demonstrates, a particular decision may no longer be positioned in a spatial or temporal sense as a natural consequence of some activity.

Many decisions are being predetermined by computer programmers when they create the programs. Their perceptions and aspirations become, in part at least, elements which drive a decision. Its process is transferred from the environment into the logic of the program. This is in a spatial sense because part of the decision is made away from the decision environment. But, more importantly, it is also in a temporal sense because the program itself was made in the past and hence possibly based upon conditions different from now, and certainly based upon different perceptions.

In short, in computer-driven systems, people other than the employees are contributing to an organization's decision processes, and are more than likely not competent to do so. Weizenbaum was in no doubt about the undesirability of our increasing reliance upon computers.[21] He saw that society's increasing reliance upon the computer to help make important decisions has dangerous consequences. Firstly, a decision support system is not generally understood by the users and therefore they are relying on something for which they do not know the ground rules. Hence their decisions are, in effect, transferred to those who write the programs since not knowing the ground rules the users can only act passively. Thus it is the program developers who in effect determine the outcome, that is the decision. Secondly, because the ground rules are developed in the past and somewhere else, they are independent of the users. The programs are therefore immune to environmental change. Organizations are making decisions predetermined by outdated criteria and ground rules. For Weizenbaum this could lead only to disaster.

8.5.3 Conclusions

Decisions and computer processes are closely intertwined. They are affected by the implementation of new technology as much, if not more, than many other parts of the organization. Weizenbaum talks of a computer-created gap (a black box) between the outcome (the decision) and the rules upon which it is based, and of an inability to correct such things. I would suggest that the impact goes beyond even this.

Because the decision and its process is such an integrated part of any firm, through it – acting as a dynamic of the organization – many of the perceptual effects of computer technology are being transmitted like some cancerous entity through the structure of the organization.

8.6 Summary

Contrary to the belief of many business studies students, the decision is not the private property of the manager. We all make decisions in one form or another. The manager's decision is seen as something special because the consequences of its outcome are probably so much greater. However, to a great extent, knowing this does not help us to understand the organization any better. The decision, like any other aspect of the firm, is an integrated part of the business process, and therefore we have to understand it in this context. It is not a separate thing, almost an activity to be developed and learnt separately from all other aspects of organization.

We identified within this chapter three major approaches to business decision analysis and then looked at them in terms of a perceptual aid (a model) for organizational analysis. Decision as an action was considered to be unfruitful for further analysis of an organization because of its rejection of context. The last of the three, decision as a dynamic, is to be discussed in the next chapter. The remaining theorectical approach was to see a decision as a process. Much of the chapter was thus devoted to an analysis of this approach. It is not a cohesive body of thought and comprises three identifiable themes. The first is the classical paradigm. This we determined treats the decision as a separate, prescriptive entity independent of the organization environment. We concluded that it is an approach which does not promise to further an understanding of the firm.

The other two paradigms – contextual and political – are in some respects similar in that they recognize the importance of the environment. The contextual approach, however, determines an identifiable and manipulable decision process. The political approach, on the other hand, sees the environment as being so complex and turbulent, and the decision process so disjointed, that no certainty could be established about consistent characteristics of decision processes within.

Apart from understanding these paradigms in terms of how appropriate they each are for an analysis of organization, the other object was to use them as a vehicle for assessing the impact of information technology. The lack of detailed research in this area tends to disallow any rejection of one in favour of another. However, it was argued that the different theoretical approaches did not contribute equally to the assessment of the impact of a computer, the implication being that the political paradigm was perhaps the most suited to capture the essence of information technology and its effect on the decision process.

Throughout this chapter it has been argued that decision processes are affected by computer technology, if for no other reason than simply because in order to make a decision information is required. Thus the better the technology is for generating such information the better the decision. Certainly the practitioner has regarded the relationship between the computer and the decision in this way and specifically on two levels. Firstly, the computer as a substitute for the decision-maker; secondly, the computer as an aid to the decision-maker.

Whether the computer is an aid or substitute depends upon the nature of the decision itself. Simon identified programmable or easily repeatable, operational decisions on the one hand, and non-programmable, strategic-type decisions on the other. The computer can carry out the former but not the latter. This encouraged organizations to split their decision processes so that their computers could accommodate as much of the programmable areas as possible. What management ignored in doing this was the profound effects such action would have on the way their firms took decisions.

The decision processes must reflect the logic of the other elements of an organization for there to be equilibrium. By splitting the decision processes, computer requirements were probably met but, through the linkage mechanisms discussed in previous chapters, the mismatch between the decision and its environment became manifest in poor work practice and control.

In particular, two areas of impact were identified. Firstly, the concertina effect, which was seen as computer technology through deadlines, etc. driving the rate of the firm's decision-making process. Managers simply no longer had the time to make quality decisions because the computer wanted an answer now. Secondly, the positioning effect which identified the transformation of the decision from the user manager to the program developer. Weizenbaum, in particular, argued that people were making decisions based upon program support they did not understand and therefore whose criteria they could not change. As such the decision outcome was predetermined by the logic of the ground rules upon which the decision support system was based.

The implementation of information technology, therefore, profoundly affects the decision processes, and through that has an impact upon the organization as a whole. Because decision processes are changed does not mean the effect will stop there. Through the balancing mechanism that every significant organization possesses, the altered decision process will change the organization. Management should be extremely cautious in implementing management information systems (MIS) and decision support systems because it is more than their decisions they affect. In the next chapter we discuss just how far this impact can go.

REFERENCES

1. Simon, Herbert. *Administrative Behaviour*. Free Press, 1976.
2. Ofstad, Harald. 'An inquiry into the freedom of decision'. Norwegian Universities Press, 1961.

3. Drucker, Peter. 'Management'. Heinemann Professional, 1974.
4. Vickers, Geoffrey. *The Art of Judgement*. Chapman and Hall, 1965.
5. Vroom, Victor. 'A new look at managerial decision making', *Organizational Dynamics*, vol. 5, 1974, pp. 66–80.
6. Lang, J., Dittrich, R. and White, S. 'Managerial problem solving models: a review and a proposal', *Academy of Management Review*, 1978.
7. Robbins, Stephen. *Management*. Prentice Hall, 1988.
8. Simon, Herbert. *The New Science of Management Decision*. Harper & Row, 1960.
9. Maslow, Abraham. *Motivation and Personality*. Harper, 1954.
10. Alderfer, Clayton. *Human Needs in Organizational Settings*. Free Press, 1972.
11. McCelland, David. *The Achieving Society*. Van Nostrand, 1961.
12. Quinn, J.B. 'Logical incrementalism', *Sloan Management Review*, Autumn 1978.
13. Lindblom, Charles. 'The science of muddling through', *Public Administrative Review*, vol. 19, no. 2, 1959.
14. Pugh, D., Hickson, D. and Hinings, C. *Writers on Organizations*. Penguin, 1986.
15. Cohen, M., March, J. and Olsen, J. 'A garbage can model of organizational choice', *Administrative Science Quarterly*, vol. 17, no. 1, 1972.
16. Pettigrew, Andrew. 'Information control as a power resource', *Sociology*, vol. 6, issue 2, 1972.
17. Pareto, V. *The Mind and Society*. Harcourt Brace, 1935.
18. Mosca, G. *The Ruling Class*. McGraw-Hill, 1939.
19. Parry, Geraint. *Political Elites*. George Allen & Unwin, 1977.
20. Wright Mills, C. *The Power Elite*. Oxford University Press, 1956.
21. Weizenbaum, Joseph. *Computer Power and Human Reason*. W.H. Freeman, 1976.

FURTHER READING

Ansoff, H. Igor. *Corporate Strategy*. Penguin, 1985.
Clough, Donald. *Decisions in Public and Private Sectors*. Prentice Hall, 1984.

CHAPTER 9
The decision as a dynamic

9.1 Introduction

The previous chapter examined the concept of a decision in a reductionist way. That does not mean that it ignored the organizational aspects. The examination, for example, of Pettigrew's model of political interaction demonstrates the importance of organizational forces. The methodology used, however, tends to treat the decision process as a discrete phenomenon, and therefore does not create to the fullest extent the necessary links to enable an appropriate understanding of the decision's fit within the organizational context.

Clough amongst others argued strongly for the integration of the decision, as well as technology, into any theoretical model of the firm.[1] The spirit of Clough's message is widely accepted in that decisions are seen as meaningful only within the context of their firms. The point, however, is more profound than mere integration, otherwise models such as Pettigrew's would have been adequate.

We are keen to identify elements of an organization and to put these into little boxes, linking them with arrows as if to demonstrate some relational significance. Yet nothing is said of the mechanism which makes all this possible. In other words, through what processes do all these elements interact?

Within the body of this chapter it will be argued that the decision provides a vital dynamic between such elements. To be appropriate, however, it must not be examined solely as an integrating force but rather as a dynamic, or enabling mechanism, which may or may not be integrating.

9.2 Organizational dynamic

We all make decisions, some of which have a considerable impact upon our lives. There could be other decisions which in themselves are not particularly important but collectively have an impact. Whichever, there is a sense of movement attached to all decisions: a sense of changing or reaffirming direction. For example, when we move jobs or emigrate or even decide which house to buy, these are all focal points in our lives which tend to drive us towards ultimate objectives or destinations. They are also constraints because they determine, to a greater or lesser extent, the direction we must go until the next focal point.

In hindsight we might be happy or sad about some decisions. Looked at individually, one particular decision may give much cause for regret and yet a deeper analysis reveals that such a mistake eventually lead to a substantial improvement. One bad decision, for example, could cause an individual to be dismissed from one job which enables her to get a far better one. We intuitively know that our lives make sense through an examination of not one but a whole range of decisions, and more importantly how they relate to one another. It is only by doing this that we could answer the question, 'Where did I go wrong?'

Similarly with organizations. They are collections of decisions taken over a period of time and driven by particular focal points. If we are to understand them and how they have achieved a certain position at some point in time, then we must look not to one decision or its process – no matter how integrated that analysis happens to be – but to a series of decisions interacting with the elements of the organization. For example, British Leyland, as it was, apart from having the Austin Maxi decided not to invest heavily in the hatchback market in the early to mid 1970s. This is despite having two models, the Princess and the Marina, which could have easily accommodated a hatch. This seemed to be in the face of a growing demand for hatchbacks such as the Golf. There are two ways of looking at this decision:

1. As a single process. Over a period of time, and taking into account certain variables, one decision was made not to make hatch versions of the Marina or Princess. In the light of market trends this would seem on the face of it a stupid and uncommercial decision.
2. As a series of decisions. There were many decisions taken which could have effectively constrained BL from making a hatchback version of their two current models. One collection of decisions, for example, led to the building of the production line in a way which

at the time did not envisage having to produce hatchback Marinas (a tooling problem). When it later became apparent that they needed more hatchback models their decisions about what to do were constrained by those past tooling decisions. The firm was thus faced with actions and decisions taken in the past which were as real as those taken in the present.

9.2.1 Decision upon decision

The British Leyland example highlights the error of any temptation to treat a major decision as an one-off process. Such a perspective does not necessarily preclude any decision process being more or less integrated with the organizational environment. It would not, however, recognize the temporal (time related) constraints that other past (or indeed future) decisions may have on the present ones. Every decision is based upon previous decisions. To understand them, and especially how they fit into an organizational environment, they have to be viewed as a historical flow.

Most models of organization, such as Leavitt's[2] or Davis and Olson's,[3] ignore this aspect by relating solely to the present. There are no mechanisms to encourage us to view organizations, particularly their decision processes, as time-independent phenomena. The decisions, very much like the elements of organization, are seen as the consequence of the here and now so that a decision is a now phenomenon rather than one linking into both the past and the future.

Figure 9.1, for example, is typical of this genre. It comprises an organization of five major systems (tasks, technology, structure, people and culture) each linked with one another, and therefore each dependent upon, and affected by, one another. It is by no means definitive in the sense that there are many other models with substantive variations. It does, however, serve to demonstrate a point.

The model in the figure indicates many relationships between the various elements but it makes no statement about how they are manifest nor how they are formed in the first place and continue to develop. How, for example, does the identified interaction between the systems tasks and people manifest itself? There is, after all, a two-way arrow connecting them. Our instinct tells us that such an interaction is logical and sensible. We know that people must perform tasks, and how they perform them will affect the nature of tasks, but in turn those tasks will affect the way the employees themselves perform. For example, an accountant will bring to her job her own perceptions and methodologies which mold the job into a unique application printed by her

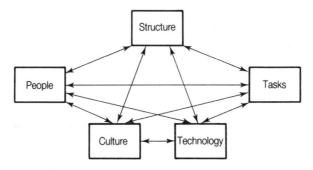

Figure 9.1   An example model of organization

characteristics. On the other hand, the job itself constrains the actions of the individual: an accountancy function will determine an individual to perceive his or her environment in a particular way.

Similar relationships can, of course, be identified between the other systems. Most models, including Leavitt's, do this quite adequately, but they ignore the dynamic mechanisms involved. To say there are links is obvious. But how do these links work? In other words what makes one system respond to another? Within systems models, for example, we talk of regulatory forces, such as feedback, which control relationships between systems and link each in terms of their framework to other systems. In an organizational system this is no different.

9.2.2 Decisions make it more complicated

In our acceptance of the importance of decisions within an organization we have established an extra veneer of complexity. We know that people make decisions within firms as everywhere else, but we also have models that describe and prescribe the decision and its processes in detail.

In the majority of cases, though, these models are maintained, and perceived, separately from their organizational counterparts. This affects the way we regard the decision. It is as if decisions are taken in a different dimension, and fed back, metamorphosed, into the organization. We have, on the one hand, a firm and all its activity, whilst on the other we have decisions somehow separate and to one side. We talk of decisions being integrated into the environment and demonstrate quite strongly how, but at the end of the day we do not have one composite model of organization and decision process. We have decision models with organizational undertones or organizational models sometimes (but very rarely) with decision process undertones. The Leavitt model has neither: decisions at best are only implied.

How, then, does this theoretical dichotomy affect the nature of our models? In a few words it makes them static and one-dimensional. These models are not working models as it were, they are static snapshots without temporal or relational mechanisms. Those aspects are explained as side issues outside the body of the model. Yet to understand the essence of an organization a model must be able to capture both temporal and spatial positioning. That is, an action within the organization is affected by other actions in the past or in another part of the firm. Perhaps no model can ever hope to do this perfectly, but at least the inclusion of decisions into one composite model of organization may further this end.

9.2.3　A possible solution

To recap, models of organization are not particularly realistic because they do not incorporate the decision process in an appropriate way. Such a process is the dynamic of organizations, driving and compelling them to change or to maintain their status quo, and linking one area to another in whatever perspective we choose to take. But the decision process also enables the firm, through the model applied, to have its own historicity.[4]

The decision as an organizational dynamic is not a simple concept to explain because much of it is abstract. It could be usefully understood in terms of integration of the decision process into the interactive relationships of all the elements of the organization. In Leavitt's model, for example, the two-way arrows established between the systems as links, can be viewed as decision processes.

How does this help? The short answer is that it enables us to understand organizations for what they really are. The conceptual frameworks of these models need not necessarily change significantly, but the emphasis within them could well shift. The links are no longer inert abstractions to be explained away as a side issue but an integral part of the process. The reason for this is that decisions are taken (on the whole) by people, and organizations comprise (on the whole) people, certainly organizational cohesion is gained through their perceptions. Thus to perceive decisions as the linking mechanism of a firm is to pull the perceptual/people aspect of organization back into focus once more.

In terms of the model presented in Figure 9.1 there are two implications. Firstly, all abstract systems such as structure, tasks and technology must involve people, because they can only gain form by people's perceptions. In other words, there would be no technological system without people to give it life, just a pile of junk. Therefore there is an implied human involvement in all these abstract systems and so the decisions are quite obviously emitting from them and linking into other abstract systems via their own human elements. At the end of the day firms cannot be firms without their employees.

Secondly, notwithstanding the above argument, the emphasis on a people activity (decisions) as a linking mechanism does tend to place a greater importance on the people systems in any organizational model. As such it seems reasonable to assume any decision process originates from this system. In other words, the link between the systems of an organization is not only the decisions of that organization but also its people system. This system in such a role forms an interface between all the other systems.

We could reflect this new perspective in a reformed model as shown in Figure 9.2. The organization is still represented by five major systems, each still dependent upon and affected by one another. However, the difference within Figure 9.2 is to portray the people system as the catalyst for all other interaction. For example, the relationship between the culture and structure systems is defined by the people system. The way that a firm is structured can have an effect upon its culture: thus formally structured firms generally give rise to formal cultures and so on. Conversely, the established culture of an organization can help or hinder its development and design. In all cases, people are needed to give it meaning, since the relationships between culture and structure are not established in reality but in people's minds and therefore appear real. Thus the people system, or perhaps the mind system, must come between both the other systems to give them their form. The argument is similar for the other system relationships.

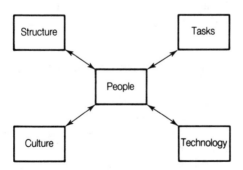

Figure 9.2 Organization model revised

This perspective is not a return to the central individual in the classical management ideal for the following reasons. Firstly, the people system may be located centrally in any model so that inputs/outputs from other systems have to pass through its domain. But that does not mean such a system need have any more or less influence on the other systems. The nature of such relationships is defined by the particular model presented. An example of a model using the people system as part of the linking mechanism can be found in Kast and Rosenzweig's book.[5]

Secondly, the concept we have of the people system, if not indeed of the whole organization, is too simplistic. Since the organization can only take form within the minds of its people, their system is the arena in which all aspects of organization are given meaning. To reiterate an earlier hypothesis, such transformation from cognition to activity comprises two domains: the physical and the perceptual. The physical domain represents the mind-independent (the 'out there') aspects of organization, whereas the perceptual domain represents the coming together of minds to interpret a part of the world in a particular way. The decision provides a way, through the organizational elements, to link the perceptual and physical domains.

This does not allow the individual self-determination in the classical management sense; their minds, nevertheless, form the organization, compelled and driven by forces beyond their perception and control. Like the madman, they are not entirely responsible for their own actions.

It also means, in apparent contradiction of Figure 9.2, that organizational models, to be a valid systems representations, should not portray a separate people system. In this instance it has been used merely as a demonstration of the importance of the perceptual organization and as a direct comparison to established models such as Leavitt's. In truth, people are the organization, they are the technology or the structure because their minds give these things form, and therefore no model should put them into their own discrete entity.

9.3 The organization and its decision process

The decision must be an important factor in any model of organization. Indeed, an organization model is lifeless without the decision process to give it dynamic qualities. There are many models to be had; the decision should play a part in each, although in many cases any inclusion of decision processes would be contrived because the analytical framework of most models has not been designed to be dynamic or systemic. The decision, and its process, is thus shown as a dependent variable rather than as a determining one.

It has already been argued that a general model of organization must be systemic. The three major systems of an organization have been identified (information network, structure and political process) which together give a model true systemic qualities, rather than contrived ones from a collection of systems which do not reflect a sustainable model. There is no people system because all three systems are people systems in that they take form within the employees' minds. Nor are the organization's decision processes a system of the model since they are not identifiable as a collective, but rather immersed once again in the other three systems. But decisions are an important enabling mechanism by transforming perception into action. It is essential therefore that the decision is fully integrated into the organizational model.

With such an objective this section will gather together the many strands of the discussion on decisions so far developed to form a composite model. This will be presented in two dimensions. Firstly, an examination of the relationship between each of the three major systems of an organization and the decision process. This will take the form of a specific proposition to be discussed. Secondly, since our particular interest is in technology, by applying to that a technological overlay, determining especially the impact of information technology.

9.3.1 Information network

Proposition. The decision acts as a focal or control point for information flow on the information network.

The information network of an organization is the channels of communication, both formal and informal, between all its elements and systems. It is, therefore, the transmission mechanism for the organization's information, enabling it to get from one system to another. Many, such as Stafford Beer,[6] see the decision playing a crucial role in this environment. Rather than being the consequence of some perceptual activity Beer sees the decision as an active mechanism in the organization's dynamics. In Pettigrew fashion (see Pettigrew[9]) Beer sees the decision being an activity on a important focal point of the information network.

Decisions could be imagined as perceptual roundabouts changing the direction and type of information flow. Not only that but they also allow the modification of information and hence organizational action through past experience. People bring to their decisions a knowledge of other decision outcomes. It is through these perceptions that the information network becomes more than a here and now entity. It is linked in time to all those other previous decisions creating in effect an organizational historical continuum. This is saying more than that a firm has a past: it is recognizing that within the organizational process there is continual interaction with the past through its decision process. This point was highlighted by Pettigrew.[7]

> Technology overlay. Because technology and human activity are integrated processes (see Chapter 3), the decision process can be affected by a change in technology. In terms of an information network this is manifest through a relocation of its decisional focal points and thus effectively alters its characteristics.

We have already seen suggestions such as Clough's[1] that technology and decisions are inexorably linked. To the practitioner the principle of this argument is accepted even if the mechanisms are not always perceived. He would readily agree, for example, to White's point that the greatest concern for any designer of an information system should be the match between the system itself and the information requirements of the user.[8]

In most cases White's sound advice is not followed. Other constraints interfere which prevent it being achievable. The link between any information system and its users are the decisions that those users make. All action is preceded by a decision, no matter how petty, and information (or data) fuels that process. Thus when we talk of user requirements we are talking of the ability of the user to make appropriate decisions. The information network involved must therefore fit like a glove to the user's decision-making needs. If it does not then, similar to a glove which does not fit, there is no comfort in the match.

Decision positioning

In a similar manner to Pettigrew's gatekeepers,[9] the location of an individual decision on the information network will bring to it greater or lesser value. How great or small that value is will be based upon its position relative to other decisions. In the analysis of any information network, therefore, the positioning of decisions as focal points is important and dependent upon three factors:

1. The technology involved.
2. The political process.

3. The structure of the organization setting the constraints to any interaction.

The last two are discussed later in the following sections. As far as technology is concerned, the impact upon decision positioning is obvious but often not considered. If the technological process is an interface between us and our environment (see Chapter 3) then our perception of that environment will be affected by it and hence our decisions. Technology demands action of some form; the action in its turn demands decisions. The decisions will then 'follow' the technology to where it has been placed in the organizational system. Such a positioning will affect our environmental perception and hence the decisions we make. The argument is circular but demonstrates an intuitive logic that if we rearrange our technologies within a firm, we may well end up changing the characteristics of its decision-making process.

For example, the technology involving a manually driven cashbook requires the allocation of a decisional focal point. That is, do I enter this figure or not? A computer-driven cashbook on the other hand will tend to split this one focal point into several minor ones. That is, they are located now not only with the cash clerk but also in the computer department. The nature of the two types is different. The first is unified and located in one area. The latter is diverse and located in two areas (see Chapter 8).

It should be stressed that this can happen with all forms of technology not just computer technology. There is an implication in Woodward's work, for example, of this phenomenon.[10] A change in production line technology can change the decisional focal points and hence the nature of management decisions.

If, then, the nature of decisions and their location within the information network change, it is reasonable to deduce that the characteristics of the information network itself also change. The overall number of focal points may increase or decrease thus affecting the flow of information. There could be a change in who can access particular information or the number of persons creating it, and so forth. All these aspects serve to alter the established patterns of flow which comprise the network.

The impact of this (see also Research 9A) on employees' perceptions is to compel them to act differently, sometimes pathologically. To seek to accommodate the change they may implement new structures around them or use information generated in different political ways. It may be that they themselves perceive their environment to be different and thus act accordingly. For example, if there are

---

RESEARCH 9A

NBS project experience tends to confirm that changes which led to a readjustment of the information network also had an impact upon employee perceptions. Many employees complained of more, or fewer, individuals in the decision process – if it were an implemented computer procedure the numbers tended to increase. Others mentioned the changed impact of their decisions giving them more, or less, ability. The general theme seemed to be one of unease and an awareness that they were making decisions in different ways, and in many cases not always in appropriate ways.

---

more decisions to be made in any given process because of changing technology, then over a similar period it will seem to an individual that his time to make a decision is considerably less. This is the concertina effect mentioned in Chapter 8. To the individual, they may be making the same decision as before, but they perhaps do not realize its increased diversification after the introduction of new technology. They only see the consequence of less time.

Management action

The consequences for the management of any organization are that to change the established technology may change the way employees make decisions not only through the direct impact of technology but also through the changing nature of the information network.

Returning to the argument of Chapter 2 (that data and information are separate entities) an extra layer of complexity can be added. By implication, the concept of data is attached to the physical aspects of an organization. It exists irrespective of whether it is perceived or not, like any physical object in an organization. It is a fact that there is a red carpet in the managing director's office whether it is seen or not. On the other hand, information is the consequence of a cognitive process and thus aligned to the perceptual aspects of a firm. Knowing that the managing director's carpet is red is important when ordering curtains for her office. You must be aware of that fact and find it important enough to act upon.

There are two factors to consider in relation to this added dimension. Firstly, how does such a dichotomy between data and information affect the information network? Are there two levels, for example, one physical and one perceptual? Secondly, in the light of the first point, does such a problem affect the focal points of decisions?

Decisions are perceptual processes, so can they operate only in a perceptual environment?

The answers to both these questions depend upon how the firm treats its information, in particular whether the members believe the firm itself owns the information or not. The collective belief of the employees will determine whether there is a difference between data and information, which will affect the way that decisions are taken. How much linkage there is with either the physical or perceptual domain will in the end depend upon the perceptual interpretations of the people involved.

9.3.2 Structure

> Proposition. The design of a particular firm will determine the position and particular characteristics of focal points on the information network.

The previous section highlighted the effect that technology, in particular information technology, can have upon the decisional focal points. The organizational structure too has a strong influence on their nature and positioning. This is because the structure sets the framework into which everything else, including the information network, must fit.

The way that functions or hierarchies are arranged, for example, will determine the points at which decisions are to be made (focal points), which would then reflect on the information network itself. In other words, gatekeepers within the information network are, partially at least, generated by the design of the structure. A manager is there because a department is there and so on. His/her ability to control information will determine the position of a decisional focal point and its effectiveness.

> Technology overlay. If the information network is changed by technology relocating decisional focal points, then the organization's structure must also follow suit in response to that or there will be an imbalance.

The principle that technology and structure are linked is well established. Woodward portrayed one type of relationship in her work.[10] Udy demonstrated a strong causal relationship between different technological characteristics and organization structure characteristics.[11] Perrow also unequivocally identified such a relationship by stating that technology shapes the structure of tasks and their co-ordination.[12]

What is being suggested is merely an extension of this. We have already concluded that the positioning of decisions within any process reflects the structure of that process. But we have also determined that technology can change the position of decisions within a process. By inference, therefore, if the decision positions are changed by technology then the structure should change also, otherwise there would be a mismatch.

For example, a particular manual cashbook system has one decisional focal point. This reflects the structure of the system in that one person enters up the cashbook and makes the decision. If the cashbook is put on the computer the number of focal points increases. The manual cashbook structure is no longer viable because that person would have now to span several functions. Therefore the structure has to adjust to accommodate this, otherwise the new system would not be workable.

Much of this may seem trivial. It is obvious to many that if a new system is introduced, work practices must change. What is not so obvious is that those changes must reflect not only the need for structural change but also the need for change in the information network. The link between the two is the positioning of decisional focal points.

The bottom line is that there are structurally imposed forces which push for a particular decision positioning profile within the information network. There are forces imposed by technology which also push for a particular decision positioning profile. The outcome tends to be a compromise or balance which is reflected in the nature of the information network. There is, therefore, by definition a balance between an organization structure and its information network. Any further change is potentially dysfunctional unless allowed to re-establish an equilibrium.

What must be realized is that if there is a change in one of these aspects (structure, technology or information network), there must a corresponding change in the other two. This is particularly critical in the case of computer technology implementation but is more often than not ignored, if perceived at all. It is the decision process, especially its positioning as focal points, which is the linking mechanism. Management ignore that at their peril.

9.3.3 Political process

Proposition. The positioning of decisional focal points will by definition give rise to the positioning of decision owners. Dependent upon the relative positioning of one focal point to another will be the power of that decision owner.

The relationship between information, power and the political process is well discussed in this book and elsewhere. Those who have information which is valued in a particular organization can achieve considerable power from it. The ability to gain possession of valued information is itself dependent upon an individual's position within the organization. This is not only in a hierarchical sense but in a locational sense as well. If their function commands a certain position within the information network which can trawl and control valued information they are, in effect, gatekeepers. As gatekeepers they can control decisional focal points either directly or indirectly. Pettigrew in proposing the concept of a gatekeeper saw this as being an important factor in understanding any political process.[13]

Others in the organization accept the gatekeeper's control of important information and are thus willing to accede to his influence, which gives him power. The basis of his power has arisen from the fact that he has been placed in an earlier position on the information network which enables him then to feed either other gatekeeper functions or decisional focal points with that information. Power, therefore, is relative to its particular gatekeeper or decisional focal point on the information network.

For example, Janet, John and Fred are members of an organizational information network (in other words they are employees of a firm). Their positioning is such that Janet receives information which John and Fred are dependent upon. Janet has power over John and Fred either because she can feed through selective information or because she owns a portfolio of decisions important to the other two.

Positioning on an information network is not just through physical location but rather a combination of both physical and perceptual aspects. Janet's position relative to John and Fred may be because she is their manager or it may be because she is the secretary to their manager. The positioning, therefore, is defined not only by organizational structure but also as a consequence of other factors such as personal credibility, knowledge and so on. A firm's hierarchy, for example, is an attempt to fix individuals' positioning on the information network.

Gatekeepers and decisional focal points are not necessarily one of the same thing. The two aspects are on many occasions combined whereby a gatekeeper owns a series of decisions which are focal points. On the other hand, a gatekeeper can also supply and not own focal points. The difference between the two reflects the different characteristics of the power relationship. The former is more likely to have objective power in that he/she is an important person placed formally in a good position in the hierarchy – a manager, for example. The latter is more likely to possess subjective power in that he/she is in an important position on the information network but not necessarily an important person. This person – the boss's secretary, for example – is generally a supplier of information to others who control the decisional focal points.

Power comes to the managing director not because he is the son of the owner, although that may have important implications, but because of his position in the information network and the decisions that he owns. The owner herself is important because she owns decisions which could close down the firm. But within the context of the organization she is not powerful because those decisions do not relate to the internal political process. Power, therefore, shifts in tune with the political process which itself can change if there is a change in the information network.

> Technology overlay. If information technology can affect decisional focal points and their location in any information network, then both the political process and the information network will change as a consequence. Structure will also have to change to maintain a healthy balance.

This is the logical consequence of the discussion in this chapter. The link between the political process and information technology is the condition of the information network expressed in terms of power relationships. Change the technology and those power relationships may well change too. As we have seen, if the decisional focal points are relocated by certain technology, their owners or gatekeepers will either gain or lose power. This will then affect their dealings with others and hence the political process.

A prime example of this happening can be seen in the shifts in power relationships in any department which has recently adopted computerized systems. New centres of power are quite often established to reflect the new ways. Who was once important in the old system is by-passed and new gatekeepers created. The important decisional focal points may still be with the same people but they have to look to these new gatekeepers. Or more drastically, they could have been relocated to others.

9.4 Summary

This chapter has demonstrated how integrated the decision process is with the organizational mechanisms by presenting the decision process as a dynamic of organization in terms of it being an important linking mechanism between elements of the firm. The logic is simple. We talk in general terms of this part of the organization affecting that part, but we do not explain how it happens. More importantly we do not incorporate this into any model of organization.

The decision process should, therefore, be expressed as an organizational dynamic rather than as a separate entity to be linked into any model. The manifestation of the decision dynamic is to be found in terms of its location in the information network. This then dictates how powerful an owner of a particular set of decisions may be. If they are located where their decisions are valued for one reason or another then they may have objective power. If they do not own important decisions but control information for important decisions then they are gatekeepers and have subjective power. They can also be both gatekeeper and decision owner and thus possess both objective and subjective power.

Power is thus determined by decision location and ownership. The political process is a consequence of these relationships. But both the information network and the political process exist within the structure framework provided. They are both constrained by it and indeed constrain it – in other words the relationship is two-way. Not only will the way the decisional focal points are located on the information network determine the organization's structure, but the structure itself will also constrain the positioning of these focal points.

So we now have a fully integrated model. Each element of organization is dependent upon the other for its equilibrium, with the decision process as its linkage. If we then apply something like information technology to this otherwise peaceful scene the destabilizing effects are more than likely to be greater than anticipated because its impact will cover more than what is immediately obvious. The three major elements of organization are so sensitively linked that any change in one will cause a corresponding change in the others: unless, that is, managements not understanding such ramifications prevent any natural adjustments by artificially maintaining the status quo in any of the three elements.

One of the major implications from this model is that a healthy organization is a balanced organization. That is, the three elements of organization are held in equilibrium by countervailing forces. But the concept of balance is a difficult one, it means many things to many people. As an essential aspect of the model being proposed in this book, it is discussed in greater depth in the next chapter.

REFERENCES

1. Clough, Donald. *Decisions in Public and Private Sectors*. Prentice Hall, 1983.
2. Leavitt, Harold. 'Applying organizational change in industry: structural, technological and humanistic approaches', in *Handbook of Organizations*, J.G. March (ed.). Rand McNally, 1965.
3. Davis, Gordon and Olson, Margarethe. *Management Information Systems*. McGraw-Hill, 1985.
4. Tranfield, David. 'Management information systems: an exploration of core philosophies', *Journal of Applied Systems Analysis*, vol. 10, 1983.
5. Kast, F. and Rosenzweig, J. *Organization and Management*. McGraw-Hill, 1986.
6. Beer, Stafford. *Decision and Control*. Wiley, 1966.
7. Pettigrew, Andrew. 'On studying organizational cultures', *Administrative Science Quarterly*, vol. 24, Dec. 1979.
8. White, Don. 'Information use and needs in manufacturing organizations: organizational factors in information behaviour', *International Journal of Information Management*, no. 6, 1986.
9. Pettigrew, Andrew. *The Politics of Organizational Decision Making*. Tavistock, 1973.
10. Woodward, Joan. *Industrial Organization: Theory and practice*. Oxford University Press, 1980.
11. Udy, Stanley. 'The comparative analysis of organizations', in *Handbook of Organizations*, James March (ed.). Rand McNally, 1965.
12. Perrow, Charles. 'Departmental power in industry', in *Power in Organization*, Mayer N-Zald (ed.). Vanderbilt University Press, 1970.
13. Pettigrew, Andrew. 'Information control as a power resource', *Sociology*, vol. 6, issue 2, 1972.

CHAPTER 10

A question of balance

10.1 Introduction

As practitioners in organizations we know that things are not always changing or dynamic; that there are periods of calm in which we work out our particular roles. The suggestion, therefore, seems to be that for some time at least an organization is in equilibrium, whereby the forces of change are counterbalanced to produce a period of stability.

But what is the nature of this stability or equilibrium? How does it come about? And what mechanisms create it – are they purely arbitrary or determined? Answers to these and other questions are important because how stable, or indeed unstable, a particular organization happens to be can have a considerable effect upon its characteristics. For example, many organizations experiencing periods of flux and instability are characterized by a more decentralized and informal management structure. This tends to be supported by the conclusions of Burns and Stalker who determined that a more loosely structured firm was preferable in times of change.[1]

This chapter explores the concepts of balance and equilibrium and determines their importance to any theory of organization. There will then follow an analysis of how the impact of information technology can affect both these aspects. We shall then be in a position to discuss the completed model in Chapter 11.

10.2 What is balance?

The concept of balance often conjures up ideas of something good. In politics, the idea of balance has been widely discussed, especially within the context of power relations producing a balance of power.

Since there is a large discussionary framework to be found in the political science literature, we shall use this as our starting point.

Claude, for example, defined the balance of power as having many meanings but felt the most appropriate was an identification of an international arena with a steady state.[2] He sees this being made explicit in the usage of a balance of power system. Opposing power forces interact within such a framework and, although not necessarily in equilibrium, are in a state of balance so that one power cannot dominate.

In this sense, then, balance is seen as an abstract goal of a political system. But it is also an important mechanism of the system, indeed a dynamic which compels the system to adopt a set of predetermined characteristics. One would always expect to find a fairly fluid situation which lacked hegemony and there to be a number of actors (nation-states) who could form into various alliance configurations. The balancing nature of such a political system requires those particular characteristics in the same way that the perfect economic market requires there to be many actors with a given set of attributes.

10.2.1 Seeking a definition

When we talk of an organization being well balanced we seem to be implying that it is in a steady state and not experiencing flux. Such an implication is also accompanied on many occasions by the idea that to be well balanced is to be totally dynamic and unresistant to change. In other words, to be well balanced an organization must possess a fluid structure capable of adapting to potentially dysfunctional environmental forces and thus enabling it to maintain a steady state, which in turn requires minimal management intervention. However, Miller has implied that such an assumption is erroneous.[3] He saw many management books encouraging firms not to resist change and to structure for continual adaptability.

The problem that Miller envisages arising from this is the possibility of a firm losing its overall direction and becoming bogged down in day to day incremental change. Others such as Quinn[4] and Lindblom[5] take the opposing view and see a firm as being able to achieve its objectives only through small and not large change. Their apparent contradiction highlights some interesting aspects of balance and equilibrium. At the end of the day, however, both sides are arguing for the same thing: for a 'well adjusted' organization which does not experience catastrophic, and dysfunctional, fluctuations.

The lowest conceptual common denominator for each approach is different. The incrementalist's viewpoint sees organization stability in terms of a balance. That is, the forces of change are dynamic and continuous and are allowed to find their natural balance with minimal interference. In this spirit, incremental decisions are the least disturbing. On the other hand, quantum theorists rest their case not on balance but on an organizational equilibrium. To be in such a state firms must, at least occasionally, be static. In other words, the environment does not always impinge upon the organizational structure. Equilibrium, and not continuous adjustment, brings about stability during which time a firm may flourish. Every so often, however, the environment (which is continuously changing) and the particular firm are out of balance so that major adjustments are needed.

There is an important difference which is more than mere semantics. Each approach requires different management action. The incrementalists by implication require non-interventionism. The quantum theorists seek greater involvement for the manager by allowing him/her the ability to determine the periods of equilibrium and adjustment. This suggests, therefore, that there is an important distinction between balance and equilibrium which reflects potentially large differences in management's strategic policy.

10.2.2 In pursuit of equilibrium

The political scientists were amongst the first to recognize a distinction between balance and equilibrium. Claude, for example, believed that a balance of power was being confused with equilibrium.[2] Some of the characteristics, such as a steady state, may seem the same but there are different forces operating. Many business analysts seem also to be guilty of the same confusion in not considering a difference, or indeed that it is important. If equilibrium is mentioned at all, it is seen as a neutral balance where the firm has achieved a temporary stability. The assumption seems to be that all firms need or seek equilibrium, and that in a steady state they must have achieved it.

In a world where balance and equilibrium are synonymous this is perhaps not an unreasonable assumption. A firm must, in the longer term, be balanced; to be otherwise would place it in a state of flux and not allow management to control it effectively. Therefore, if to be balanced is to be in equilibrium, firms must seek equilibrium. Any other option would mean jeopardizing long-term survival.

In the world of the political scientist, however, balance is not the same as equilibrium. They see the latter as a static concept, a unique point whereby the forces of change are equally opposing. Balance, on the other hand, is a dynamic concept representing many points whereby the forces of change are not equally opposed but rather cease to change

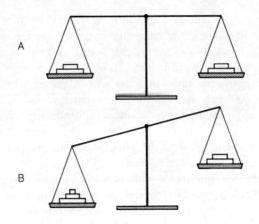

Figure 10.1   Goldsmith's scales

or be dynamic, albeit temporarily. An analogy of weighing scales is a useful approximation to demonstrate this (see Figure 10.1).

If both pans in the figure were filled with an ounce of gold each then they would be perfectly balanced and in equilibrium. If each were again filled with yet another ounce of gold so that there were now two ounces in each, the pans' relative positions would not change and they would still be in equilibrium and balanced (see diagram A). If we were now to add a further ounce to just one of the pans so that there were three in one and two in the other (see diagram B) the scales would move out of equilibrium to a new position of balance but without equilibrium. If we take half an ounce from either pan a new position of balance would be established which did not have equilibrium. Both pans do not weigh the same so that they cannot be in equilibrium but they are balanced because they are not moving.

There are, therefore, three possible states that a political system could be in. Firstly, in equilibrium and balanced; this is the most static of the positions and could be dominated by hegemony. It is not necessarily best. Secondly, balanced but not in equilibrium. Forces of change are greater on one side than on the other but the configuration of their interaction prevents any further change for the moment. Lastly, not balanced and not in equilibrium, representing a period of complete adjustment such as might be found in war.

10.2.3 *Organizational application*

With a few modifications such a model could be transferred from a political arena to an organizational one. A firm is not necessarily a balance of power system, although some may well be. In many respects, however, an organization is more complex. For instance, it may be realistic to determine a group of states acting as a group possessing one goal. With most organizations this cannot be so. In other respects firms are simpler: they generally have one dominant elite (although possessing many others) which can usually be identified in line with their management groups. A balance of power system is not so easily analysed. So it is with caution that such a concept is used and the differences and potential difficulties should be recognized.

Nevertheless it can be applied with positive advantage. If we think of an organization as possessing a balance of forces rather than being a balance of power system *per se* then we would be thinking along the right lines. This in effect means that an organizational system does not have a specific, predetermined goal (to balance its power) but rather that the goal is to balance its many contradicting internal forces in order that it can survive in the short run.

The organizational system is subjected to a dynamic balance which can be located at one of any different combinations of forces. It need not necessarily be in equilibrium which is just one point where all forces are equal. So that as with the political interpretation of balance, our balance is differentiated from equilibrium. This is indeed what differentiates the political balance from the already established idea of balance in organizational systems theory.

In the next section we pursue the application of balance in an organization. In particular, we distinguish between organizational balance and equilibrium, and determine their importance for management.

10.3 Organizational balance

A cursory look at the literature covering organization systems theory would quickly indicate an acceptance of the concept of a steady state, albeit on many occasions a purely temporary one. Unlike a physical system, however, this state is not unchanging, it is seen as an equilibrium moving from one state to the next and is termed equifinality. An organizational system is seen as developing or changing along a ratchet-like historical process whereby there would be times of stability followed by times of change. The control mechanisms of the firm would thus guide it from one point in equifinality to another.

10.3.1   Stability is essential

These steady state periods are seen as being essential if an organizational system is to maintain its validity. In other words, a system which is not valid in the longer term breaks down into entropy (chaos). However, during the calm periods firms are able to re-establish their credentials as proper systems and also prepare themselves for the periods of change or upheaval which may follow. Such turbulent periods are seen as inevitable because of the open nature of the organizational system. Therefore, to survive, a system must change, but in doing so it risks entropy. And so to survive a system must also resist change in order to gain a steady state; a paradoxical situation which has confounded many organizational systems theorists. To this extent antagonists such as Silverman have rejected it as a viable explanation of organization.[6]

10.3.2   Inadequacies of systems theory

The major weakness of organization systems theory is two-fold. Firstly, it is treated as a theory rather than a methodology (we discussed this point in Chapter 5). Secondly, the assumption that a system may be in a steady state or not – one or the other with nothing in between – is problematical. To remain balanced, and therefore valid, an organization needs forces which compel it to continual change (with a neutral net effect – to be otherwise would result in its decay). On the other hand, the organization must also adjust to its environment, which means change and thus by implication abandoning its balance. Systems theory does not seem to be able to reconcile the two opposing needs with its one concept. It requires the firm to abandon its balance in order to change. The resulting difficulty has been caused by the muddling between balance and equilibrium. As a consequence both are treated as the same thing.

The solution may lie in the usage and definition of these concepts found within the political model discussed above. Thus armed, we can now talk of organizational balance and organizational equilibrium instead of equifinality. By adopting two potential steady states rather than the one we have allowed an organization the ability to be appropriately balanced but not necessarily in equilibrium. An organization can thus maintain an internal stability whilst in a state of change. This is essential because many firms are quite obviously effective even within periods of change, contrary to the implication of organization systems theory.

10.3.3 An inexorable link

This two-fold perspective of balance and equilibrium also equates with ideas about change in an organization. Such aspects are dealt with in greater depth in Chapter 11, but at this point it would be useful to establish an overview. We have already discussed change in relation to equilibrium. Both concepts are inexorably linked. To move from one equilibrium to another requires change; or to put it the other way around, to be changing is by implication not to be in equilibrium.

Unfortunately, change is not as simple as the prescriptive analysis of people like Lewin would suggest.[7] Lewin sees change being either active in an organization and therefore controllable, or not active and therefore needing no control: one type of change which seems to move the firm from what it is to what it is not. Others, however, do not agree.

10.3.4 At two levels

Watzlawick *et al.* have identified two levels of change.[8] What they term first-order change is change which takes place or can be stimulated within the system. This is within management's control, so that changing the in-house performance of an organization falls within this category.

On the other hand, to change the behaviour of the firm's market or industry is a second-order change and is beyond the direct control of management. Kenwyn Smith[9] and subsequently Stuart Smith and David Tranfield[10] developed this theme further by determining first-order change as morphostatic and the second-order change as morphogeneric. The implication is that there is change and yet more change. The first sort of change is potentially controllable (although not always successfully) in that it possesses a logic which lies within the control function of an organization. The second sort of change is much more fundamental. Its logic lies beyond the boundary of just one organization and that is why it is considered to be generic. Indeed, there could be many layers of change potential affecting increasingly higher levels of social organization.

10.3.5 A similar relationship

We are able to view in a similar fashion not only the relationship between balance and equilibrium but also between those two and the different levels of change. To put it crudely, we could state that balance is to do with the operational aspects of the firm – the management and control of the entities which comprise the organization so that they are the most efficient and the most effective. Equilibrium, on the other hand, is located more at a strategic level since it is affected not only by internal forces but also by forces from the environment.

This rough approximation allows us to link quite nicely with the concept of change. This is not to suggest that the Smithian morphostatic change or the Watzlawick first-order change is merely operationally bounded, but the implication is that such a level of change is within the control of management. Thus change within this framework involves an adjustment of an organization's balance not its equilibrium. This is so because we have established balance as the steady-state effect of opposing forces within the first-order framework of organization. By definition, therefore, to not be balanced is to be changing. And such change must relate to the same framework of interaction, namely the first-order level.

The same logic can be applied to the relationship between equilibrium and the second-order level of change. To move or re-establish an organization's equilibrium requires change in a level of interaction beyond management's control.

For example, using Leavitt's[11] model we could assume that the four elements (technology, tasks, structure and people) are balanced so that one element is not affecting change in the organization. We could also assume that the organization is in equilibrium.

Management now wish to introduce a computer into their administrative processes. There will be an impact upon the four elements of the firm which will throw them out of balance with one another. Management, if it was wise, would recognize the impact and thus effect change on all the elements and not just the obvious one, technology. Such a change is at a first-order level and is required to re-establish the balance.

But such an impact may also throw the firm out of equilibrium. This could be manifest in that the firm is no longer effective in either its market or industry. To regain directly such an equilibrium is beyond the control of management: it could not change the market, for example (assuming the firm is not a monopoly). The trick would be for management to stimulate at first-order level the right balance combination which will induce equilibrium at the second-order level.

10.3.6   Many combinations

The above is, of course, but one example of the multiplicity of relationships between balance, equilibrium and the two levels of change. For example, change may not always be stimulated by management action, it may occur on the second level thus throwing the firm out of equilibrium and perhaps also out of balance. The point to be made is that this relationship is dynamic in that, although untouchable and very abstract, it is the consequence of the forces of change within the organization which are always present and thus cannot be ignored. What must be done by management is to arrange these forces as much as they are able in order to gain a steady state. It is only in such periods of stability that firms can consolidate their resources and become effective.

RESEARCH 10A

NBS analysis of many firms within the north-east of England and across the spectrum of organizational type tends to support the idea of the impact of change upon two logical levels.

The first-order level is easy to find. It is there in all management plans and refers to actions such as organization structural or production changes, new initiatives, policy directives and so on. It is also positively responded to (rightly or wrongly) as an outside force such as a change in market demand. Managers are at ease in this level because they perceive themselves as being able to control effectively (again rightly or wrongly).

The second-order level is considerably more difficult to find. Because of its long-term effects the impact may not be seen as anything special in a short-term analysis. In other words, managers may not see second-order change because of their short-term perspective. The manifestations of such changes are no less real, however, and may perhaps be seen in inexplicable downturns in the firm's effectiveness, for example, or a management structure which no longer matches the needs of its organization.

One firm in the North-east suffered this latter effect. It was considered a large employer and was a producer of national brand name consumable products. We found that it had experienced second-order change pushing it from equilibrium and alienating the established management process from the emerging organization structure generated by the changing environment. Its disequilibriate and dysfunctional characteristics made it a perfect candidate for takeover – which is precisely what happened.

10.3.7   A management problem

The two levels of balance and equilibrium confront management with two sets of problems and perspectives. Balance reflects, as it were, the health of the organization itself. In many respects, as well as being operationally driven it is also a short-term concept. Firms could not survive for very long in a state of imbalance: their cohesive forces would begin to break down and they would no longer function efficiently or effectively since they would be in a state of perpetual change. On the other hand, it is possible to have an almost infinite number of positions of balance, so that although balance must be achieved, if managed properly it is relatively easy to find.

To establish equilibrium, however, is considerably more difficult. Indeed, many firms may never really achieve it, or may have lost it through inadvertent management action and never regained it. In the long run they are doomed to decline or fade away. Thus a firm can survive, certainly in the short run, in a state of disequilibrium, but the change which is occurring at second-order level is still, nevertheless, having a dysfunctional effect. And unlike balance, within any given set of forces there is only one equilibrium (there can only be one point where all the negative forces exactly equal all the positive forces) and as such, is harder to find.

It would seem, therefore, that as in all other aspects of an organization the two levels of change-impact are in some way interrelated. An event stimulated at one level may have implications on the other. This has consequences for management because they might well be creating an effect within the structures of their organization which they had not anticipated.

10.4   A quick management appraisal

It is the second-order level of change which causes the real problems for organizations. Management focus is very much on the first-order level, it is to that which it responds. Its action, however, stimulates further change on both first- and second-order levels. The first level they are likely to be able to control, but on the second level the situation has been made doubly complex with change occurring on change. Thus the initial first-order change actions will more than likely not now be effective in inducing an appropriate change on the second-order level. And so it goes on, management is like the proverbial tiger chasing its tail, never able to quite catch up.

10.5   Balance and information technology

To recap, balance is the steady state achievable after a first-order change. In many respects it could be seen as an operational change consequence, whereby the aspects of change are located within the specific firm's control boundary. Equilibrium, on the other hand, is only established or re-established after a second-order change. This is a far more fundamental concept and is associated with strategic aspects of organization.

10.5.1   Degrees of change and impact

The implementation of information technology into any firm will affect it on both change levels. Its introduction will initially affect the firm's balance; by how much will depend upon the degree of impact. For example, a new tooling machine on the factory floor which significantly alters the production process will have a considerable impact on that particular firm and thus affect its balance. A new typewriter for the chief engineer's secretary is unlikely to have much impact on the firm and thus unlikely to affect its balance.

What the management of the firm described in Case Study 10.1 experienced when it introduced its new piece of technology were the effects of a first-order change which was sufficient to throw them into imbalance. In particular, the neutralizing effects of the control mechanisms on dysfunctional forces of change were rendered inoperative. Its actions to adjust the control mechanisms seemed to be correctly done since it would appear that another new balance was established.

In this respect information technology is no different from general technology. If we used a microcomputer as an example we would see that its impact may or may not affect the firm's balance depending upon the degree of that impact. Were we to introduce a microcomputer into a

---

CASE STUDY 10.1

A small firm based in the north-east of England which makes precision machines introduced into its line a chemical coating process for the parts of its machines. This was previously done by external contractors. The firm found that its impact was more than anticipated, to the extent that it had to alter drastically the management control mechanisms embracing the production line.

CASE STUDY 10.2

A small engineering firm with five administrative staff introduced a powerful microcomputer into the office. This was very much a technology-driven rather than management-pull decision in that the machine was far too powerful for its needs.

The impact it had on that little firm was catastrophic. The change in work practices it induced led to some of the staff leaving who had been there for many years. It also created an imbalance between what was being produced and the monies being collected. Bespoke software demanded new procedures which just did not slot in with the existing production process. The net effect was that the firm was brought almost to bankruptcy.

large organization we would probably find that its impact would not be sufficient to create an imbalance. On the other hand, if we were to introduce this same computer into a very small, owner-run firm, for example, then we are likely to find its impact to be considerable and quite easily bringing about an imbalance. Case Study 10.2 illustrates the point.

In a large firm the effect of the changes described in the case study would have been barely measurable. The change factors would have been the same in either case (i.e. the microcomputer and its required new work practices) but because the impact was different the consequences would also have been different. Balance is associated with first-order change, but the impact of that change has to be such that it can disturb the forces already at work.

Thus the consequence of a particular change stimulant cannot be consistently determined since it depends upon the size and characteristics of the environment upon which it is having an impact.

10.5.2   The individual has a role

Case Study 10.2 demonstrates the importance of individuals within the organization as part of the balancing mechanism. This is not solely through human aspirations but because all the change forces we have been discussing can only be understood, or misunderstood, by people and thus interpreted into organizational activity through them. Lorsch and Morse hinted at such a relationship when they implied that to be a member of an organization an individual has to be in equilibrium with the forces of that organization.[12] To pursue the full implications of this statement one would have to examine the environment and the socialization process. For our purposes, however, it does demonstrate that in some way people are acquiescent to, if not compliant with, the organization for which they are working. That is, they have come to terms with, and more or less accept, a particular set of organizational requirements and/or constraints placed upon them. If that relationship changes then Lorsch and Morse suggest that the individual's equilibrium is displaced.

This is more fundamental than the acquiescence of an individual. How they are as people, their characteristics, their perceptions and so forth, play a major role in molding the cohesive and destructive forces in an organization. So that, in Case Study 10.2, workers resigning because of the implementation of new technology is more than just the consequence of resistance to change (which no doubt it is); it is part of a greater overall change process which at the very least will affect the balance of the firm.

Such a conviction is based upon the important relationship (discussed in Chapter 3) between the individual and technology. As we saw, any piece of technology is to a greater or lesser extent an interface between the individual and the environment. We could say that a balance exists between the technology and the individual; this is more pertinent when applied to an organizational context. If a good part of the organization is formed in the individual's mind then their relationship with certain sets of technology will also determine how they see the organization and therefore how it is to be. On the other hand, how they see their firm will also affect how they relate to their technology. The relationship is thus a complex circular one, where no single aspect can be taken in isolation.

10.5.3 Individuals are the organization

There is considerable ignorance of these complex relationships. An individual leaving as a result of change is seen solely in those terms. In many cases it could well be; but in just as many others it is part of a chain of interlocking events, each having an effect on the other. An employee is part of the organization. Her perceptions and her relationship with the firm's technology (albeit minuscule in effect) feed into a group cohesion and steady state which is the organization.

Quite often an organization is devized by the management alone and without the support of the individuals who are designated members of it. It is then little wonder that these things are rarely successful; an organization is not simply a set of rules and regulations. Managers are the organization's shepherds and no more, they alone cannot form an organization.

The understanding of this is particularly important when considering the implementation of information technology. We have seen how more than any other type of technology it can affect our perceptions of the environment. Therefore, by merely introducing it into a firm and developing different work practices around it we have disturbed the balance in the organization. Our perceptions have changed because of it and we no longer act in the same way. We may try to understand our work environment in terms of the old ways and find ourselves at odds with the new order. Or indeed, the technology itself may make us see things differently which do not fit into the established way of working. We seem to operate in both a perceptual and physical organization, each affecting the other, driven by conflicting forces and linked by technology.

When an organization is thus in a steady state all these aspects are balanced, the perceptual with the physical, the individual with the technological and a complex array of many other forces. Any change is potentially dysfunctional to this because it will create imbalance and at best, in the process of moving to another new balance, develop a period of uncertainty.

10.5.4 Change affects perceptions

The impact of information technology is, therefore, not far short of catastrophic. Managers have to be skilful indeed to see their firms through such periods of change. As we have seen it has considerable impact upon our perceptions through the technology link. Our changed perceptions will compel realignments in organizational forces and the consequence can only be imbalance. No other technology can have such an immediate and potentially dangerous effect, yet we treat it as if it were merely other technology without realizing the havoc this may wreak.

The irony is that one of the first casualties of such impact is management control itself. As we have seen, management is essentially about controlling access to information by acting as gatekeepers. Information technology allows each of its users to see beyond these gates and access the lusher informational pastures beyond. The incumbent management structure becomes no longer necessary and managers are quite often by-passed. Their power diminishes. This in turn affects the way people within the organization interact with one another, which in turn affects the functional structure (departments, etc.) of the firm. And so it goes on, spiralling downwards in ever-increasing imbalance.

10.5.5   *The nature of the outcome is not certain*

The introduction of information technology may not require just a one-off adjustment to gain a new balance. Much, of course, depends upon the size of its impact in relation to the firm involved (see above), but if it is sufficient then it would seem that an almost unstoppable process is induced, something akin to a complete structural eruption of the organization. In the end (if there ever is an end) much will depend upon management action and how sensible and sensitive it has been to whether the firm will survive or not, let alone come out better.

Much will also depend upon the cohesive characteristics of the organization. We saw earlier that how a firm treats its information/data is important in determining the way it coheres. As such the balance of an organization, being the consequence of forces which are themselves influenced by these cohesive characteristics, is also thus affected by the way that information is treated. This is particularly pertinent when examining the impact of information technology.

There are three aspects which must be considered in this instance. Firstly, there is the technology itself; secondly, the way information is treated in any particular firm and thus the ideal structure to accommodate that; lastly, the structure of the organization. There will exist a series of balanced positions between all three which will enable the firm to achieve a steady state. To change any one of these would be to lose the balance and thus the firm's steady state. One force (or more than one), such as technology, could then become more dominant than the others and attempt to drive the organization towards a state which would most suit it but not necessarily the firm.

This situation does not necessarily preclude a balanced state; many healthy but technology-driven organizations are located at just such a position. But it is more likely, however, not to be a balanced state – or at best a temporary one – because of the domination of one force over the others. That is why many technology-intensive firms are so vulnerable to change (Case Study 10.3 is an illustration of this).

Balance, then, is never guaranteed, no matter how established it happens to be. In most cases management action is governed by a parochial perspective and does take into account that an action in one part of the organization may affect others. The tendency is to implement the technology first and to ask questions afterwards. The characteristics of the market, its producers and its sellers tends to encourage such an approach.

CASE STUDY 10.3

A particular organization in the north-east of England is very much technology-driven. The processes are dreamed up by the engineers and the rest of the firm is fitted into them as an afterthought.

There was, however, at this time a precarious balance, in that although dominated by one force (technology), steady state had been achieved. This was quickly upset with the attempt to go for computer integrated manufacture (CIM) by linking (via information technology) all the islands of technology.

The firm was quickly to discover that far from improving its competitive edge by such a change it was losing it. Production targets were not being met and the 'place did not seem as well oiled as it used to be', to use the words of one senior manager.

This firm's particular problem with information technology, despite appearing to be a good candidate for its implementation, was that it treated information as a resource. Paradoxically, this was worsened by the fact that the firm's structure suited such an arrangement. Since information technology tends to push structures towards a more perceptual cohesion, its impact on this firm was all the more substantial.

10.5.6 There is no easy prescription

Balance is such an abstract concept. It is no defence to depend upon the established ways just because they have been there for some time. Organizations are dynamic entities, and even with an inert management they undergo change frequently. It often seems to be the case that whether an organization re-establishes balance and thus a steady state is more by luck than explicit management judgement.

Even knowing about balance is not always helpful. What any manager would want to know as the bottom line is: 'How do I know when my firm is out of balance?' Unfortunately that is not easy to answer.

10.6   Equilibrium and information technology

The other aspect of steady state in an organization is equilibrium. The changes which affect equilibrium are second order and therefore not directly influenced by management. The irony is, however, that it is just this kind of change, leading to a shift in or the establishment of the equilibrium, that managements are most keen to achieve.

Nowhere is this more the case than in the implementation of

information technology. There is increasing talk of using computers and their systems not as tools but as strategic weapons to achieve a competitive advantage.[13] The point is that it is not that the technology produces more information and of better quality but rather that it produces the same thing in a more complex fashion and at a reduced cost. Because the initial learning and implementation curves of the new process are too costly for others to adopt, they are quickly excluded from the market.

10.6.1 Competitive advantage and change

In terms of the model presented in this chapter, managers are trying to achieve second-order change through policies and strategies aimed at competitive advantage. The failure of many of those policies is due to the reasons already discussed: that is a second-order change is not directly achievable. In the management's view, the computer is yet another weapon in their armoury for such goals. The managers interviewed for Research 10B saw the computer as being able to affect directly the relationship between their organization and its particular environment. To this end they were developing policies compatible with such expectations. What actually happens, however, is far more complex.

10.6.2 The reality differs

Information technology initially affects the balance of the firm. This impact first shows up in areas which are not always foreseen by management. They either do not know what is happening and therefore no corrective action is taken, or they may well understand the impact and take the necessary action. These are all first-order change stimuli, and through management response a new balance may or may not be achieved.

RESEARCH 10B

The NBS research project in the north-east of England showed that up to 70 per cent of senior managers saw investment in expensive computer systems (i.e. as opposed to one micro on the desk) as being an essential part of increasing their firm's effectiveness in their industry/market.

Unfortunately such first-order activities may have further reper-cussions on the second order. If the firm is established in equilibrium it is highly likely that a changing balance will also throw the firm into disequilibrium. The logic of this is that given the resource framework of a firm there is only one point of equilibrium which corresponds to only one point of balance. If, on the other hand, the firm is not in equilibrium, such first-order activities could serve to drive it further from such a point.

Another complication can be added to this: the responsive and initiating action of management. Throughout all this they are acting as if they are effecting a second-order change when in reality they are effecting change at the first-order level. Nevertheless, management's action does have profound implications for the second-order level. By acting as if they were initiating second-order change, managers develop inconsistencies at first-order level which could in the longer term change the relationship between the firm and its environment, which is a second-order change.

10.6.3 The unachievable equilibrium

It may at first seem that managers have achieved their objective of gaining the required second-order change. In reality they have achieved something different. Their previous objectives (to use information technology to increase their competitive edge) were set within the logic of a different organizational framework and therefore not in sympathy with what they have now.

In such a situation the firm has doomed itself to an inability to gain equilibrium. This is because there is no direct relationship between the internal forces of the firm which are still acting under the previous logical relationship and the new potential equilibrium which is located in a different logical relationship. To use the previous analogy it is like having to use two sets of scales, one for balance and the other for equilibrium. Figure 10.2 demonstrates this point.

The line AB in the figure represents the series of balanced possibilities available to a particular firm. Given that range of possibilities AB provides a logic framework of which there is only one equilibrium possibility (E_1). Subsequent change drives the firm to a new equilibrium (E_2) which is located on a different logical framework. However, management action maintains the old logic framework (AB) and thus there is a mismatch between the actions of employees and their organization.

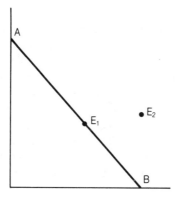

AB = Balance possibilities
E₁ = Equilibrium relating to logic framework AB
E₂ = New equilibrium outside logic framework AB

Figure 10.2 Unrelated balance and equilibrium

10.6.4 Another worldliness?

In many cases such a dysfunctional split would not be sustainable, forces would be pushing the firm back into one logical framework. Information technology, however, possesses a unique set of characteristics which would enable such a split to be permanent. It is not a 'normal' technology in the sense that it is not constrained by the existing organizational framework. Through the individuals who use it, information technology can generate other logical (perceptual) frameworks of organization beyond the existing one.

From one respect, at least, these frameworks are real: like any other they can govern the way that individuals act and react. They are also second-order logic because they are not of the first-order organization that we are familiar with. As such, two organizations are created out of the one: the first being as we know it and accessible (first-order), the second an abstract phenomenon linked just as strongly to the organization but on a second-order level and hence beyond the direct control of management.

This relates to a discussion in which every organization was identified as having two parts: a physical and a perceptual aspect. We could also determine that the former possesses a first-order logic and the latter a second-order, so that all these factors have the potential to exist in every firm. What information technology does through its introduction and continued use is to drive the emphasis of the firm's logic towards the perceptual, second-order end. In so doing it establishes the possibility of an equilibrium point outside the logical boundary of the existing organizational framework. Given this, such an equilibrium would be impossible to achieve for any organization.

In short, the implementation of information technology, by its very nature, will not allow a firm to gain its equilibrium. This is not a desirable situation especially for the long-run stability of the organization (see discussion earlier in chapter). To avoid this, management should not drop information technology – there are many successful firms which owe their position to its introduction – but should abandon technology-push policies and adopt a more imaginative and further-reaching implementation strategy.

10.7   Summary

In many respects this chapter is the logical completion of the earlier chapters; it is also a departure from them. In the first sense this chapter ties together the loose ends of previous chapters by converting them into a working dynamic model. Whereas in those initial chapters we were looking at the forces of organization (the bricks), here we have been looking at a composite force which binds them all together (the mortar). These abstract concepts may be difficult to grasp, they nevertheless deserve close attention because to succeed is to grasp hold of the fundamental workings of an organization.

We have developed the proposal that organizations are a complexity of contradicting forces. This chapter determined, however, that although there must be dynamic interaction within all organizations which often leads to contradiction, there must also be periods of stability (steady state) if an organization is to survive and develop – to remain healthy. However, organizations must also establish equilibrium. This has much to do with the concept of change. To be in equilibrium is 'to be what is' and not changing. To be changing is, on the other hand, 'to be what is not' and therefore not in equilibrium. But there are two logical levels of change, and one equilibrium point cannot cover them both.

It was proposed that first-order change was associated with a more physically-orientated perception, change within the particular social system. It is controllable and can be induced by management, and because of this is linked with the operational level of an organization. But to have change one must also have non-change. At this level we called such an identifiable phenomenon balance. That is where all the forces within the organization are neutralized by their own interaction so as not to produce change. There are many points of balance. And since it reflects the health of the operational machinery of the firm, we decided that in the short term a firm must be balanced more often than not.

A considerable amount of change also occurs at the second-order level of logic as well. In simple terms this is change outside the social system. For an organization this would be likely to involve aspects in its environment: but it is not just aspects physically beyond the firm (there are environmental changes which are first order for example), it is conceptually distant as well. That is, because we are constrained by the first order we cannot directly manipulate occurrence of change on the second-order level. Yet in the same way as first-order change and the organization must be stable on second-order level when it is not changing.

We call this equilibrium. For any given framework of organization it is a unique single point position, unlike the multiple points of balance. This is because there can only be one fundamental point of no change (equifinality) which must involve all systems beyond that of the specific social system, the environment for example.

Second-order change can be self-induced or induced by changes occurring on the lower level; quite often, therefore, they are stimulated by management. However, because of the complexities involved in achieving an equilibrium it is likely that many firms will never achieve it. In the short run, firms do not need to be in equilibrium since their environment is always dynamic and if they possess an internal, first-order balance, they will be seen as responsive to outside change. But in the long run a firm must be in equilibrium at least for some of the time if it is to survive. Every system must reach its point of equifinality.

The relevance all this has for management is quite profound. All actions for change or non-change have repercussions throughout the organization which are beyond what is initially obvious. Management actions on the first-order level may work through to second order, for example, and permanently throw the organization into disequilibrium. Managements must realize, therefore, that their firms are intricate networks of dependencies. What they do in one place which seems relatively minor may have serious implications somewhere else, although the two may not necessarily be linked in time or understanding. Nowhere is this argument more pertinent than in the implementation of information technology. Managements are introducing computers into their firms solely upon the grounds of efficiency criteria without fully realizing the effect they may have on their effectiveness or indeed their very existence.

REFERENCES

1. Burns, T. and Stalker, G. *The Management of Innovation.* Tavistock, 1961.
2. Claude, Inis. *Power and International Relations.* Random House, 1962.
3. Miller, Danny. 'Evolution and revolution: a quantum view of structural change in organizations', *Journal of Management Studies*, vol. 19, no. 2, 1982.
4. Quinn, J.B. *Strategies for Change: Logical incrementalism.* Irwin, 1980.
5. Lindblom, Charles. 'The science of muddling through', *Public Administration Review*, vol. 19, 1959.
6. Silverman, David. *The Theory of Organizations.* Heinemann, 1970.
7. Lewin, Kurt. *Field Theory in Social Science.* Harper & Row, 1951.
8. Watzlawick, P., Weakland, J.H. and Fisch, R. *Change: Principles of problem formation and problem resolution.* W.W. Norton, 1974.
9. Smith, Kenwyn. 'Philosophical problems in thinking about organizational change', in *Change in Organizations*, Paul Goodman & Associates (eds). Jossey Bass, 1982.
10. Smith, Stuart and Tranfield, David. 'A strategic methodology for implementing technical change in manufacturing', paper given to the British Academy of Management, inaugural conference, Sept. 1987.
11. Leavitt, Harold. 'Applied organizational change in industry: structural, technological and humanistic approaches', in *Handbook of Organizations*, James March (ed.). Rand McNally, 1959.
12. Lorsch, Jay and Morse, John. *Organizations and their Members.* Harper & Row, 1974.
13. Parsons, G.L. 'Information technology: a new competitive weapon', *Sloan Management Review*, Autumn 1983.

FURTHER READING

Goodman & Associates (eds). *Change in Organizations.* Jossey Bass, 1982.

CHAPTER 11

Virtual organization

11.1 Introduction

The previous chapters have developed, in part, the fundamental elements of a model which perhaps would allow us a more enlightened understanding of the perceptual organization. It is now time to bring all these aspects together within a conceptual framework and to establish a working mechanism for future analysis.

Firstly, we need formally to differentiate between physical organization and perceptual organization. Throughout there has been reference to both these aspects. We have, for instance, discussed the three major elements of a firm in terms of both the perceptual and the physical but without definition.

The following sections will, therefore, present a formal definition. We will then re-examine the three aspects of organization (information network, structure and political process) and apply them to our newly-formed definition. This will enable us then to turn our attention towards the concept of virtual organization itself. In so doing we shall identify one piece of work already done in this direction and then look in detail at the dichotomy existing between the physical and perceptual aspects which create virtual organization. Lastly, we shall put the model together and see how it works.

11.2 Physical and perceptual organization

This section identifies the difference between the physical part of the organization and its perceptual part by presenting a perceptual pattern. It is essential, however, that an appreciation of the difference is grasped so that the mechanisms of the model developed herein are fully understood.

Everyone has his or her own ideas about the two concepts physical and perceptual. The instinct we all seem to have that the world of the organization relates to its physical aspects is reasonably sound. The abstract, perceptual aspects, though, we tend not to understand, nor even try to do so. Yet even in our ignorance we can all in some way identify a dichotomy between the physical and the perceptual. How much we act upon such, albeit limited vision depends considerably on the individual.

11.2.1   Gaining some credibility

The humanist and psycho-social approaches have gone a long way to giving the perceptual aspects credibility in an organization. McGregor,[1] Maslow[2] or Likert[3] have given academic weight to management thinking which is now receptive to aspects of organization other than those of profit or resource. The creation, in the larger organizations at least, of vast personnel, training and industrial relation functions shows to some extent that the individual employee has been given a higher profile in management strategies. Many managers will have gained qualifications or experience which will have exposed them to ideas about motivation and human personality and how they can be used to greater effect in the search for efficiency and productivity. These are aspects which cannot be seen but are accepted as reality. They are perceptual things; part of the perceptual organization.

On the other hand, the physical organization needs very little introduction. It is that part of the firm which we are all the most comfortable with. It is the activity, production and resource allocation that we see around us in the performance of our working lives. In its most simplistic interpretation it is the buildings and the products. But it also comprises more complex aspects such as management and technology. Because we can easily identify it, management see it as the part which matters, its impact can be readily understood and thus seem more important. They know also that our feelings are important to them; some of the enlightened may even be aware that we could all see the world differently, in the sense that our perceptions act as a filter between us and reality. But at the end of the day our nature demands the familiarity and contentment which we find in viewing our physical world as set and indisputable.

11.2.2   An inexorable link

Physical and perceptual are indeed different sides of the same coin. We cannot separate them and are erroneous in trying. We cannot comprehend our physical environment without perceiving it. Therefore what affects one will affect the other. Our perceptions will determine the reality we can identify in the physical world. If those perceptions change, then so will our physical world and vice versa. To others the physical world may well not have changed, because their perceptions have not changed. Thus reality could have two different meanings to two different people. In short, none us can identify a total reality because each of us has differing interpretations of it. Yet in organizations we attempt to do just this by implying a common reality.

There is a two-way communication process between the physical and the perceptual; one which is inexorably linked and irrefutable. A simple example will demonstrate this relationship. A classroom comprising a teacher and her pupils could be conceived as a simple organization: it meets many of the criteria set in terms of goals and common purpose. More important for our purposes, there is also a physical and perceptual aspect. The classroom itself, the organization of pupils in rows and the teacher at the front, the textbooks, the blackboard, the curriculum taught along with teaching methodology all form the structure. These then are the physical aspects. They are the most obvious factors confronting the members of this particular organization, and as such they are the most controllable,

However, this classroom (like any organization) would not have meaning if it were not for its members and perhaps to a lesser extent third parties, perceiving it to have such meaning. It is no more than a room with a group of people in it of which one happens to be an adult and the rest children of about a certain age. The adult may also possess more useful knowledge than the others and spend all her time transmitting it to them. They all have books, pens, paper and so on which they use from time to time. This is the physical world as it appears to any observer, but it is meaningless and lacks purpose to those who do not understand the concept of classroom.

Something is obviously missing. It is the perceptual agreement of all involved parties, through socialization processes, that this is a class-room. It is dependent upon everyone knowing the *raison d'être* of the group, knowing rules, the culture and the norms and being able to place themselves (cognitively, temporally and spatially) into the group. It therefore involves not only knowing what your fellows are doing and reacting to them, but also the interpretation of your physical environment and the consequential development of perceptual patterns/ maps for action in that environment.

These are the perceptual aspects of the classroom. They are the factors which give our organization depth and meaning – its reality. But because the physical aspects of the classroom can be translated only through the perceptions of the teacher and her pupils, it is likely that each is subtly different. The extreme would be between the teacher and the rest. Standing at the front with a completely different role and so exposed to scrutiny, her interpretation of the classroom is not the same as the greater anonymity of a pupil sitting in the back row. For one thing she would continually be confronted by a sea of faces looking and listening to her; whereas the back row pupil may see a mass of necks and one person standing at the front. These two perceptions highlight different roles and hence different necessities for action. In turn these will affect the organization of our classroom because each person's differing perceptions are influencing the realities of that organization in different ways. Take any one person away and the organization will be slightly different.

11.2.3 Dividing line

If physical and perceptual organization are so inexorably linked, at what point are we able to identify their distinction? Can we indeed draw a line between them?

This is one of the major difficulties, the two cannot be separated, they are meaningless on their own. The world may exist whether we do or not, but physical reality is made real to us only through our perceptions, and these are only meaningful (objective) for us if they are of something physically real. The two are interdependent and cannot be separated. There is rather a molding of one into the other where the boundary between them is blurred. Physical resource may be organized in a certain way, for example into departments, but the logic we attached to that in order to stimulate action is founded in our perceptions.

It is difficult for any existing model of organization to truly reflect this state. That is why I believe that writers have so far failed to capture the real nature of the firm in our theoretical frameworks. We have already seen that the humanist/social psychology approach places considerable credence on the perceptual organization as the major construct of any firm. But in so doing they ignore the physical aspects by not placing their specimen employee into context.

Structural/sociological theorists have also attempted to grasp perceptual and physical sides to their organization models. The most notable of earlier writers was Parsons in his construct of a social system comprising a network of interlocking subsystems such as personality and culture.[4] It was left to the systems theorists to develop his work further. Parsons was concerned with the major system – society – first and foremost and only looked at subsystems as a means to understand that, of which organizations were a part; systems theorists, however, were primarily interested in organizations. In one form or another they envisaged our business enterprises comprising a hierarchy of systems (see earlier chapters) which in their turn comprised a mix of perceptual and physical, such as tasks or technology.[5] In particular, Kast and Rosenzweig identified a psycho-social system within an organization.[6] Unlike the previous examples mentioned, this system is purely abstract and has no physical attributes. It is perhaps the nearest thing we have to a true perceptual organization.

11.2.4 Problems arise

There are definite problems with the models just cited. Although they do acknowledge a strong perceptual element which is seen to be working closely with all physical aspects, it is nevertheless tied in with and dependent upon the physical part of the organization. The psycho-social system is defined as the culture of the organization and its norms, and in particular the ability of the organization's employees to 'place' themselves within its context. In many respects, however, it can be all things to all persons, a sort of theoretical dustbin in which to dump abstract things. This imposes consequential problems upon the workings of perceptual organization.

An examination of the Kast and Rosenzweig model quickly demonstrates this. It becomes quite apparent that the physical organization dominates any relationship. The psycho-social subsystem exists in name only, the terms and concepts within are not given their own form. They are merely expressions to overcome certain nasty things in organization which cannot be easily ignored or explained away. What we in fact have is not true perceptual organization but a sham of it, not really reflecting the realities of the relationship between it and physical organization.

This is the greatest failing of the systems model of organization. The nature of its approach, through the study of interaction between parts, demands that to be successful, and for the model to work properly, all the parts must be identified. The absence of an autonomous but interdependent perceptual organization denies the model its validity. As such it fails to give us a complete picture of organization. In particular the failure to identify a dynamic perceptual factor gives us an ability to understand only consequences and not accompanying causes. This is simply because to know how something has come about one must be able to understand the complete picture, whereas to analyze the effects of action alone, as in the systems model, one needs only observation and a partial framework in which to place it.

11.2.5 Further development

To a great extent the development of a more appropriate perceptual organization would go a long way to answering criticism from Silverman and his fellow social action theorists.[7] They believe that functionalist models (which include systems theory) emphasize consequence rather than cause in social phenomena.

In particular, when conducting an assessment of the impact of something like information technology, it is not enough merely to observe consequences of such phenomena; one has to understand the root causes. To do that it is not sufficient to conduct this analysis in terms of the information technology alone since within the organizational context nothing can be considered in isolation. This includes not only the linkages of the many parts of the physical organization, which many models already encourage us to look at (see previous discussions), but also the linkages into perceptual organization.

Later in this chapter a model is developed to demonstrate this point, that is to highlight a link between the physical and perceptual organization. The advantages of this over other systems models, or indeed any other model of organization, is that its composition will be non-specific to a particular set of phenomena and thus highlight consequence and causal effect of any impact such as information technology. The next section discusses the theoretical background to such a model.

11.3 The work of Abbe Mowshowitz

There is a substantial piece of work by Abbe Mowshowitz in which he examined the social impact of office automation.[8] Much of it was a hard analysis of computer implementation and its effect upon office design. But contained within a few lines towards the end he introduces the concept of virtual organization by highlighting the distinction between logical and physical location within computer technology. There is nothing new in this, but more interestingly he goes on to propose that a social organization may indeed possess the same logic.

We could understand Mowshowitz's logical location as a rough equivalent to our perceptual location, although it is recognized that there are certain differences (highlighted below). The basis of his idea is well acknowledged in the computer fraternity: that is, an interpretation of the data in physical terms, identifying its whereabouts in the computer, does not reveal anything about its informative value. In those terms alone it is just a mass of nonsensical electronic signals. But the way the signals are stored can have meaning if interpreted through another medium, such as a program. The signals cannot be seen in the physical sense, their location in relation to one another may be completely random; there are, however, logical links established through a program which creates meaning. This meaning forms a sense, unseen but logical, and every bit as real as any physical observation.

An Impressionist painting can provide a good example of how perceptual form can achieve greater logic than physical form. Close to, the painting has no real sense: its brush strokes are seemingly random. Only by standing back can one appreciate the painting for what it is. This is because the logic of the painting can be perceived only in a certain form. In this sense the logical location of the brush strokes is more important than the physical location.

11.3.1 Computer and organization

For his example Mowshowitz used a business organization. Because a computer and its control mechanisms are a form of organization he saw a firm as possessing the same logical characteristics. There are similar aspects, which we have already discussed, in which perceptual organization forms a greater logical cohesion than its physical counterpart.

Mowshowitz, however, did not pursue this as a descriptive model of organization. He believed that such an analogy was useful in understanding the impact of information technology on organizations. If computer networking is employed then its effects could be minimized by 'managing on the basis of virtual organization'.

To him there was often a contradiction and conflict between the needs of the firm as a whole and the needs of its computer organization. He found, as many have (see previous chapters), that computer installations tended to break down the predominately physically-orientated control mechanisms. On the other hand, such controls were very restrictive for the perceptually-driven needs of computer organization. It seemed that neither side could win. Organize from a management perspective and the computer would lose out; organize from a computer perspective and the management would lose out. What he was seeking, therefore, was a form of prescriptive methodology to enable management to manage but at the same time to allow the computer to realize its full potential.

He envisaged the solution in managers' better understanding of their environment, and thus encouraged the elements which enabled them to maintain their control but at the same time stimulated the necessary structures for computer organization. This is possible because implicit in his hypothesis is the division of a business organization into two fundamental dimensions, the virtual and the physical. The former acts as a sort of perceptive sponge, soaking up the subversive intrusion of information technology and thus protecting the physical structures of organization from its destabilizing effects. The latter – the physical – is the firm as the traditionalist would understand it to be, the functional/structural aspects and its general resource profile. The trick for management was to ensure that both thrived.

11.3.2 Unused potential

Unfortunately, Mowshowitz did not explore the concept much further, and although he called it a model it was still incomplete. He was interested only in his proposition as a means to analyse the evolution of office automation and its social implications for the workforce. Mowshowitz did not consider his hypothesis a model of organization and therefore did not pursue the much more interesting aspect of his concept: that is, an organization as a dichotomy between two realities, each determined in importance by internal and external forces and existing in continuous competition with the other but in equifinality.

Had he done so I believe that he would have had the beginnings of an effective framework for measuring the impact not only of office automation but also of any change aspect. Indeed, I would suggest that we would at last have had a composite model of organization. But since he did not develop any of these aspects, Mowshowitz's interpretation is extremely limiting and does not highlight the true relationship between the perceptual and physical elements of an organization. The perceptual aspects he identified were based upon the logic of a particular physical relationship which taken at face value had no real sense (i.e a painting seen close to). There were no suggestions that these could be veils between human action and their physical world. As such, therefore, no dichotomy was ever really identified. The model, if it could be called such, was left shallow and overly simplistic.

In the remainder of this chapter I wish to go beyond Mowshowitz and develop a truly working model. Firstly, its components are defined and explained.

11.4   The organizational framework

Within the boundaries of this model there are five relevant dimensions:

1.   The organizational arena.
2.   The elements of organization.
3.   The enabling mechanisms.
4.   The organizational states.
5.   The organization's environment.

Each is an integral part of the model and cannot be excluded, since to understand the parts one must understand the whole, and to understand the whole one must understand all its parts. There is an interdependence between them all and any exclusion would not only render the model ineffective but also miss the essence of any organization.

The following sections discuss each of these five dimensions in greater detail. To a certain extent we have covered much of this in previous chapters, therefore there will be some reiteration. However, the model itself and the way that it uses all these components are new.

The organizational arena

The organizational arena is perhaps the most abstract of the five dimensions and represents the physical aspects of the organization along with its perceptual aspects. We have already examined these in detail throughout several previous chapters. For example, when we talk of a firm's resources or its functional division we are referring to its physical nature. On the other hand, when we refer to its psycho-social factors such as its culture, the norms operating or an individual's perception of his/her work environment, we have the firm's perceptual nature in mind.

This arena, though, is more than just a framework for these two aspects. It is also a dynamic mechanism which allows for their continual interaction and adjustment. From a systems viewpoint it is basically one system with two subsystems, where all things in the organization have either physical or perceptual characteristics. As such it is also the most fundamental of all our five dimensions since all aspects must be embraced by it.

The elements of the organization

The next system comprises the organizational elements. This in turn comprises three subsystems which we have already met:

1. Information network.
2. Structure.
3. Political process.

These are the major building blocks of any organization, constituting the aspects which are immediately apparent in any examination. Together they form the framework in which we carry out our working lives. They form the departments in which we work, the communication systems that are established between each of us, and the mechanisms we have developed to help ourselves act and succeed (or destroy opponents) within the organizational arena. Such aspects can be located physically or perceptually depending upon their characteristics. This then is the link between this particular dimension and the previous one. (For a deeper analysis of the three individual aspects, refer to previous chapters.)

The enabling mechanisms

An organization, or indeed any social entity, is a living entity, responsive and continually changing. Although increasingly discredited, that school of theorists which regards organizations as organisms did at least capture the essence of their form.[9] To create a framework of organization and to place it in an arena is not sufficient to understand it. The parts must be wound up, as it were, like a clockwork toy, and given life. It is only in their dynamic state (which is their natural state) that we can appreciate what it is they are supposed to be doing. Similarly, only when a clockwork toy is moving can we appreciate its full potential. That is why models which attempt to represent an essentially dynamic entity, such as an organization, in a static way are bound to fail because they do not relate meaningfully to the major operating force – movement. Unfortunately, organization theory is replete with such models.

There are two important mechanisms of organization which give it those essential dynamic characteristics: the technological process and the decision process. (A detailed discussion has been conducted on both these aspects in previous chapters.) They involve particularly the human element of organization, and it is only through human activity and perception that a firm can achieve form. The technological and decision processes are the manifestation of that.

Firstly, the technological process, combining all aspects of human knowledge and skill with the firm's physical and perceptual resource, is the essence of human activity, especially in a formalized collective such as an organization. As we have seen, it allows a firm or individual to exist and survive within its particular environment. It is, therefore, an essential part of any living organization.

Secondly, the decision process links human perception to action. People must make decisions in order to act. For the organization this is particularly important since the collective decision process enables it to respond to changes in its environment.

As such, both are agents of change. Any living mechanism must adapt as its environment and own internal logic demands. A firm may not truly be an organism since it also represents relationships, both perceptual and physical, far more complex than any single organism can simulate. Nevertheless there is a form of life (beyond the obvious human element) within any organization which cannot be denied and is thus supportive, in part at least, of the organismic metaphor.[10] For all living creatures, change control (homeostasis) is important, and therefore no less so for any organization. In this respect, the technological and decision processes are essential.

The organizational states

An organization must exist in both time and space in a certain condition. In previous chapters we identified three states:

1. Changing.
2. Balanced and in equilibrium.
3. Balanced and not in equilibrium.

There are, therefore, three concepts – change, balance and equilibrium – to be considered. Each is important for understanding an organization because depending upon what state a firm happens to be in at a specific time will be its characteristics. We have already seen that a firm is not static but dynamic, even when it is not experiencing change. Thus to place that within an appropriate theoretical framework one has to know the net effect of all those dynamic forces, hence the three organizational states.

The organizational environment

The final dimension of organization is its environment: that is, the total area external to an organization which has an influence upon it in some way. This, of course, comprises its market, but it also comprises the organization's particular industry if it happens to be a business organization. Beyond these there are not only the political and social processes (government, local/national customer bodies, etc.) but also their customs, norms and established procedures. The externalities which their employees or members bring into the organization can form part of its environment because they are, by definition, external influences which can be brought to bear upon any firm. It should not be forgotten that an organization's environment can be both physical and perceptual: it is anything outside its accepted internal boundary which can affect it.

Every organizational environment is different. There may be many similarities, especially in organizations in the same industry or market, but there are also spheres of influence which differ in the same way that firms differ in their people content. For example, two banking organizations may operate in similar areas and are thus affected by the same environmental mechanisms, but they will each have interests in other areas which will in their turn have different influences. Their employees, for example, are different and thus have different interests. One manager may know the prime minister personally which will affect the organization. The other may be a keen golfer and always absent, thus presenting his firm with a different environmental effect.

It is, therefore, difficult to generalize about any organization's environment and maintain credibility. Much depends upon the level, and intention, of the analysis. Governments and their economists have quite often gone wrong because they have either generalized too much and lost meaning or were too specific.

For the purposes of our model, the environment is an exogenous influence; therefore in the setting of the framework, at least, it can be generalized. That is not to say that we assume that all firms possess the same environmental influences. It is, however, important that we include such influences, albeit in a general sense, because they can shape the internal forces of the organization. A law limiting the number of public houses that a brewery may own is just such an example of this.

11.4.1 A general discussion

The above five dimensions represent the total organization. Everything that we experience whilst working within them must come under one or more of those headings – there is nothing else. In addition, these dimensions are not specific to any type of organization, although given the nature of this book we shall be concentrating upon the business organization. They are, therefore, representative of both physical and perceptual mechanisms which form the organization.

As we have already seen, two of these dimensions (the organizational arena and the organizational states) are purely abstract concepts. That is, they describe the condition of an organization in order to understand the consequences of that condition more fully. For example, a balanced organization may well appear more healthy than one which is not balanced. Or again, the nature of the relationship between physical and perceptual in the arena may favour certain forces over others (a point we explore later).

The remaining three dimensions are identified within the framework of an organization rather than in its condition. As such they can have both physical and perceptual aspects. The environment, for example, is as much a part of an organization as are its elements because the organization can be shaped by its forces. Those forces can be physical such as location, transport or government laws, or they can be perceptual such as societal norms.

Always dominant in the relationship between these dimensions is the split into their physical and perceptual sides. How that forms will dictate very much how they will operate as subunits and as a total unit. The first two dimensions (the arena and the state) promote, as it were, the conditions for this to occur. The enabling dimension allows for a link between the two sides (physical and perceptual), whilst the last two are the framework affected by it.

To understand this better we must therefore examine an organization not only in terms of these five dimensions, but more importantly in terms of the split between the physical and perceptual aspects. I have termed this the dichotomy of organization.

11.5   The dichotomy

Every organization, large or small, no matter what type, either has a dichotomy in its form (that is, a split between the physical and perceptual organization) or possesses a potential for it. In general, the larger the company the more prevalent this dichotomy is likely to be. This does not mean that small businesses do not have perceptual aspects, but dichotomy refers perhaps to a more formal relationship found in larger organizations. Thus the strength of either the physical or perceptual aspects is such that they can be viewed as entities in their own right. The perceptual force available from small businesses is unlikely to be powerful enough to be of any consequence.

Therefore when we speak of a dichotomy we are referring to something more than a collection of things physical and perceptual. Of greater importance are the relationships within both these aspects which make them cohesive units. In this way Mowshowitz used the term virtual in order to avoid confusion with the simply perceptual, and to demonstrate it as being something logical and relational rather than merely cognitive. I shall use the term virtual in the same spirit. However, I shall endeavour to go beyond Mowshowitz and present virtuality as an interdependent entity, as much a part of an organization as its physical counterpart.

The remainder of this section is devoted to an examination of the two sides of this dichotomy.

11.5.1 Virtual organization

Virtual organization, or virtuality as Mowshowitz termed it, is the most profound and complex of the two. It is much more than some perceptual world attached to the structures of a business firm, and indeed it is considerably more than even Mowshowitz suggested as a basis for technological and structural integration, although it does perhaps lend itself in part to either hypothesis. Virtuality is indeed organization in its own right, competing with its physical counterpart for resources as well as – and perhaps more fundamentally than – the perceptual domination of the actors within their parameters. The particular formation of a virtual organization can affect how actors perceive their environment and thus their allocation of resources to it.

For example, organizational culture, an element of virtuality, could affect the way the employees perceive their market and thus how they allocate resources to it (e.g. marketing, production, etc.). A firm may pride itself on being in the forefront of innovative production, and market itself as such. The reality may be totally different.

It should be stressed that virtual organization cannot exist independently, there must be interdependence with the physical organization. In the final analysis, like every other part of the organization, its meaning depends upon the perception of its members and third parties who are themselves as much a part of the physical world.

A different perspective

Sociological phenomena such as culture or norms have not been rejected. These are aspects of any society or organization. They are, however, viewed from a different perspective – that of virtual organization. The traditionalist, functionalist interpretation of such concepts is tied into the physical framework. The culture of an organization is set and controlled by the physical environment for example, whereas within the content of my proposal the ingredients of aspects such as culture are driven by the perceptual mechanisms of organization.

A more general view

This wider definition allows the development of an appropriate framework. But if virtuality is also a mode of organization in the purest sense, we have to attach something else to it beyond a collection of employee ideas.

We need to establish an homeostatic mechanism (such as in any physical organization) whereby virtual organization can achieve a limited existence and thus interdependence with its physical counterpart. For the moment if we can accept that such a mechanism can exist within virtuality, then it should be possible to demonstrate its importance. Put simply, I believe that an homeostatic mechanism would transform the virtual organization into something more than a psychosocial subsystem.[11]

Different models do not create different organizations, the reality is the same whatever model we use, only our perception of that reality will be different. A model including virtual organization, however, gives us greater analytical flexibility because perceptions are no longer constrained by the physical dimension but form a competing logic within the organization. This has particular significance when examining change.

Self-regulation and limited independence are, therefore, important for the physical and virtual organization, particularly so if virtuality is to be differentiated from the psycho-social subsystem. This is because the psycho-social subsystem is construed a subsystem of physical organization, its regulation and survival are dependent upon it and as such no more than a perceptual extension of it. Therefore, to have virtuality mimic such characteristics would be to condemn it.

To stress again, virtual organization is a separate system which nevertheless interacts with the physical system within a commonly defined environment.

Side effects

There are two general implications which arise from this approach.

Firstly, the physical and environmental aspects of the organization have to be redefined. This is caused by virtuality encroaching upon the traditionalist framework. Virtuality creates links with 'out there' beyond any contact with the physical organization and thus affects the established concept of organizational boundary. And similarly, the now separated physical organization has its own set of relationships which are not accessed by its matching virtual system. As such the environment can no longer be defined solely in terms of economics or geography, its boundary is now set by the degree of physicalness and virtuality within the organization and the nature of the balance existing between them.

The second implication is that in presenting this model an otherwise physical concept, homeostasis, has been linked to an abstract form, virtuality. In theory there is nothing which should prevent this from being done. But the mechanisms for homeostasis are generally translatable into a physical form such as one would find in a biological organism or social group. It is, therefore, unusual to relate such a concept to an abstract system whose self-regulation is independent of any physical interpretation.

Virtuality must, however, possess some enabling mechanism which will allow homeostasis to be achieved. Such a mechanism is found in both the technological and the decision-making processes which allow virtual organization to respond to change and maintain a steady state. This is not done consciously, of course, since it is only people who can think and act with meaning, not systems. It is the consequence of an interplay between forces which, if controlled effectively, will tend towards a steady state.

Further levels

The virtual organization, like every other system, comprises subsystems and elements. What these elements are depends upon the individual characteristics of the organization. But there are some general pointers which have relevance in all forms of business. These would include concepts such as power, communications, knowledge, information, and self-perception.

It should be stressed that these are not separated from the elements of organization previously described. They form part of the virtual organization, but they can also be part of an organizational element. Thus the first of these, power, for example, is part of the virtual organization but it is also part of the political process.

Power

This is an important element because simply defined it is 'the capacity to produce intended effects',[12] or 'the ability to influence the behaviour of others in accordance with one's own ends'.[13]

Individuals or groups have goals and objectives, the achievement of which is in part dependent upon their power. The more they have the better able they are to gain their ends and thus influence the organization. Power is a perceptual mechanism in that it is based upon the perception of others. A powerful woman is only powerful because others are dependent upon her and thus perceive her to be so.

Through this perceptual framework interaction evolves which extends beyond the initial parameters set by the original actors, developing a historical continuum by which others respond and initiate their own action, thus adding to the framework. What is established in virtuality as a consequence is a motivating force which provides a link with the organizational arena.

Communication
Communications, in the abstract sense of networks, provide the means to integrate individuals into a perceptual network. As a collective through communication, albeit fractured and divisive at times, people can maintain a higher level of cognitive activity because they are more sensitive to the wider environmental boundaries than they would otherwise have been. This is important for virtuality since such an ability provides a perceptual cement giving the system a uniqueness within its own environment.

Knowledge and information
Knowledge and information can be dealt with together. In many ways they are the most fundamental of all the generalities. They represent our humanity and thus the organization itself, for what is organization other than a collection of resources transformed in some way by our knowledge and information? Knowledge and information, therefore, provide the framework for virtuality, attaching to it characteristics which will be identified solely with that particular organization.

Self
Lastly, the perception of oneself is another generality which needs to be included in virtuality. It allows for individuals to have perceptions about themselves and their position relative to the rest of the organization, which in many cases may not be as the majority see them. This is not critical since people act upon their own perceptions and therefore contribute further to the illusion of themselves. As for virtuality the importance is probably quite apparent. Employees will be interacting not in accordance with how they really are, but in accordance with how they think they are – the difference is perceptual.

The profile of this selection should indicate the nature, at least, of the characteristics of virtuality. However, the concept is difficult to grasp completely. Virtuality is not like a building or the people in it, which is the sort of idea we normally conjure up when thinking of organizations. On the other hand, its effects are just as real. The result is an abstraction which can determine physical aspects of organization and so affect its health and viability. This is possible because perceptual processes can and do live beyond their moment of conception. Once created, through communication they become part of a larger resource which is tapped by others, and thus easily utilized. As such, a continuum exists independently, in one sense, from physical organization. It is this which is the basis of virtuality.

The virtuality point

Virtuality is probably not applicable to all organizations. It is likely that there is a certain critical size, which I term as the virtuality point, at which an organization can sustain virtuality.

Before that point organizations may well operate at a low level of perceptual interaction. After that point, like a newly-created sun, virtuality becomes self-regulatory and thus able to maintain itself. The critical size of organization may vary from industry to industry, dependent upon many factors, but it is suspected that throughout organizations generally their virtuality point has been considerably lowered by the introduction of information technology. What could have been achieved in this respect by a much larger organization in the past, in terms of information generated to create virtuality point, is being easily achieved by smaller organizations with the use of information technology.

It would seem that virtuality is good for an organization. Given the right blend of characteristics, virtuality can stimulate a continued growth. This should be possible because the information and so on generated through the virtual organization would increase by a type of multiplier effect, which in turn would have a knock-on effect upon the firm's physical resource.

There are, however, certain conditions within the organization and its environment which would make this effect more likely to happen (discussed later).

11.5.2 Physical organization

The other side of an organization is its physical dimension. This side is to most of us its most understandable and familiar, acting as it does in a space–time continuum which fits nicely with our own perception of reality.

However, that is not to say that the physical organization is defined merely by its organizational objects – the office building, chairs, machines and so on. There are still abstract forms to be accommodated which can give purpose and cohesion to the otherwise lifeless lumps of metal, wood and building materials. In particular, people, who form the workforce, would be no more than a social collection without them, but with them they can be resourced and organized into an efficient transformation process.

Therefore by abstract forms within physical organization, I mean concepts such as mission, structure, management, hierarchy and information systems. The last item, information systems, details its physical organization and not its logical organization, which is included in virtual organization.

Technology revisited

The physical technology (machines, etc.) used in the transformation process can be termed as resources. Technology is partially covered by this heading. As a book value in the business firm it is seen as a resource because it provides an important potential input. There is more to technology, though, than just the machinery. Knowledge and technique have to be applied to it before it becomes productive. Technology, then, in a physical sense is a resource; in a perceptual sense, through knowledge and technique, is part of virtuality, and as a dynamic process (in other words entities working in real-time situations) is an enabling mechanism. This perhaps demonstrates more than many other aspects how integrated the organizational elements are between the physical and perceptual sides.

The output

The output of an organization has also to be considered when looking at the physical organization. Its form will vary from organization to organization. If it is a manufacturing firm then one would expect to find an output at the end of the process which is physically identifiable, such as a car or a piece of machinery. If, on the other hand, the firm is in the service sector, such as a bank, then the output is not so tangible and could indeed be described as having virtual characteristics. The distinction between these two examples could give a clear indication of the way ahead.

From what has been said it could be deduced that perhaps some outputs are more orientated towards one side of the organizational dichotomy than the other. For example, a bank's output is information in one form or another, and this would be inclined toward virtuality, whereas a car manufacturer's output is located at the physical end of the continuum. This has implications for organizational effectiveness.

11.6 The completed model

The mechanics of the model are now complete. This section presents a static view of it, like a snapshot, so that we may understand more clearly how the pieces fit together. The following section then presents a dynamic perspective. Since we have already examined each element in depth, the presentation here will be an overview.

Figure 11.1 is the diagrammatic representation of the model.

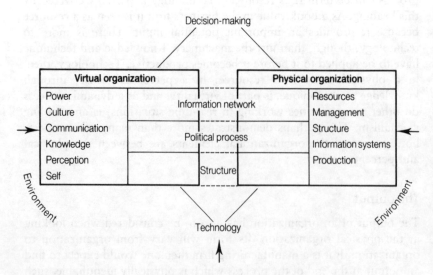

Figure 11.1 The organization

11.6.1   Familiarity

Referring to the figure, there is much within this model that is still easily identifiable with other established ideas. The environment is portrayed as being the major area of influence. As such it is shown to surround, almost to embrace, all other aspects. In systems terminology, the organization is an open system, that is one which interacts with, responds to and is changed by its environment.

Another characteristic of this model is the two blocks headed virtual and physical. These represent the dichotomy between the abstract, perceptual aspects and the more concrete, physical things. Both blocks are of equal size to represent equal importance and interdependence. They can be regarded as two equal parts of the same organization, or perhaps a little more contentiously, as two competing suborganizations with a certain degree of independence.

Each block is divided into two. The first section in both shows a typical cross-section of the elements of which they are composed. Thus aspects like power and knowledge are virtuality-orientated, whilst resources and production are physically-orientated. Neither list is by any means definitive. In the same way that Easton[14] argues for simplicity in his model of a political system without sacrificing workability, I too suggest that it is the principle rather than the specific we seek. With each particular organization the content of either virtual or physical organization may differ in some way, but the operating forces will nevertheless work on the same principles.

The other part of both the virtual and physical blocks are, as it were, mirror images of one another. They both comprise the three major elements of organization (information network, political process, structure), either being virtually-orientated, hence located in the virtual block, or physically-orientated. Each is represented in the model as linking both the virtual and physical blocks to demonstrate that there are both virtual and physical qualities in all three elements. The physical aspects in the information network, for example, can comprise the equipment and the functional layout, whilst the information itself comprises the virtual side of organization, and so on.

11.6.2   There are difficulties

The locations of the components of both the virtual and physical organization have been oversimplified since they cannot be represented in two dimensions in any other way. For example, virtuality factors such as power and knowledge are not separate from but part of the organizational element, political process; or physical aspects such as management and resources can also form part of the political process. The boundaries between all components are not as definitive as the model suggests: there is a great deal of blurring and overlap between them all.

Our world is like a prism which changes through different perspectives. We view it one way and power aspects or production aspects on their own come to the fore. We view it another way and another system such as structure is more clearly seen. No model can fully represent such fluidity. To a great extent it has to be assumed.

Lastly we come to the enabling mechanisms: the technological and the decision processes. They are represented as being outside both blocks because they are seen as linking mechanisms. The process of making a decision, for instance, links the physical with the perceptual. An individual may decide to rearrange company resources in some way and in so doing not only physically change the company but also change employees' view of it. Or the technological process converts people's understanding of their world (virtual) into action in the physical world. They are the links of communication and the life blood of the two worlds. Each, through these processes, feed the other. Neither can exist without the other, but nourishment (in a metaphorical sense) is passed on from one block to the other after environmental stimulation. So these two processes are an important transmission mechanism and any effect in one block finds its impact in the other through these.

It should be stressed that we are examining processes rather than technology or decisions *per se*. Thus, like every other component within an organization, they are located in either virtuality or the physical dimension. Technology has physical attributes as a resource but it also has perceptual attributes in terms of knowledge and technique. Decisions are the consequence of virtual aspects but they are also linked to physical organization through the structure and functional order; in this sense they are no different from other elements. Their processes, however, are different and this is what makes them enabling mechanisms.

We now have the completed model. We have looked at each element and how they relate to the others. What remains is to wind the thing up and see how it works.

11.7 The working model

The advantage of taking a systems approach is that we can quite easily adopt different levels of analysis without forgoing theoretical linkage with those already established. In the case of our model, we have been looking at the firm in terms of its subsystems, in particular the virtual and physical organization. It is now time to take a step upward, as it were, and to examine the firm as a whole interacting within an external environment, the system and its suprasystem. But we shall take with us the experience gained from the previous sections and see how it applies to this wider dimension. In so doing it is hoped to demonstrate how business organizations can be affected by the relationship between virtuality and physical organization.

11.7.1 Enter physics

We need to convert our model from a lifeless description on paper to a working process. The principles, the elements and the relationships remain fundamentally the same but our perspective is different. The interpretation of our model as a machine is depicted in Figure 11.2.

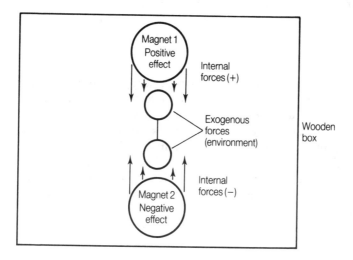

Figure 11.2 The metaphorical model

The boundary

Imagine, firstly, that all the components of our machine are contained within a box. As can be seen in the figure, this box represents the organizational boundary. What cannot be represented by such a box is the nature of the boundary itself. This is very much determined by the characteristics of business within which the firm operates, covering aspects like the market, custom, tradition, management practices and so on.

The forces

The organization boundary is also important because it can contribute to the nature of the internal forces within the total organization. The reader will recall that these forces are the consequences of interaction between the elements of organization. In our demonstration these can be represented by two magnets, each placed against the side of the box, north and south. The magnets are strong enough to dominate their half of the box with a decreasing influence in the other half. Thus their influence will be dependent upon two factors; firstly, in which half of the box any potentially controllable body is located, and secondly, how near the centre that body is. The nearer the dominating magnet, the greater that magnet's control.

There are two magnets, one on either side, to reflect the positive and negative effects that these forces may have on an organization with given characteristics. One magnet is always representative of the positive effects, the other always the negative effects. However, one type of force may not always be negative or positive. It could be positive in one firm and negative in another. Much will depend upon the individual firm.

For example, the same management stance within a banking organization would have different effects in a manufacturing firm because their different structural and market characteristics, etc. bring different influences to bear upon the structure of each. As such, this management stance might prove suitable for one and not the other depending upon whether the particular force was favourable to the particular organizational characteristics or not. I, therefore, regard the positive effect as being good for a firm and the negative effect as being bad.

A mechanism

Lastly we need to establish a mechanism within this model to represent the relationship between the virtual and the physical organizations. This is done by two spheres balanced on a fulcrum as shown in Figure 11.2. Each sphere represents one of the organizations, and has the rather dubious physical property of being able to increase or decrease its influence in relation to the other by physically increasing or decreasing its size. Thus the larger one sphere is in relation to the other, the greater the influence it has over the other. Any such change takes place through exogenous force stimulation, that is a change factor created either in the environment or within the firm which has an impact upon the internal consistency of the organization (e.g. changing market conditions, production techniques or management policy). The whole mechanism is then perched on a fulcrum and can turn a full 360 degrees, attracted by the positive or negative magnets at either end.

How the models works will depend on three factors: the degree of influence of one sphere over the other; the attraction characteristics of the internal forces, and the type of exogenous forces involved.

The idea of the contraption is to establish, with a given set of internal forces, the equilibrium and balance location of both spheres. The nature of the mechanism that controls them will mean that each will be in opposition or contradictory to the other. Therefore if, for instance, the virtuality sphere was located in the positive half of the box (as in Figure 11.2), the physical organization sphere would in turn be located in the negative half. This is not due to the limitations of the demonstration, but a deliberate attempt to reflect the antagonistic and competitive relationship between the two organizations. They cannot exist without each other but neither can they exist together.

One exception to this, however, is when both spheres are equidistant from the extremes (along the horizontal, east/west) and thus still opposing one another though not in contradiction but in neutrality. This is one of the major conditions for equilibrium. In most cases, however, this state will not be achieved and the spheres will be in contradiction, the degree of which will be determined by their proximity to the opposite poles. The extreme is when the two spheres lie vertical to the plane, one aligned fully to the positive and the other fully to the negative.

So what can we gain from this that will be useful to our assessment of organization? The dominant organization (physical or virtual) will always be attracted to the side of the box most reconcilable to its characteristics; by default, therefore, the weaker one will align to the other side. Within the framework of our metaphor we could then state that wherever the dominant sphere is positioned (negative or positive) its influence upon the organization's effectiveness will be reflected by such positioning. For example, if the dominant sphere was virtuality and was located in the positive side of the box, then virtuality would have positive effects upon the firm in question.

The game can also be extended by changing the magnets and box, thus representing a change in the characteristics of the organization, and making a consequential effect upon the forces of the organization. The virtual/physical mechanism would then act differently. There would still be only one equilibrium point accompanied by its innumerable balance points, but how these are achieved may be in slightly different ways.

11.7.2 Constant opposition

The model portrays an organizational environment dominated by the relationship between virtuality and physical organization. By their very nature, in that each is located at opposite ends, they must be in contradiction. Their characteristics and their relationship are governed not only by the technological and decision processes (see previous sections of this chapter) but also by a range of elements and subsystems which themselves create the internal and exogenous forces. And with those given characteristics virtuality and physical organization form a dynamic status quo (equifinality) which changes in accord with their environment.

Their physical movement as represented in the model is obviously metaphorical, but it does demonstrate the shifting patterns of dominance one organization can have over the other. Extending the metaphor slightly, whether the virtual sphere is positioned in any particular part of the box will depend upon the interplay of forces which influence it and its competitor. If negative forces happen to be in greater sympathy with the dominant sphere then it would be located in that region. In other words, the location of the dominant organization determines the eventual characteristics of the total entity. Wherever, in reality neither organization (virtual/physical) would be located physically, but abstractly through a series of complex relationships which can only be identified in each individual case.

11.7.3 A mismatch?

But what if the dominant sphere does not suit the business characteristics of the organization in question?

We use a banking corporation as our example. We know, for instance, that the nature of its business makes subsequent characteristics more akin to virtuality rather than physicality. This is because they deal in perceptual exchange rather than physical exchange in terms of product. This then forms part of the characteristics of the bank's external environment. But if through management action the banking corporation is more physically inclined than it should be (in other words, if the dominant sphere was physical organization) we would then have a situation whereby the firm's characteristics, dominated by the physical organization, are contradictory to its environment which is dominated by more perceptual aspects. It is predicted by this model that physical organization would align itself, to a greater or lesser degree, to the negative effects. As a consequence the bank could experience factors contradicting its effectiveness, such as inertia, lack of growth despite investment, and large scale inefficiencies. None of these could be adequately explained by traditional theory because it is likely that, on the face of it at least, the structures of the firm seem reasonably sound.

11.7.4 Conclusions

This model should convey the impression that organization is dominated by the relationship between the virtual and physical organizations. There is really nothing extraordinary about such a proposal. The nature of our lives in all aspects, whether political, social or whatever, is in terms of a conflict between what we perceive and what is really there. Political theory in particular recognizes this fact, but it is just as valid to apply such ideas to organizations since if we accept these conflicts in the larger environments, we are no less human for being in subunits of that environment.

Of course, management will not be able to identify aspects of organization conveniently labelled virtual or physical, nor will a force or element marked one or the other interact in unison with its fellows similarly marked. This is the danger in presenting such a model. The best that can be said is that there is a group of forces which have a tendency to act in a like fashion and thus have similar effects which can be artificially labelled for convenience. If we did not do this, how else could we simplify complexity?

What we have are organizations dominated by conflicting forces which can be seen by us to have either virtual or physical characteristics. Nothing is neutral: a desk can create a physical force and a consequential perceptual one, albeit rather minor in its effect. So that merely moving the furniture around can have an impact in the organization. Obviously things of greater importance will have a greater impact and more far-reaching effect. Being a fully open system, the organization is laid bare to all influences. Therefore, managers must treat any change with extreme caution, since it may potentially have a great impact; and there is no impact so potentially disastrous in such an environment as that of information technology.

11.8   A new perception of information technology

Quite apart from an interesting new aspect of organization that we gain, this approach also enables us to examine to a greater depth the impact of information technology upon any business enterprise. We have already discussed the reasons that traditional views of organization will not allow us to understand the true characteristics of the relationship between the organization and its information technology. To put it briefly once again, it is because such technologies are driven by our perception which is thus not always containable within the structural formation of any organization. Consequently our perspective within a traditional, theoretical framework could blind us to the more appropriate paths of analysis. That is not to say that the traditionalist view is now incorrect, merely that it does not highlight those things necessary to the understanding of the impact of information technology.

What this proposed model does that the others do not is to emphasize a dichotomy between the physical and the perceptual aspects of organization. In so doing it enables us to appreciate just how fundamental the introduction of computers and the like can be, reaching far beyond the efficiency criteria usually laid down by management.

11.8.1   Not all gain

To date we have assumed that the introduction of such equipment is a win/win situation, generally by improving efficiency and thus increasing the firm's effectiveness. As we have seen through the model, however, this may not be the case.

For example, a manufacturing firm with a traditionalist management approach introduces a computer-driven production line. We shall assume that prior to the introduction of the computer the firm is in the fortunate position of being in equilibrium as well as being in balance. That is, in terms of our metaphor, the two spheres representing both physical and virtual organization are in neutrality lying east/west. However, given the nature of the firm's activity (production) we shall also assume that its dichotomy is dominated by the physical organization. This is still in keeping with the firm's equilibrium state, since all forces generated will produce a neutral effect. Change can occur but within the framework set by the equilibrium. We therefore have a firm which is stable internally and also, because of its dominant physical organization, in harmony with its production-orientated industry.

Against this background, if we now introduce the new computer-driven production line, we can not only analyse the effects of a new technology but also use a working example to gain a further understanding of the proposed model. For simplicity we restrict our perspective to the organizational suprasystem but at the same time recognize the complex interplay of forces whose identification and construction have gone towards the content of the greater part of this book.

11.8.2 Functional impact

The immediate, and perhaps most obvious, impact is a functional one, in that departments and line function are reorganized. As such, the effects are initially found within the physical organization, but like the ripples in a pond radiating out from the impact of a stone, the effects spread through to all parts of the organization. In general, however, we perceive only the first effect, in the physical organization, since it is the most akin to our abilities to understand. We, therefore, make our plans and strategies relating to information technology within that framework alone. Unfortunately, the greater impact, and thus the need for the most control and understanding, is to be found in the virtual organization.

Already the firm has been destabilized and knocked out of equilibrium. This is not unusual, any large impact would do this. In many cases balance is quickly restored with equilibrium following some time later. In such cases the physically-orientated management action is generally all that is required. In cases, however, where the virtual organization has been significantly affected such action is not appropriate and thus will not restore equilibrium.

11.8.3 Transmission

The physical impact of the information technology is translated into a perceptual impact through transmission by the enabling mechanisms. Once planted there, the characteristics of information technology encourage considerable growth of the virtual aspects of the organization. Depending upon the size and vigour of the system implemented, the virtual organization could indeed become larger than its originally dominant physical competitor. If this happens then the firm is in lose/lose position rather than the assumed win/win one mentioned earlier.

In terms of the metaphor, we would see a shift from the neutral east/west position towards a north/south one where virtual organization is placed in the negative end rather than the positive. This is because the characteristics of this particular firm's environment are more physically orientated and thus more appropriate to physical organization. However, because information technology has created a dominant virtual organization the firm is now driven by negatively based forces which serve as a major dysfunctional influence upon the stability of the organization.

Managers then find themselves in a classic position. They see effectiveness declining when it should be increasing, despite, perhaps, an increase in production. The criteria they have employed for implementation, being physically orientated, concentrate upon efficiency. Their perception of what is happening is also physically constrained. Therefore their actions for solving the problems are targeted at the physical organization. This only serves to exacerbate the problem.

11.8.4 Action can worsen the situation

Since they possess no effective means of analysing what is going on, managers all too often put it down to their company's inability to utilize their new technology. They develop yet more physically-orientated training programmes to overcome their perceived difficulties. In fact it is more likely caused by the firm's inability to internalize their new technology. But managers, because they do not understand, rather than abandon the project or restructure the organization in a more suitable way (both of which could prove costly), hire consultants who recommend yet more technology, which only exacerbates the problem still further. This type of vicious circle is all too common.

Many firms do not even start in equilibrium prior to information technology implementation. Most are internally balanced but their dominant organization (whether physical or virtual) has generally been driven into a positive relationship with its environment. If the firm, such as a bank, is a virtuality-dominated organization then the introduction of information technology could serve to exacerbate that differentiation, although consequential balance is more easily achievable. On the other hand, a firm that is physically-orientated may never achieve balance in this situation because its naturally obtained leadership has been usurped by the virtual organization.

In any event, and there are many combinations, it is highly unlikely that after system implementation an organization will ever again achieve equilibrium (as opposed to balance) without drastic restructuring. Managers are, therefore, faced with three options:

1. They can reject all large computerized systems and maintain traditional methods. The increasing desire for growth and efficiency seems to make this option impractical.
2. They could accept that equilibrium is no longer an achievable state for their organization and be prepared to manage in that environment. This is not as good an option as it sounds. The consequential forces evolving from a perpetual state of disequilibrium would be considerably more complex.
3. They could decide to restructure the organization completely so that a new equilibrium state is once more achievable. The short-term cost of this may be too high a price to pay for many management teams. But the long-term benefits do make this the best of the three options.

The last two options are indeed to do with the management of change. The first option is to do with no change or, perhaps more cynically, inertia. Having said that, the first option may in many circumstances be the best.

11.9 Summary

In this chapter we have developed the working model. I not only presented its components in a static mode but also, with the use of a metaphor, demonstrated how these components worked together as a whole. It became obvious through doing this how much every organization (provided it has grown beyond its virtuality point) is dominated by the relationship between its virtual and physical parts: so much so that the organization itself is shaped by the characteristics of their interaction.

The main message of the chapter is this. If a firm is static and not changing too drastically then control is no problem. But in these days of ever-increasing change that is unlikely to be the case. Most forms of change will upset a firm's balance and equilibrium. The former can be relatively easily restored with careful and imaginative management. The latter, though, may be easily lost for ever, resulting in continuous instability and decreasing effectiveness.

Lastly, the change implications of the implementation of information technology were highlighted as a special case. The perceptual aspects of it are so powerful that the effect on an organization's dichotomatic relationship is bound to be profound. Managers must recognize this. They must also recognize that it is not a solution merely to introduce information technology. It will never have a neutral effect, it will always upset established forces and require sensitive and professional control. Solving efficiency problems with information technology is like putting a lion in the sheep pen to keep the wolves away. It can work, and sometimes very successfully, but the knack is to ensure that the lion does not eat the sheep in the meantime.

REFERENCES

1. McGregor, Douglas. *Leadership and Motivation*. MIT Press, 1966.
2. Maslow, Abraham. *Motivation and Personality*. Harper, 1954.
3. Likert, Rensis. *New Patterns of Management*. McGraw-Hill, 1961.
4. Parsons, Talcott. 'An outline of the social system', in *Theories of Society*, Talcott Parsons (ed.). Free Press, 1964.
5. Leavitt, H. 'Applying organizational change in industry: structural, technological and humanistic approaches', in *Handbook of Organizations*, J. March (ed.). Rand McNally, 1965.
6. Kast, F. and Rosenzweig, J. *Organization and Management*. McGraw-Hill, 1986.
7. Silverman, David. *The Theory of Organizations*. Heinemann, 1970.
8. Mowshowitz, Abbe. 'Social dimensions of office automation', *Advances in Computers*, vol. 25. Academic Press, 1986.
9. Watson, Tony. *Management, Organization and Employment Strategy*. Routledge and Kegan Paul, 1986.
10. Morgan, Gareth. *Images of Organization*. Sage, 1986.
11. Kast, Fremont and Rosenzweig, James. *Contingency Views of Organization and Management*. Science Research Assoc., 1973.
12. Frankel, J. *International Relations*. Oxford University Press, 1964.
13. Organski, A. *World Politics*. Knopf, 1958.
14. Easton, David. *A Systems Analysis of Political Life*. Wiley, 1965.

CHAPTER 12

The way ahead – a management problem

12.1 Introduction

As part of the interview procedure for our full time MBA at the Newcastle Business School we conduct a group session. This is where the six or seven interviewees gather around a table and are presented with the following problem:

> Your submarine is stricken at the bottom of the ocean. You know that rescue is at hand but before they are able to reach you the air will have turned fetid. In order for your group to survive you must therefore eject two members from the submarine!

The group is then asked to decide out of those present who the two shall be. This group of strangers then sits around a table and enacts a potential disaster. In giving this scenario to them and in their responding to it, then, we have created a fairly strong virtual organization amongst that group. Roles are adopted and earnestly enacted; to an unknowledgeable observer it would have seemed more than strange, probably incomprehensible. The physical organization confronting such a person would be the classroom we were interviewing in, which indeed would be the physical organization of the group. Their virtual organization, however, was the submarine, but the observer ignorant of the scenario would not readily perceive that. For the group their physical and virtual organizations are in harmony, whilst the observer cannot reconcile the physical organization to the group's virtual organization nor indeed to his own perception of virtual organization.

Although this is a fairly simple situation there are lessons to be learnt for both the student and the practitioner within our business organizations. In many respects, managers are confronted with the same perceptual problems as our unknowledgeable observer. Their organizations are considerably more complex than our group of interviewees.

They do not have the benefit of a scenario forming the framework for interaction as with the MBA interview, and the numbers of people interacting within any given situation are considerably greater. In the former situation also, the actors have been tuned into the scenario and thus given their virtual organization; the links are therefore strong by their acceptance of it, and they are able to respond to it quite happily. In a business organization, however, people are still primarily driven by their physical organization and would not be happy to respond to virtuality.

This then brings us to the point of the chapter: to discover how the model of physical and virtual organization will help the manager. Unlike those in our submarine, most managers are not aware of their virtual organization. Like our observer, they will interpret what is going on through their physical organization. In the same way that our unknowledgeable observer would not be able to act either effectively or appropriately in such a situation, so too are management teams not acting properly because they appreciate neither the existence nor characteristics of their virtual organizations. Therefore, merely to understand the virtual organization will probably make a manager more efficient.

12.2   More than a model

In some respects the two-organizations model is proposing that managements adopt a new culture within an organization. That may seem contradictory to this work's implied sociological approach rather than one of prescription. This has not altered. But there are inevitable consequences from all types of analysis which are bound to change our perception of the environment. As a consequence, subsequent action will also change. For example, if a running man is informed that a few yards ahead there is possibly a cliff, even though he has never seen it himself nor has any way of verification other than by contact, he is bound to slow down to a walk. His changed perception through new information has changed his action. In this respect all models of social interaction will have an impact upon the arena that they analyse. It is an old problem of the social analyst.

Therefore, although the prime motivation of the model is to understand the phenomenon of organization, the side effects of that could be to change an observer's perception of it. And as people begin to act differently – the virtual organization already affected – the transmission mechanisms will feed this through to the physical organization.

It is hoped that, as a consequence, an organization's culture will become more virtually-orientated than it is perhaps at present.

12.2.1 Effects upon management action

For practical purposes such a culture would result in management action more sensitive to the organization's perceptual needs. What type of action that should be will be presented as a general discussion in this section.

Mintzberg, for example, classified management activity into three major roles:

1. Interpersonal.
2. Informational.
3. Decisional.

A greater awareness of things perceptual within an organization will alter the way a manager approaches these functions. His/her inter-personal skills would be governed, as they should be now but perhaps are not acknowledged to be, not just by functional relationships but also by perceptual ones. Managers are trained to be figureheads, to lead and to liaise very much from a physical perspective. They are perceptually positioned in the physical organization as heads of functions: I am a marketing manager or I am a manufacturing director and so on. General information is also placed functionally, such as information technology, purchasing and supply and so on. But every manager is also a manager of the perceptual dimension. There is no choice about this: because a manager may not understand or know about the virtual organization does not mean that he/she is not involved. Indeed, every employee is an actor within virtual organization and all training programmes should take that into account.

A firm's information network is far more complex than the physical links between one computer and the next, or the electronics of a telephone system or indeed some management hierarchy. And yet managers are trained to deal with information on solely that level. They are expected to monitor and disseminate information upwards as well as downwards. They seem not to be encouraged to be sensitive to the virtual information networks of their organizations.

Decision-making and how to do it is seen as another major management role. Its importance is reflected in the number of management training programmes there are to improve those skills. Once again, however, these are physical organization centred. They are seen as a consequence of physical interaction in terms of resource control, and indeed quite often they obviously are since it is difficult for us to perceive our environment in any other way than through the physical dimension. And yet decisions are very much a part of the virtual organization: their impact is both spatial and temporal and through transmission mechanisms they can affect all aspects of organization.

12.2.2   The solution

The consequence of this argument is for a change of emphasis in management training to enable individuals to understand the importance of virtuality. The virtual organization is more than an academic exercise, it is a force which can compel an organization to adopt certain, quite often undesirable, characteristics. Managers must know of its existence and be sensitive to it. The training they receive and the methods of action they prescribe must be sympathetic to managing a complete restructuring in order to accommodate the virtual organization. At the same time the firm's efficiency must be maintained to at least the minimum acceptable levels. As any manager would probably complain, this would not be an easy task.

As such, the more likely course that managers will take, because of its short-term advantages, is to maintain their present organization structure and thus hope to control the increasing complexity. The skills and the knowledge they would require to do this successfully would have to be considerably broader. It is unlikely, however, that in the long run they would succeed, even with the necessary skill base. Nor is it an argument to say that to date firms have survived without fully appreciating virtual organization. Someone can walk through a minefield without knowing about the mines and survive, but the risk is still there.

12.2.3   Why should I change?

Apart from the analogy of the minefield, there is a counter-argument which comprises several levels. The first point to be made is that many firms have not survived which might otherwise have done so. My experience in the business environment has shown that a significant number of firms have collapsed because of internal dysfunction. Their product seemed acceptable, markets were there, it was just that they could no longer remain a cohesive unit. There is, as yet, no formally logged explanation of these phenomena, many easier solutions having already been proposed. However, an illness which is not fully understood cannot be denied. Imbalance and disequilibrium in many cases was the illness of failed business. We do not as yet fully appreciate their meaning, but we should not try to deny their effects.

The second point is that even if business organizations are doing reasonably well without knowledge about the effects of virtual organization, and obviously many are, this does not mean it will always stay that way. The increasing use of complex technology systems has made the effects of an untended virtual organization even more acute. We have reached the point where management must be able to manage both organizations – physical and virtual – otherwise these systems will increasingly drive their organizations into dysfunctional activity.

This returns us to the old argument of effectiveness or efficiency. The latter is to a great extent achievable in the physical organization, the production of more widgets per resource input and so on. Effectiveness is not, on the other hand, so easily defined, being more within the domain of the virtual organization. Information technology is introduced on most occasions on the form of efficiency criteria, leaving the firm's effectiveness to follow on behind. Quite often it does not.

Prior to the introduction of a computer system within a business organization there may be a balance between the two organizations. This is probably not due to positive and knowledgeable management activity but rather a consequence of natural force interaction within that firm. The impact of technology subsequent to introduction will drastically upset that balance which then requires positive management action which is not always forthcoming. We then have the seemingly paradoxical situation of increased efficiency accompanied by decreased effectiveness.

The final point takes us to a certain extent onto a macro level of analysis. Because they do not understand virtual organization UK firms generally may not be as competitive as many of their competitors abroad. I am not suggesting that foreign firms know about or understand the concept of virtual organization, rather that in some cases their organizational culture is more in keeping with, perhaps more sensitive to, things virtual. I would further suggest that it is because of this that they are often more successful than UK firms.

A classic case is cited by Peter Drucker (management) who compared western business organizations with their Japanese counterparts, who are recognized as being more effective. It would be naive to put their success down to merely a more conscientious workforce. That may or may not be part of the equation. What is more important is that their societal culture is more conducive to the formation of a business organization. The often quoted Samurai and rice grower relationship allows for a successful management of these firms. On the one hand, the worker is happy to work for a particular organization (all the individual's life, and from generation to generation is not uncommon) because to do so reflects their relationship with formal authority into which they have been socialized. On the other hand, the management, through this same social mechanism, feels a patriarchal sense of responsibility towards its workers. The net effect seems to be a well functioning and happy firm.

Without the benefit of an empirical study on this particular issue, NBS research nevertheless tends to support the view that there is a difference in attitude between UK-based Japanese firms and western-managed business organizations. The management culture within the Japanese firms seemed to be more sensitive to aspects other than resource manipulation. There is evidence of stronger links into the virtual elements of an organization through a management acceptance of having to deal with the employee as a whole person rather than as a physical resource. In other words, the Japanese organizational culture could allow for a more effective utilization of the virtual and physical organization. If this is so, then in any competitive situation the Japanese firms could have a head start. For this reason alone it is worth understanding virtual organization.

This book, therefore, issues a challenge to all managements which cannot be ignored. That is, to understand and use appropriately their virtual organizations or to go under. This understanding cannot come about overnight. It is socialized into all of us to conceive in the physical perspective. To change this needs training and education. If we are to survive the onslaught of computers and perhaps our foreign competitors this needs to be attended to sooner rather than later.

12.3   The evidence

Virtual organization is an abstract thing, its relationship with physical organization can only be measured by consequential action and therefore we are effectively seeking to analyse a world constructed in the human mind. We cannot take a psychological or humanist approach, that is to set aside a group of individuals and study them either in or out of context. To do that would miss the whole point of the relationship between the two organizations. People have to be studied not only within context but also within their functional positions. To take them out of that would be to create a different relationship and thus create a different virtual organization. But not to take them out means an impossible task for the analyst in gaining the necessary data.

The problem is not easily surmountable. There is no quick and effective way of gathering the necessary data. In many respects the practitioner is best able to test the model through day to day experience and a feel for the organization.

The specific objective of the NBS research project was to analyse the impact of information technology on the structural characteristics of organizations. In particular we were interested in the implications for human behaviour. This allowed us to gather data on a range of interactions before and after computer implementation. The construction of such data into workable models led me to perceive the organizational context in terms of the physical and the perceptual. We found that the efficiency criteria of computer implementation generated physically-orientated relationships such as output management and structural change, whereas the effectiveness criteria of computer implementation generated the perceptual relationships such as political change and culture. It was obvious that the two were linked, particularly since managers seemed not to be attending to the effectiveness criteria and yet that part of the organization was not static in terms of change. This suggested that linkage mechanisms between the perceptual and physical aspects were indeed working.

It was but a small step from this to create the model presented in this book which formally recognized the dynamics of the two domains and satisfied the NBS's objective to understand better the impact of information technology upon organizations.

Information technology is important in the modelling of an organization because its poignant perceptual characteristics have a greater impact upon virtuality than other phenomena. The two sides cannot be separated. The effects of computers cannot be understood without virtual organization, whilst the computer has increased the need to understand virtuality.

12.4 The future

Where do we go from here? Empirical research alone is not practical for reasons already stated. The Silverman *et al.* action research approach has greater promise. This is where the individual analysts are involved within the organizational process and are insiders as opposed to outsiders. But then we shall get only their side of the story. This could be broadened further by having many analysts in one company, but then the numbers would encroach upon the characteristics of the firm and also possibly be an inconvenience. An examination of an organization over a period of time could be carried out in a similar manner to the research conducted by Burns and Stalker. The results, however, would at best be only the consequence of the relationship we seek and not a reflection of its mechanisms. NBS research has already achieved this.

It is, therefore, down to the practitioner, the employees of our business organizations. They are the physical and virtual organizations, it is through them that any organization has form and reality. An easy thing to say, but it requires their considerable participation and understanding in any research that is conducted. But more than this, the virtual/physical dichotomy is an action. As such, it cannot be analysed like a piece of furniture. In many respects it has to be accepted as being there and action then taken in accordance with that perception. An act of faith it may be, more likely a 'suck it and see' approach. Unfortunately the nature of our social entities do not allow us the convenience of a comfortable and well defined research framework.

Index

INSIDE INFORMATION TECHNOLOGY
A Practical Guide to Management Issues

Tony Gunton, Independent Consultant, London, England

This book deals comprehensively with the issues facing business organizations as they strive to tackle the problems of managing information as a corporate resource. Managers at all levels have to consider the business opportunities that information technology can provide/support. The book develops the theme from a discussion of technological developments and corporate experience, and reviews their impact on information systems, users and managers, through to the less defined activities carried out in corporate strategic planning.

Inside Information Technology is divided into six parts:

- Deploying equipment
- Assessing the technologies
- Managing information and information policy
- Selecting suppliers/procuring equipment
- Developing applications
- Managing skills/supporting end-user computing

Contents

1. Distributing processing power
2. Overcoming geography 3. The rise of generic computing 4. New dimensions to information 5. Applications in summary
6. From data files to database
7. Supporting the knowledge worker
8. Information management in practice
9. IBM and the systems business
10. Technological Tower of Babel
11. Policy for procurement 12. Advances in programming 13. New ways to develop systems

1990   302 pages
hardback   ISBN 13–931452–0
paperback ISBN 13–931346–X

Business Information Technology Series

Business
Information
Technology
Series

MANAGEMENT STRATEGIES FOR INFORMATION TECHNOLOGY

Michael J Earl, Director, Oxford Institute of Information Management, Templeton College, Oxford, England

'There is probably no other single book which covers the subject so thoroughly, comprehensively and competently, drawing on up-to-date practical experience and backed up by appropriate research.' CIS JOURNAL

As IT becomes a source of competitive advantage and an important support for many firms' strategies, it has also *created* new strategic choices for many companies.

Taking these facts as the theme for his book, which is based on contemporary research and experience in business, Earl uses real world examples from Europe and the USA to demonstrate how to formulate IT strategies and how to manage IT and the information systems function in large organisations.

Key features include:
- early chapters suggesting both **why** and **how** exploitation of IT must be connected to business strategy formulation
- subsequent chapters re-examining some traditional problems of information systems management from this strategic perspective
- an overall managerial, analytical and practical, rather than technical, approach

Contents
1. The IT Era 2. Information management 3. Information technology and strategic advantage 4. Formulating information systems strategy 5. Formulating IT strategy 6. Formulating IM strategy 7. Organizing IT activities 8. Controlling IT activities 9. Change strategies for strategic change

1989   218 pages
hardback   ISBN 13-551664-1
paperback   ISBN 13-551656-0

END USER FOCUS

Tony Gunton, Independent Consultant,
London, England

'...a worthwhile book. It is a mine of useful diagrams and check-lists...for business people who need to see system specification in a more global context.' HICOM Reviews

This lucid and comprehensive account of the information technology revolution focuses on the fast-growing range of technologies — personal computers, office automation, departmental systems — where end-users themselves directly exploit the computing power at their disposal. Information is provided to enable managers, consultants and future managers to cope with all aspects of change such as attitudes, organisation structures and the huge investment in outdated systems.

Valuable features include:
- useful tables and charts for illustration
- a quick reference guide giving a compact visual representation of the key points made in each chapter, plus page citations for easy cross-referencing
- case material from leading companies such as Bank of America, Dupont, ICI and Hughes Aircraft is featured.

Contents
INTRODUCTION: Why are End User Systems so Important? MAKING IT ALL ADD UP: Appraisal Mechanisms PLANNING THE INFRASTRUCTURE: Planning Approaches BALANCING TOUGHNESS AND TENDERNESS: Controlling the Interfaces Between people, Technology and Information ENABLING END-USERS TO HELP THEMSELVES: Information Centres NOT JUST PROJECTS, MORE A WAY OF WORKING: Identifying the Targets, Setting Project Goals SHAPING TECHNOLOGY TO THE BUSINESS NEEDS: A Formula for an Adaptable Architecture Conclusion

1988   213 pages
hardback   ISBN 13-100843-9
paperback   ISBN 13-100835-8

Business Information Technology Series

PROFESSIONAL SYSTEMS DEVELOPMENT
Experience, Ideas and Action

Niels Erik Anderson, Finn Kensing,
Jette Lundin, Lars Mathiassen,
Andreas Munk-Madsen, Monika
Rasbech, Pal Sorgaard

Presenting a coherent framework for
evaluating and planning systems
development projects, this book
addresses and suggests solutions to
the practical problems that can arise.

**Part One   Theory of Systems
Development**
● presents and clarifies the concepts
and ideas applied throughout the book
● includes authors' research
conclusions in the form of
fundamental principles for systems
development

**Part Two   Systems Development in
Practice**
● planning ● project evaluation ●
cooperation with the users in analysis
design

**Part Three   Changing Working
Practices in Systems Development**
● strategies for changing working
practices: change agents, training ●
learning from experience ● applying
the book in practice

Contents
1. System development — many
possibilities 2. Situations and action
3. What is systems development?
4. Project establishment — a sound
investment 5. Planning — the key to
success 6. Project evaluation — see
the problems in time 7. Baselines
improve project management
8. Cooperation with users
9. Description — vary working
practices and perspective 10. Avoid
permanent firefighting
11. Strategies for changing working
practices 12. Learn in the project
13. The book in practice

1989   283 pages
hardback   ISBN 13-725540-3
paperback ISBN 13-725524-1

Business Information Technology Series

INFRASTRUCTURE
Building a Framework for Corporate Information Handling

Tony Gunton, Independent Consultant, London, England

'Managers who realise that they must take policy decisions to protect and capitalise on their investment in technology will find much to ponder in this excellent distillation of Tony Gunton's consultancy experience ... it is enjoyable to read and by no means a dry technical reference work.' ICL TODAY

This practical book explains **why** an information technology infrastructure is needed, **what** the main policy and design options are, and **how** to make the important choices.

Part One examines the forces shaping the infrastructure — business pressures, user and organisational needs, the supply industry — in order to define the requirements and principles which should be applied to its design. **Part Two** shows how these requirements and principles can be turned into a workable business information systems infrastructure, appropriate for a particular organisation with particular needs.

Contents
1. Applications and customer needs
2. The demands of the organization
3. Engineering for the 1990's
4. Procurement — the insoluble problem
5. Information power — the workstation
6. Distributing processing power and information
7. Managing the interconnection problem
8. The corporate network.

1989   228 pages
hardback   ISBN 13-465535-4
paperback   ISBN 13-465543-5

MANAGING THE HUMAN RESOURCE

John Westerman, Independent Consultant, and Pauline Donoghue, Human Resource Manager, Digital Mobile Communications, London, England

This practical and action-oriented book promotes the development of comprehensive corporate strategies for the management of human resources within the information technology environment(s) of the 1990s. The approaches discussed are proven management techniques for developing a culture where business and human benefits are achieved to mutual gain.

Detailed and extensive surveys in industry and commerce form the research basis for the book, involving executives from ● life assurance ● banking ● retailing ● financial services ● regional health authorities ● international airlines ● automotive and instrumentation manufacturing

Contents

1. Introduction 2. HRM problems and an overall approach to the task 3. Is there more to strategies than just planning? 4. Can we prepare for change? 5. Why invest in training for information technology?
6. Motivation — Is it more than stick and carrots? 7. Improved utilization of human resources — yes, but how 8. Manpower planning and the IT environment 9. Putting everything together. Appendices.

1989   184 pages
hardback   ISBN 13-547316-0
paperback   ISBN 13-547324-1

AN INTRODUCTION TO COMPUTER INTEGRATED BUSINESS

Lesley Beddie and Scot Raeburn, Napier Polytechnic, Edinburgh, Scotland

'...by avoiding gratuitous jargon, and making extensive use of diagrams, Beddie and Raeburn manage to demystify and clarify even the most foggy areas of their subject... excellent for college students... lecturers will also find it particularly useful, as exercises and bibliography are appended to the end of each chapter.' MICRO DECISIONS

Written for the non-computing student of information technology in business, this book concentrates principally on applying computer systems on a small scale. It explains the difficulties that will be met and the technique that must be applied as soon as machines are linked together for shared use, or when systems are linked across departmental boundaries.

Other features include:

- guiding the reader through analysis and design of stand-alone systems to the more complex multi-user systems

- exercises in most chapters to stimulate interest
- an illustrative case study integrated throughout the text showing how ideas are developed and applied

Contents
1. Systems concepts 2. Vertical software 3. Horizontal software packages 4. Designing small applications 5. Growth and complexity 6. Further systems concepts 7. Design for larger applications 8. Making connections 9. Security considerations 10. Acquiring systems.

1989   279 pages
hardback   ISBN 13-479726-4
paperback   ISBN 13-479718-3

FORTHCOMING TITLES

Information Technology in Personnel Management

Barry Allen, formerly of Hoechst (UK) Ltd
ISBN: 0-13-465170-7 (c)
       0-13-463589-2 (p)

Information Systems and Corporate Goals

Alastair de Watteville, Formerly a director of Hoskyns
ISBN: 0-13-463670-8 (c)
       0-13-463662-7 (p)

Electronic Data Interchange: The Information Management View

Paula Swatman *et al* (eds), Curtin University, Perth, Australia

Prospective authors are invited to submit proposals for Series titles.

Please contact:
Michael Cash
Acquisitions Editor
Simon & Schuster International Grou
Prentice Hall, Wolsey House, Wolsey Road,
Hemel Hempstead, Herts HP2 4SS, England.
Tel: (0442) 231900
Fax: (0442) 52544

All of the titles detailed on the previous pages are available from y usual bookstore, or in case of difficulty please contact your local Prentice Hall/Simon & Schuster office.

Prentice Hall
SIMON & SCHUSTER
INTERNATIONAL GROUP